# Five Percenter Rap

**Profiles in Popular Music**
Glenn Gass and Jeffrey Magee, Series Editors

# Five Percenter Rap

## God Hop's Music, Message, and Black Muslim Mission

Felicia M. Miyakawa

Indiana University Press | Bloomington and Indianapolis

This book is a publication of

**Indiana University Press**
601 North Morton Street
Bloomington, IN 47404-3797 USA

http://iupress.indiana.edu

*Telephone orders*  800-842-6796
*Fax orders*  812-855-7931
*Orders by e-mail*  iuporder@indiana.edu

The paper used in this publication meets the
minimum requirements of American National
Standard for Information Sciences—Permanence
of Paper for Printed Library Materials, ANSI
Z39.48-1984.

Manufactured in the United States of America

Miyakawa, Felicia M.
    Five Percenter rap : God hop's music,
message, and black Muslim mission / Felicia M.
Miyakawa.
        p. cm. — (Profiles in popular music)
    Includes bibliographical references (p. ) and
indexes.
    ISBN 0-253-34574-X (cloth : alk. paper) —
ISBN 0-253-21763-6 (pbk. : alk. paper)
    1. Rap music—Religious aspects—Islam.
2. Five Percent Nation. I. Title. II. Series.
    ML3531.M49 2005
    782.421649—dc22          2004021159

1 2 3 4 5 10 09 08 07 06 05

We ain't just rappers
We changers of black situation.

**POOR RIGHTEOUS TEACHERS**

# CONTENTS

# Acknowledgments

This book is the product of more than five years of research and writing and would not have been possible without the help of several institutions and many individuals. Early stages of this project were supported by a Dissertation Year Fellowship at Indiana University (Bloomington). A grant from the Jack and Linda Gill Foundation enabled archival research in New York City. My early forays into this topic led to a presentation at the Rock and Roll Hall of Fame and conference papers given at meetings of the Society for American Music and the American Musicological Society. I with to thank my colleagues and friends from all of these venues for their stimulating questions and comments.

At Indiana University I was blessed with a stunning group of mentors. Jeffrey Magee, J. Peter Burkholder, Portia Maultsby, and Massimo Ossi guided me from ABD to Ph.D., and in the process helped me develop the foundation for this book. I truly could not have done this without their help. I am also indebted to the late A. Peter Brown, who, despite his misgivings about rap music, did everything within his power to support and promote my research.

During the course of this project, I had the good fortune to be part of two writing support groups. My Indiana group included Judy Barger, J. Peter Burkholder, Mark Butler, David Griffioen, and Luiz Lopes. In California I communed with Francesca Draughon, Kara Gardner, and Mina Yang. My thanks to all of these folks for keeping me on task and providing me with vital feedback.

I am also grateful to Harry Allen, for his encouragement, and to Joe Schloss, Albin Zak, and Akiem Allah Elisra (DJ Kool Akiem), for their cogent comments and suggestions on early drafts of this book. Oliver Wang, Mark Katz, and Joe Schloss have become my esteemed academic hip-hop crew (watch for us at conference venues near you!). I have learned so much from them.

The editorial staff at Indiana University Press consistently amazed me. I am especially grateful to my editor Gayle Sherwood, for her steadfast belief in my project; to editorial assistant Donna Wilson, for keeping track of the minutiae; and to copyeditor Shoshanna Green, for her incredible attention to detail.

No hip-hop head is complete without her crew. Mark Butler, Nic Butler, Sarah Hill, Greg McCracken, Alisa Rata, Scott Sanders, Cory Smythe, and Jessie Thoman rejoiced in my findings, listened to me prattle on without complaining, and reminded me to have a social life. The Beaver family in California—Bill, Sue,

**x**   and Sarah—gave me plenty of opportunities to take time off and relax and provided moral and emotional support as I made my way through the book-writing process. David Beaver offered me support, ethnomusicological perspectives, puns, rhymes, and digressions when I needed them most. My family, and especially my mother, Linda Vollmer, never stopped believing in me. For that I am ever grateful.

Finally, I would like to extend heartfelt gratitude and props to the Gods and Earths who create this slammin' music. Without the music, this book would not exist.

Peace.

*Murfreesboro, Tennessee*
*August 2004*

# Five Percenter Rap

*Introduction*

# God Hop

In October 1979, rap music burst onto the popular music scene with the highly successful single "Rapper's Delight" by the Sugarhill Gang. But rap music had been growing for nearly a decade before its first commercial hit. Rap music began in African American and Latino neighborhoods of the Bronx in the early 1970s. Rap's roots are in the dance music produced and performed by disc jockeys (DJs) at parties and street gatherings. DJs were mobile: they carried with them complete sound systems, including, in some cases, huge speaker systems that could be heard blocks away. DJs used two turntables, allowing them to segue smoothly from one record to the next, a practice taken from Jamaican dance hall DJs.[1] Initially concerned with maintaining a good groove for dancing, DJs soon realized that they also needed to do or say something to interact with and control the ever-increasing crowds. Some DJs began exhorting the crowd with phrases such as "To the beat, y'all," or "Wave your hands in the air, wave 'em like you just don't care." Others drew the audience into responding to them in ways patterned on the African American tradition of call and response. But as DJs such as Kool Herc, Afrika Bambaataa, and Grandmaster Flash increasingly focused on developing technological prowess at the turntable, they could not pay as much attention to the crowd, and DJs began to have sidemen—called masters of ceremonies, or MCs—who interacted with the crowd in rhymes over the DJ's beats. And thus was born one of the most powerful cultural forces of the late twentieth century: rap music.[2]

Whereas early rap lyrics concentrated largely on encouraging and controlling the crowd, by the late 1980s several genres of rap could be distinguished.[3] Party rap, the oldest rap genre, continued the tradition of enticing a crowd to dance to the DJ's beat. As rap's popularity moved south and west, regional styles infiltrated what had been a New York City monopoly. From the west coast in the late 1980s came a genre known as mack rap. MCs of this genre, such as Oakland's Too $hort and Seattle's Sir Mix-A-Lot, positioned themselves as ultimate ladies' men and self-styled pimps. MCs and DJs from both coasts also developed gangsta rap, a genre known for its "realistic" and often violent and misogynistic lyrics. The late 1980s also saw the birth of "conscious" rap; conscious MCs and crews took black nationalism, Pan-Africanism, Islamic doctrine, education, political empowerment, and other social causes as their themes. With powerful groups such as Public Enemy fronting this genre, conscious rap voiced the woes of social inequality and racism.

Many of the most commercially successful conscious solo acts and groups of the late 1980s and early 1990s, such as Public Enemy, Brand Nubian, Poor Righteous Teachers, X-Clan, the Jungle Brothers, Queen Latifah, KRS-One, Nas, Busta Rhymes, and the Wu-Tang Clan, had at least nominal ties to Islamic doctrine. Conscious rap became less popular in the late 1990s, but a core group of MCs and crews continued to produce it throughout the decade and into the new century. Many of them are members of the Five Percent Nation, a breakaway sect from the Nation of Islam. Their rap music, known within the Five Percent Nation as "God Hop," is the focus of this book.

In a 1991 interview with Joseph Eure and James Spady, Wise Intelligent, a member of the rap group Poor Righteous Teachers, was asked, "How did you come up with the name of the group? Is teaching one of the priorities of the group?" Wise Intelligent responded,

> Indeed. Poor, righteous, teachers, the statement itself defines those Black men who gained knowledge of themselves and then take it as their duty or obligation to teach and resurrect the poor. . . . So what we're trying to get across to poor people is that, you are the fathers of civilization. You are the makers, the owners, the givers, the takers, the Gods of the universe. You are the Lords of all the worlds. . . . We know who the true and living God is, and we teach that the true and living God is the Son of Man, supreme being Black man from Asia, teaching freedom, justice, and equality to all the human families of the planet earth.[4]

Wise Intelligent's lyrics are filled with references to his self-imposed goal of teaching: phrases such as "I educate you through the teacher in me" ("Word Iz Life"); "So in the head of ignorance, I rip some conscious clip / Niggas is small, my task is educate y'all" ("Gods, Earths and 85ers"); and "Teaching is the duty of a civilized man / Teach truth to the youth / That be thirstin' for the knowledge" ("Butt-Naked Booty Bless") are but three of many examples. And Wise Intelligent is not alone in his wish to educate the black masses. From Grand Puba of Brand Nubian we hear "Each one teach one, so here I come to the drum" ("Drop the Bomb"); from the group Gravediggaz, "And this is it, the black God exists / Can you understand this? Let me teach you a lesson" ("Twelve Jewelz"); and from King Sun, "We have a duty and our duty is to teach and civilize" ("The Gods Are Taking Heads").

As even these few examples illustrate, Five Percenter rappers see themselves as teachers, bringers of a specific type of self-knowledge. But who are the Five Percenters? What do they believe? What do they propose to teach? What is the nature of the connection between the Five Percent Nation and hip-hop? And how do Five Percenters communicate their theology through the medium of rap music? These questions fueled my six-year investigation into the Five Percent Nation, and they form the basis of this book.

My study of the rap music produced and performed by members of the Five Percent Nation unexpectedly became both timely and socially relevant on September 11, 2001. As I was putting the finishing touches on an early draft of what would eventually become chapter 3 of this book, the news came in: two planes had flown into the World Trade Center towers in New York City, another plane crash had set the Pentagon on fire, and a fourth plane had gone down in Pennsylvania. Thousands of casualties were expected. Because these crashes had happened almost simultaneously, government experts quickly assumed they were orchestrated acts of terror. Reports and rumors vied for headline space in the following weeks. It did not take long for the government to identify the terrorists: Islamic extremists led by Osama bin Laden and protected by the Taliban.

As President George W. Bush and his international allies prepared for the subsequent "War on Terror," journalists and academics flooded the marketplace with information about Islam. Factoids about Islam, such as the "Five Pillars of Faith," the various meanings of "jihad," and the differences between numerous Muslim sects, suddenly became gripping topics of conversation for Americans seeking to understand the motivations of the attacks. While the war against Osama bin Laden's Al-Qaeda network and the Taliban raged in Afghanistan, American Muslims suffered on the home front. Many became the victims of hate crimes, retaliatory acts meant to clearly differentiate "us"—Americans—from "them"—Muslims.

But in December 2001 American intelligence officers found Jonathan Walker Lindh, an American youth, among captured Taliban forces in Mazar-e Sharif. Reporters quickly learned that Lindh, born and raised in California, had converted to Islam while still a teenager and allegedly had joined with Taliban troops to fight against America. Lindh's presence among the Taliban soldiers challenged America's "United We Stand," us-versus-them mentality. The American press now had a new question to answer: who or what was to blame for Lindh's unthinkable treason? Searching for the earliest pernicious influence, the one that had originally led Lindh astray, numerous sources settled on the same culprit: rap music. A *Newsweek* headline, for example, implied a direct line of causality: "How did John Walker Lindh go from hip-hop to holy war?"[5] The article's authors proposed that hip-hop music was at least partly to blame for Lindh's degeneration because hip-hop lyrics first introduced him to Islam. They went on to single out the popular rapper Nas as one of the influences Lindh later rejected when he converted to orthodox Islam.

Lindh's story attracted my attention not only because it put a human face on the war, but also because it put rap music on trial again in the American public sphere. This time, however, the issue was not "gangsta" violence, misogyny, or foul language. This time the public eye turned to rap lyrics that endorse Muslim spiritual values, values assumed to be similar to those held by the terrorists responsible for the September 11 attacks and thus anathema to America's fight against terrorism. A great number of American rap musicians do claim Muslim ties, but just as there are many branches of Islam, "Islamic" rap bears no single face. Indeed, most "Islamic" rappers follow either the Nation of Islam or the Five Percent Nation, both of which orthodox Muslims consider heretical. Rap lyrics may have first introduced the young Lindh to Islamic thought, but rap cannot carry all the blame for the series of complex events and decisions that led Lindh to the Taliban.

A year after the September 11 attacks, the Five Percent Nation and rap once again made news headlines together. In October 2002, the suburbs of Washington, D.C., were terrorized by a sniper (dubbed the "Beltway Sniper") who killed ten people and wounded three others. While police forces under the leadership of Montgomery County police chief Charles Moose searched for clues to the sniper's identity, the media offered theories based on messages left by the sniper near crime scenes and in phone conversations with the police. Phrases such as "word is bond" and "I am God" led the media to speculate that the perpetrator was associated with the Five Percent Nation. Mark Goldblatt's report for *USA Today*, for example, said, "The Associated Press has reported that notes left at two shooting scenes contain language and symbols associated with the Five Percenters, who splintered off from the Nation of Islam (NOI) in 1964 and consider themselves a culture, not a faith."[6] Examples of lyrics from Five Percenter artists and groups such as Busta Rhymes, Killarmy, the Wu-Tang Clan, Nas, Sunz of Man, Brand Nubian, Rakim Allah, and Poor Righteous Teachers were dredged up to support the theory.[7] The snipers were eventually identified as John Allen Muhammad and his young associate Lee Boyd Malvo, and reporters soon unearthed Muhammad's former membership in the Nation of Islam.[8] There is no evidence, however, that either Muhammad or Malvo were ever associated with the Five Percent Nation. Yet months after the snipers' strikes, Five Percenters still felt compelled to defend themselves and their beliefs. In the *Village Voice*, for example, Dumar Wa'de Allah, the Nation's national representative, proclaimed,

> We are not that type of people; we are civilized. We are not a violent people. We are not a hate group. First and foremost, we teach freedom, justice, and equality to all the human families of the planet Earth, and I want to emphasize

that, and second, our knowledge that we advocate to the world has nothing to do with violence. We are here to stop violent behavior that is taking place among our young people.[9]

In the same *Village Voice* article, rapper Busta Rhymes echoed Dumar Wa'de Allah's protests: "we don't advocate no violence."[10]

America's understanding of Islam has improved somewhat since September 11, yet we remain largely ignorant of the Five Percent Nation. The misguided media focus on the Five Percent Nation in the Lindh and Beltway Sniper cases merely provides recent examples of persistent misunderstanding and misrepresentation of the Five Percent Nation. This book is a long-overdue study of the Five Percent Nation from historical, cultural, theological, and musical perspectives. Such a kaleidoscopic approach is necessary given the Five Percent Nation's complex theology, historical ties to major movements and moments in American history, and deep involvement with popular culture. Five Percenter theology is multiply grounded in Black Muslim traditions, black nationalism, Kemetic symbolism, Masonic mysticism, and Gnostic spirituality. But the Five Percent Nation's history is also tightly entwined with hip-hop's history. The stories of both Lindh and the Beltway Sniper are just two modern examples of this relationship.

This study is divided into two parts. Part 1 deals with the particulars of the Five Percent Nation's history and theology. Chapter 1 traces the cultural and spiritual history of the Five Percent Nation, beginning in the early twentieth century with Noble Drew Ali's Moorish Science Temple and extending through the legacies of W. D. Fard, Elijah Muhammad, Malcolm X, Louis Farrakhan, and Clarence 13X, the founder and leader of the Five Percent Nation. Chapter 1 considers not only the impact each leader had on the development of the Nation of Islam and the Five Percent Nation, but also the social and cultural context within which each new incarnation of Black Muslim theology took shape. Chapter 2 offers an in-depth introduction to Five Percenter theology within the context of its Nation of Islam origins, considers the impact of Five Percenter theology on the daily life of its adherents, and offers historical and social explanations for the close ties between hip-hop music and culture and the Five Percent Nation.

Part 2 of the book turns to the tools God Hop musicians use to support their mission of bringing their message to the masses. Chapter 3 examines how Five Percenter MCs hide their lessons within God Hop lyrics, which are often thickly coded with seemingly-obscure references to theology. In chapters 4 and 5 I argue that Five Percenter MCs and producers support their teaching efforts through careful, conscious musical choices. Chapter 4 considers how flow, layering, rupture, and groove are used in the construction of God Hop. Chapter 5 is a detailed study of sampling practices in God Hop. Here I illustrate how sampling, as yet another tool in the hands of God Hop musicians, not only provides musical and aesthetic interest as the samples interact with other layers in a musical texture, but also introduces crucial intertextual meaning. Finally, chapter 6 examines album packaging. Here I consider the role of album art, liner notes, "shout-outs," "skits" between tracks, and album organization in the overall goal of spreading doctrine.

Despite the close ties between the Five Percent Nation and hip-hop traditions, this book is not intended as a comprehensive survey of rap history. Many excellent treatments of regional, national, and international hip-hop history have been published in recent years. Instead of covering the same historical ground, I take these studies as my starting point. I invite those readers interested in hip-hop's history to browse these sources for general background knowledge.[11] That said, familiarity with hip-hop history will add depth to a reading of this book, but is not a pre-requisite.

More importantly, this book makes no claims to being a definitive study of the Five Percent Nation. I have spent countless hours in the past five years listening to music, studying album art, wading through archival material, "surfing" the Internet for Five Percenter information, reading Five Percenter and Nation of Islam literature and decoding their lessons, and exchanging emails with a few Five Percenter consultants to produce this book, the first in-depth study of the Five Percent Nation. Despite these efforts, my study only scratches the surface of this complex culture. The Five Percent Nation is a young, vibrant, growing organization. I have no doubt that the Nation will continue to transform itself as its membership expands. Additionally, I am constrained by my position in this study, which is—and I assume always will be—that of an outsider: the Nation of Islam and the Five Percent Nation both essentially exclude whites from participating.[12] As a cultural outsider, I do not have access to every detail of the Five Percenter "way of life." And since I cannot draw on first-hand experience and insider cultural knowledge, I am limited by the availability of sources and am dependent on the good will of my consultants.

In the course of my work on the Five Percent Nation, colleagues, friends, family members, and students have frequently asked me if pursuing my subject puts me in any danger. "How do Five Percenters feel about you, a white woman, writing about their patriarchal, black nationalist beliefs?" they want to know. On the one occasion when I had the opportunity to present my scholarship to Five Percenters, I received a warm welcome. One young man thanked me for taking the time to care about them. Curiously, the only resistance to my research has come not from the Five Percent Nation, but from other outsiders who disagree with Five Percenter theology and urged me to speak out against the Nation. But readers looking for objections to Five Percenter theology will not find those objections in my study. As much as possible, I have let Five Percenters speak for themselves throughout the book. This is their story.

# History and Theology
## of the
# Five Percent Nation

# Building a Nation

The immediate history of the Five Percent Nation begins in the early 1960s with Clarence 13X's separation from the Nation of Islam, yet the intellectual and spiritual heritage of the Five Percent Nation extends much further back, to nineteenth-century black nationalist trends and early-twentieth-century social and spiritual movements. Before tracing some of the forces that shaped the Five Percent Nation's development, however, a caveat is in order. Many of the secondary sources that form the backbone of my discussion are based on oral histories of conflicting splinter groups. What follows, then, is by no means a comprehensive treatment of all possible historical theories, nor is it an attempt to reconcile conflicting testimonies. Instead, this chapter summarizes ideas and narratives taken from primary and secondary sources that have some bearing on the formation of the Five Percent Nation. Together these sources illustrate that the social, theological, and black nationalist foundations of the Five Percent Nation uniquely prepare Five Percenter rappers for their mission to teach the black masses.

### Theological Beginnings: The Moorish Science Temple

Some scholars trace the beginnings of the Five Percent Nation and the Nation of Islam to Noble Drew Ali and the founding of the Moorish Science Temple of America. Noble Drew Ali was born Timothy Drew in 1886 in North Carolina. His childhood is mysterious, shrouded in oral histories of miracles predicting his great future. One such story tells of a wicked aunt throwing Noble Drew Ali into a fiery furnace, from which Allah saved him.[1] Some accounts maintain that he was the child of ex-slaves and was raised by Cherokee Indians after his parents died,[2] while others propose that his father was Moroccan and his mother was Cherokee.[3] The Moorish Orthodox Church claims that he was raised by Cherokee Indians and was later adopted into the Cherokee Nation.[4] Whatever the case, he is said to have worn a feather in his fez to honor his Cherokee roots.[5] According to some sources, Noble Drew Ali joined either a traveling circus or a band of gypsies in his youth.[6] Oral histories also suggest that he traveled to Egypt while still a teenager, and there studied with the "last priest of an ancient cult of High Magic," who accepted him as an adept.[7]

The exotic tales and mysteries of Noble Drew Ali's youth contrast starkly with the realities of black southern life in the post-Reconstruction era. In an age when black lives seemed to be worth little or nothing, survival alone might appear to be miraculous.[8] The best way to survive was to comply with the new Jim Crow laws, since physical resistance usually meant death.[9] Denied the basic rights of education, health care, suffrage, decent food and lodging, travel accommodations, and personal safety, many southern blacks could only imagine a better future. And for some, imagining a better future meant abandoning the mores of the south and fashioning new religious and cultural practices. Religion offered one means of escape, and spiritual leaders of any religious bent were highly prized in this tenuous time.[10] Noble Drew Ali's miraculous youth, exotic travels, and rise as a spiritual leader should thus be read as one man's attempt to carve a path out of oppression and disenfranchisement. The differences among the oral accounts of his life indicate how much was at stake in the formation of a black leader.

After his return from Egypt, Noble Drew Ali founded the first of his Moorish temples in Newark, New Jersey, calling this center "The Canaanite Temple."[11] He established his official headquarters, the Moorish Science Temple, in 1928 in Chicago, and soon opened other temples in Pittsburgh, Detroit, Baltimore, and other cities in the South and Midwest.[12] Codes of conduct for Moorish initiates were strict. As scholar and Moorish Orthodox exilarch Peter Lamborn Wilson (also known as Hakim Bey) writes, "Upon joining the Temple, converts were given new surnames—'Bey' or 'El' and told to wear their fezzes at all times. Meat, alcohol, and tobacco were forbidden, as were shaving, and the use of cosmetics and hair-straighteners, and morality was encouraged."[13] Noble Drew Ali instituted ceremonial parades and new holidays for his followers and offered products such as identity documents for Moorish citizens, herbal remedies and potions, and proper reading materials, including a weekly newspaper entitled *The Moorish Guide*.[14]

The essential text of Noble Drew Ali's teachings, *The Holy Koran of the Moorish Science Temple of America* (1927), is said to have roots in his Egyptian period.[15] (For purposes of clarity, throughout this study I will use the spelling "Koran" to refer to Noble Drew Ali's writings, and the spelling "Qur'an" to refer to the sacred Muslim text revealed to the Prophet Muhammad.) *The Holy Koran* draws heavily on the legacy of "classical" black nationalism and teaches a path to spiritual enlightenment based on Christian, Gnostic, Masonic, and Islamic doctrines.[16] Crucial to Noble Drew Ali's teachings is his theory of the origin of modern blacks. He taught that modern blacks are the descendants of ancient Moroccans, themselves the descendants of the Biblical prophetess Ruth, whose progeny settled the area known as Moab. According to Noble Drew Ali, the Moorish civilization at its height (around 1500 B.C.E.) extended from the area today known as Morocco to North, South, and Central America, encompassing even the mythical Atlantis.[17] The potency of this origin theory cannot be overestimated. Placing blacks in the Americas in pre-Columbian days gives them primacy of place over later colonists and slaveholders and justifies their demand for full rights in American society, a demand rarely honored in the segregated world of 1920s America.

Although Noble Drew Ali's doctrines and the subsequent teachings of the Nation of Islam and the Five Percent Nation have much in common, historians disagree on the level of influence Noble Drew Ali exerted on the beginnings of the Nation of Islam.[18] The Nation of Islam itself denies any historical ties with Noble Drew Ali.[19] Nation of Islam scholar Mattias Gardell gives perhaps the most nuanced account of what may have happened. As Gardell explains, the "Moorish Theory" is merely one of many theories developed to explain the teachings of the Nation of Islam. He cautions that "the creeds of the Moorish Science Temple and the Nation of Islam do have tenets in common, but these are better explained by reference to an exchange of ideas and the common roots in the black nationalist tradition, specifically the legacy of Marcus Garvey."[20] Indeed, many of Noble Drew Ali's "converts" had been followers of Marcus Garvey, the charismatic black nationalist leader of the early 1920s who preached a back-to-Africa message and purchased a shipping line to transport African Americans to their "homeland." Marcus Garvey's followers found in Noble Drew Ali's teachings a common core of black nationalism. Images of a glorious past and future for blacks, racial solidarity, and separatism infused the rhetoric of both leaders. Noble Drew Ali himself was highly influenced by Garvey and in fact refers to Garvey as his forerunner in chapter 48 of the *Holy Koran:*

> In these modern days there came a forerunner, who was divinely prepared by the great God-Allah and his name is Marcus Garvey, who did teach and warn the nations of the earth to prepare to meet the coming Prophet; who was to bring the true and divine Creed of Islam, and his name is Noble Drew Ali: who was prepared and sent to this earth by Allah, to teach the old time religion and the everlasting gospel to the sons of men.[21]

Noble Drew Ali considered himself heir to Garvey's black nationalist mantle, but whereas Garvey preached a message of physical repatriation to Africa, Noble Drew Ali wanted the "Asiatic Blackman" to gain full rights in American society rather than a new society in Africa.[22] Thus for Noble Drew Ali, repatriation was not physical but spiritual and political in nature.

Like many of the leaders of the Five Percent Nation's pre-history, Noble Drew Ali died under rather mysterious circumstances. After infighting among his followers led to a series of violent murders within his congregation in early 1929, Noble Drew Ali was apparently taken into police custody for questioning and died soon thereafter, perhaps because of a severe police beating. He could also have been assassinated. Peter Lamborn Wilson has suggested a third theory: that Noble Drew Ali was "made to 'disappear' by the police in collusion with the FBI."[23] Whatever the circumstances surrounding his death or disappearance, his congregation quickly divided into multiple factions, including one led by Sheik Timothy Givins El and another led by Wali D. Fard (also known as Wali Farad, W. D. Fard, and Wali Fard Muhammad).[24] The latter became the Temple of Islam, soon to be known as the Nation of Islam.

## The Nation of Islam: Early Years

As the founder of the Nation of Islam, the teacher of Elijah Muhammad, and—according to the Nation of Islam—God in person, Master Fard Muhammad, as he came to be known, is the key figure in the Nation of Islam's early history. Little is known of Fard's early years. Scholars have traced him to multiple possible birthplaces, including New Zealand, Barbados, Jamaica, Syria, Palestine, Turkey, and Portland, Oregon.[25] Some of Fard's earliest followers believed he was born in Mecca into the same tribe that gave birth to the Prophet Muhammad, the Quraysh tribe.[26] The Nation of Islam maintains that Master Fard Muhammad was born to an Asiatic Blackman[27] and a white Muslim woman in Mecca on 26 February 1877, and was Allah in person.[28] (Fard's birthday is now celebrated in the Nation of Islam as a holy day known as "Savior's Day.") Fard based his teachings on a belief in the primacy of the Blackman, although his own race and ethnicity were ambiguous: the Nation of Islam teaches that Fard was an Asiatic Blackman, but primary and secondary sources also describe him as "a mysterious White man of Turkish origins," "an Arab from Greater Syria," a "Palestinian Arab," and as having an "oriental cast of countenance."[29]

       Fard's mission to his "lost-found" brethren began in Detroit, one of several northern metropolises that boomed between the World Wars. (The unprecedented mass northern movement of southern blacks in those decades is known as the Great Migration.) Lynchings, poor living conditions, and agricultural disasters such as the boll weevil encouraged agrarian southern blacks to seek their fortunes in northern cities where jobs were plentiful. Detroit's history illustrates the effects of this mass migration. Historian Claude Andrew Clegg notes that whereas Detroit's African American population numbered 5,741 in 1910, by 1920 it had expanded to 40,838, and by 1930 had swelled again to 120,066. Nearly all the new migrants took blue-collar jobs, many in Detroit's automotive-related industries.[30] The Great Depression brought unexpected unemployment and a new form of poverty to the migrants, many of whom were separated from family members still in the south and thus lacked the family networks necessary to survive economic hardship. Bereft of jobs and hope, Detroit's African American population was particularly ripe for Fard's teachings. He peddled cloth and other "African" goods door to door in black Detroit neighborhoods, using his trade as a salesman to gain entry into homes and reach out to his "lost-found nation." He founded his first Temple of Islam in Detroit and called his ever-growing number of followers the Nation of Islam. According to one source, Fard had amassed some eight thousand followers in Detroit by 1933.[31]

Noble Drew Ali had preached that every man should "worship under his own vine and fig tree," promoting a return to the "Old-Time Religion" (that is, Noble Drew Ali's version of Islam) for blacks but tolerating Christianity and other religions. Fard, however, took a violent stance against Christianity and other so-called white religions, teaching that "Christianity is a tool in the hands of the White slave masters to control the minds of black people."[32] Furthermore, under the leadership of Fard the spirit of black American Islam evolved from joyful race pride into a more aggressive black supremacism. Fard introduced the doctrine that whites are devils, a doctrine that would play a significant role in the teachings of Elijah Muhammad. Indeed, most of the doctrines associated with the Nation of Islam originated with Fard. According to Prince-A-Cuba, who claims to be associated with the Five Percent Nation, Fard designed secret lessons and rituals to inspire race pride in his followers.

> [The] infrastructure was built upon Fard's ideological foundation known as the "Secret Ritual," which, arranged in a question-and-answer format, became better known as the "Lost-Found Muslim Lessons" or simply as "the lessons." Within these lessons were the basic elements of an ancient mystery school. It involved secrecy from outsiders; an esoteric ritual containing keys for recognition between fellow members; a cohesive world view; and a tradition that could be explained only to initiates. Central to these teachings were the knowledge of self and the Black man's godhood. According to these teachings, the Black man was by nature divine, and in fact was the original man, ancestor of the human race.[33]

Fard drew freely from the Bible and the Qur'an and disseminated his teachings in the 154 lessons, which were orally transmitted as the "Secret Ritual of the Nation of Islam," and in his written *Teaching for the Lost Found Nation of Islam in a Mathematical Way.*[34]

The Nation of Islam teaches that Fard summoned his followers shortly before his mysterious disappearance in 1934 to tell them, "you don't need me anymore, hear Elijah," thus anointing (the honorable) Elijah Muhammad (né Robert Poole) as his successor.[35] Nevertheless, Fard's congregation again divided, this time into factions led by Abdul Muhammad and Elijah Muhammad.[36] Whereas Abdul Muhammad taught that Fard was a prophet of Allah, Elijah Muhammad and his congregation believed that in addition to bringing the truth of the Blackman's self, Fard was actually the latest incarnation of Allah.[37]

Elijah Muhammad brought his congregation closer to mainstream Islam, yet, as many scholars insist, his teachings are anything but orthodox. Elijah Muhammad presented a new origin theory to his Nation that was based on his study with Fard, teaching that blacks are the "Original" people. He spoke of an evil scientist called Yacub (or Yakub), who created the white race over six thousand years ago by means of grafting, or genetic engineering. Yacub's intention was to create a race of people wholly devoid of divinity, a race of pure evil. In order to create the white race Yacub bred for light skin (a recessive trait), and in the process of lightening black skin he also diluted the divine essence that is inherent in blackness.[38] Elijah Muhammad also taught an interrelated Gnostic doctrine, a belief in black divinity. As Gardell explains,

> There is an element of divinity a priori in each black man and woman, who "are born genetically to manifest characteristics of God." The human brain is a transmitter, a receiver of electrical energy or the power of God. If man submits to God, the power of God will begin to manifest in man, as "all Muslims are Allahs." . . . As in Gnosticism, this is not understood as reincarnation but as *representation* of the divine or the diabolic, as realization of embedded true nature and *actualization* of dormant potentials.[39]

Elijah Muhammad recorded his doctrines for his followers in several texts, including *The Supreme Wisdom: Solution to the So-Called NEGROES' Problem* (1957); *The Supreme Wisdom, Volume Two* (ca. 1960?); *Message to the Blackman in America* (1965), considered the most complete record of his teachings; *How to Eat to Live* (1967); *How to Eat to Live, Book Two* (1972); *The Fall of America* (1973); *Our Saviour Has Arrived* (1974); and *The Flag of Islam* (1974).[40] His congregation grew rapidly throughout the 1950s, prompting the construction of more temples and the appointment of ministers—such as Minister Malcolm X— to run them under Elijah Muhammad's guidance.

The rise of Malcolm X within the Nation of Islam and his subsequent turn to orthodox Islam after his *hajj* (his pilgrimage to Mecca) has been recorded in many other sources and need not be recounted in detail here.[41] Yet a short discussion of Malcolm X's last few years in the Nation of Islam will shed light on the beginnings of the Five Percent Nation. Malcolm X was appointed the first national representative of Elijah Muhammad in 1963, becoming Elijah Muhammad's primary spokesman in addition to his role as minister of Temple #7 in Harlem. Soon thereafter, a young philosopher from Malcolm X's temple, Clarence 13X (né Clarence Smith Jowers), left the Nation of Islam and founded the Five Percent Nation, later also known as the Nation of Gods and Earths.[42] (Five Percenter men are called Gods, and Five Percenter women are Earths.) Clarence 13X's departure was only one of several upheavals rocking the Nation of Islam in the early 1960s. In the summer of 1963, rumors of Elijah Muhammad's affairs with several of his secretaries and of the "love children" these affairs produced reached the ears of Malcolm X (as well as the general public, thanks to FBI leaks to the media), causing Malcolm X to question his mentor for the first time. In addition to creating a rift between Elijah Muhammad and his national representative, Elijah Muhammad's indiscretions contributed to a general dissension within the rank and file of the Nation of Islam. By the end of 1963, Elijah Muhammad had silenced Malcolm X as a result of the latter's remarks after the assassination of President John F. Kennedy, and by late February 1964, Malcolm X had left the Nation of Islam.[43]

Further complicating the situation, Elijah Muhammad's son Wallace, later his successor, waffled between orthodox Islam and his father's teachings throughout the 1960s and into the early 1970s. Wallace was widely considered his father's heir apparent. His repeated challenges to his father's teachings and subsequent cycles of suspension from and reinstatement in the Nation must have caused tension not only between father and son but also within the general congregation.[44] Furthermore, the spirit of dissension had already produced splinter groups prior to 1963. In 1958, for example, Ernest 2X McGhee left Temple #7 to found the black Hanafi Muslims.[45]

## "Arise You Gods!": Clarence 13X and the Five Percent Nation

No one knows for sure why Clarence 13X left the Nation of Islam, but given its state of affairs in the early 1960s, the splintering of the Nation of Islam should come as no surprise. Some scholars maintain that Clarence 13X left for theological reasons, disagreeing with Elijah Muhammad that Fard was Allah incarnate.[46] According to this theory, Clarence recognized an inherent contradiction in the teaching of the Nation of Islam that Fard was Allah in the flesh: since Fard was probably Arab and not black, he logically could not be Allah, since the Nation of Islam also teaches that the Creator is a Blackman. Further, the Nation of Islam teaches that there is no "mystery god," that God exists in the flesh. Yet initiates were encouraged to think of Fard as Allah, even though Fard no longer had a physical presence. Clarence 13X, entrusted with instructing other student ministers, began to share his ideas with his students until caught in the act by Captain Joseph, the head of the Fruit of Islam, the military arm of the Nation of Islam.[47] Reprimanded for teaching heresy, Clarence 13X left to begin his own sect.[48]

Other accounts of Clarence 13X's split with the Nation of Islam are far less idealistic. According to "insider" Prince-A-Cuba, "the leading rumor of the cause of Clarence's expulsion was his admitted love for playing craps."[49] Barry Gottehrer, aide to New York City mayor John Lindsay during the 1960s and a personal friend of Clarence 13X, suggests that he was expelled for violating the Nation of Islam's rules against both gambling and drinking.[50] Marital problems could also have prompted his leaving.[51] Whatever the cause for Clarence 13X's departure from the Nation of Islam, his followers soon believed that he was the latest incarnation of Allah in the flesh, and they began to call him Father Allah.[52]

According to media accounts, the early years of the Five Percent Nation were marked by gang-like activity and violent resistance to the police and other city officials. Newspaper articles alerted the New York public to the Five Percenter presence with alarming headlines. A 1965 article entitled "Harlem Hit by Five Percenters," published in the black-owned weekly newspaper *New York Amsterdam News*, described the Five Percent Nation as a new hate group. Claiming that the Five Percent Nation had between fifty and seventy-five young members, the newspaper article reported "growing concern [among] police and some community circles over rumored threat being expressed by a new young Harlem hate group which called themselves the 'Five Percenters.' "[53] The article further stated that members of the Five Percent Nation had received some Muslim training and were proficient in karate. (It is, in fact, highly likely that these early Five Percenters both were familiar with Muslim doctrine and had received martial arts training. As former members of the Nation of Islam, all of the early Five Percenters would have received some Muslim training as part of their initiation. Furthermore, Father Allah's male followers would have been obligated to join the Fruit of Islam, and all Fruit of Islam initiates were taught karate and self-defense.) Adding to the deliberately disquieting rhetoric, Clarence 13X was quoted as saying, "if we don't get some poverty money to build our own Mosque we're going to kill all white-skinned babies, bomb homes of Negro policemen and riot."[54]

Another contemporary article began with a provocative rhetorical question: "is there a new hate group in Harlem dedicated to violence against white people?" This article repeated the purported quotation from Clarence 13X and added a disturbing report of a violent outburst by Five Percenters: "The name 'Five Percenters' first was aired publicly last May when black Nationalist Clarence Smith allegedly led a group of 150 followers on a window smashing sortie across 125th St. in which one Negro man was beaten with a pole."[55]

Such sensationalistic journalism was at least partly fueled by law enforcement agencies. As Gardell effectively documents in his study of the Nation of Islam, throughout the 1960s the FBI and other law enforcement agencies infiltrated black religious and nationalist organizations, including the Nation of Islam and the Five Percent Nation, under J. Edgar Hoover's direction and the auspices of COINTELPRO (the counterintelligence program). Gardell also tracks the FBI's many attempts to cause dissension within the Nation of Islam by "leaking" invented rumors to the press.[56] In 1965, the FBI opened official inquiries into the Five Percent Nation, instructing its New York office to begin an investigation, identify the Nation's leaders, and determine its "policy."[57] Subsequent reports yielded inflammatory "data." One FBI file, for example, characterized the Five Percenters as "a 'mysterious armed group of Negro youth' who were 'prepared to die' fighting white supremacy."[58] Another report, dated 4 November 1965, described the Five Percenters as "a particularly vicious type of street gang in New York City composed of Negro Youths who have found in the Muslim form of indoctrination a mysterious ideology that seems to unite and inspire them."[59] In their various reports, FBI agents also attempted to link the Five Percenters with radical groups and communist organizations such as the Fair Play for Cuba Committee, the Revolutionary Action Movement, the Workers World Party (formerly part of the Socialist Workers Party), and even the Black Arts Repertory Theater, headed by poet, playwright, and activist LeRoi Jones (Amiri Baraka).[60] Such allegations were clearly intended to both defame the Five Percent Nation and justify Hoover's investigation.

As the leader of the Five Percent Nation, Clarence 13X also faced the FBI's scrutiny. His files include a wealth of information concerning his birthplace (given as Danville, Virginia), his medical history (including a bout of syphilis), his military service in Japan and Korea as a light weapons infantryman from 1952 to 1954, and his many military decorations (the list includes a Korean Service Medal with one Bronze Service Star, a Combat Infantryman's Badge, a Presidential Unit Citation, a United Nations Service Medal, and the National Defense Service Medal). Clarence was sent to Matteawan State Hospital for the Criminally Insane in March of 1966, following his arrest and conviction of marijuana possession and second-degree assault in June of 1965. Physicians at Matteawan diagnosed him with paranoid schizophrenia and delusions of religious grandeur, presumably because of his claims to be Allah incarnate.[61] Shortly after Clarence's release from Matteawan on 6 March 1967, J. Edgar Hoover circulated a memo declaring him (under the name Clarence Edward Smith) to be a danger to the president, given his history of mental illness, his violent past, and his membership in a "group or organization inimical to U.S." (see figure 1.1).

As these early investigations suggest, the Five Percent Nation has long been considered a gang. Even today, the majority of recent journalistic depictions of the Five Percent Nation discuss its members' incarceration rates or gang-like

FD-376 (Rev. 11-12-65)

UNITED STATES DEPARTMENT OF JUSTICE CONFIDENTIA

FEDERAL BUREAU OF INVESTIGATION

WASHINGTON, D.C. 20535

*In Reply, Please Refer to*
*File No.*   **Bufile 100-444636**   **May 16, 1967**

Director   **NYfile 100-150520**
United States Secret Service
Department of the Treasury
Washington, D. C. 20220

Dear Sir:                          Re:   **Clarence Edward Smith**

The information furnished herewith concerns an individual who is believed to be
covered by the agreement between the FBI and Secret Service concerning Presidential protection, and to fall within the category or categories checked.

1. ☐ Has attempted or threatened bodily harm to any government official or employee,
including foreign government officials residing in or planning an imminent visit to the
U. S., because of his official status.

2. ☐ Has attempted or threatened to redress a grievance against any public official by other
than legal means.

3. ☒ Because of background is potentially dangerous; or has been identified as member or
participant in communist movement; or has been under active investigation as member
of other group or organization inimical to U. S.

4. ☐ U. S. citizens or residents who defect from the U. S. to countries in the Soviet or
Chinese Communist blocs and return.

5. ☒ Subversives, ultrarightists, racists and fascists who meet one or more of the following
criteria:

    (a) ☒ Evidence of emotional instability (including unstable residence and
        employment record) or irrational or suicidal behavior;

    (b) ☐ Expressions of strong or violent anti-U. S. sentiment;

    (c) ☒ Prior acts (including arrests or convictions) or conduct or statements
        indicating a propensity for violence and antipathy toward good order
        and government.

6. ☐ Individuals involved in illegal bombing or illegal bomb-making.

Photograph ☒ has been furnished   ☐ enclosed   ☐ is not available
☐ may be available through _____

Very truly yours,

John Edgar Hoover
Director

1 - Special Agent in Charge (Enclosure(s) 1 (RM)
   U. S. Secret Service , NYC

CONFIDENTIAL

Enclosure(s) 1 (RM) *(Upon removal of classified enclosures, if any, this transmittal form
becomes UNCLASSIFIED.)*

Figure 1.1. Letter signed by F.B.I. director J. Edgar Hoover, declaring
Clarence Edward Smith (Clarence 13X) to be a threat to the president.
From F.B.I. file 100-444636.

activities.[62] Five Percenters themselves, however, consistently rebutted (and today continue to fight) the media's sensational treatment of their community. Two Five Percenters, God Allah Shah and God Adew Allah, defended themselves and their Nation in a 1976 article entitled "In the Defense of the Five Percenters," in which they argued that the media had blown the violence of a few members out of proportion.

> Once again the tides of public opinion are being shrewdly and diabolically turned against the Nation of the Five Percenters. Three young men are apprehended for alleged charges of criminal mischief and because one bears the emblem of the Five Percenters, all members of the Nation are automatically condemned as thieves, murderers, mischief makers[;] does this not seem strange? Does this not clearly disclose the diabolical scheme systematically designed to deliberately injure the reputation of the Five Percenters in the Black community, by making and printing false accusations about the Five Percenters through the media of television and newspapers[?][63]

The rise of the Five Percent Nation—and the reactions of the media and law enforcement to the group—must be seen within the context of the racially charged early and mid-1960s, an era marked by violent upheaval in major metropolitan areas throughout the United States. Riots protesting racial inequality broke out in cities throughout New York, New Jersey, Illinois, and Pennsylvania in the summer of 1964, and were followed by the 1965 Watts uprising and some additional 150 riots reported in 1967.[64] In an effort to head off violence in his city, New York City mayor John V. Lindsay decided to send an emissary, Barry Gottehrer, to the Five Percent Nation. Gottehrer, head of the mayor's Urban Action Task Force, was charged with the task of establishing a relationship with the leader of the new "gang," and with troubleshooting in case of unrest or upheaval.[65] Gottehrer later published an account of the two years he spent with Clarence 13X, entitled *The Mayor's Man,* in which he describes his initial mission: "Allah [Clarence 13X] and his group had a reputation for being unreachable, anti-white criminals. . . . The police had told us that if we could reach him, we really would be doing something."[66] Once he met with Father Allah, however, Gottehrer discovered that he was not violent ("Allah wasn't sounding like a revolutionary"), but was dedicated to his community's well-being, asking Gottehrer for help in educating his followers.[67] As a gesture of good faith, Gottehrer organized city-funded picnics and plane trips for Father Allah's young disciples.

In 1967, with Gottehrer's assistance, Clarence 13X opened a street academy in Harlem—Mecca, in Five Percenter parlance[68]—using a handful of teachers hired by the Urban League. The establishment of a school—known as the Allah School in Mecca—dedicated to Five Percenter theology followed a pattern established by the Nation of Islam, which opened the first two elementary schools dedicated to the Nation of Islam's teachings in 1932 (Detroit) and 1934 (Chicago), calling these schools Universities of Islam.[69] While the Allah School was originally intended to be a general educational institution (as were the Nation of Islam's Universities of Islam), it soon became only a place for informal religious instruction. As Gottehrer remembers,

> The academic curriculum took a beating from the start, as the Five Percenters had their own ideas. They believed that the most important thing is to have knowledge of self and, as everybody is godly, so everybody is Allah. As a consequence, they felt free to reject as much as they accepted from the teachers the Urban League hired. . . . The Five Percenters were probably no more dogmatic than extremely religious Jews or Catholics or fundamentalist Christians, but they were no less so, and eventually a different solution had to be found to the problem of their education. The kids attended different street academies, a few to each school, for their more conventional education, while Allah [Clarence 13X] kept his store front open as a place for kids to study their religion or just hang out.[70]

Although the Allah School in Mecca did not provide a general education, initiates learned doctrine and religious lessons there, consequently honing the verbal skills so essential to the dissemination of Five Percenter doctrine through oral catechism.[71] Eventually other street academies opened in Brooklyn, Queens, and the Bronx, and each of these schools has served as a meeting place for the general membership as well as a locus of indoctrination. The Allah School in Mecca still serves as the Nation's unofficial headquarters.

Clarence 13X was slain on 13 June 1969; his murder has yet to be solved. Gottehrer reports contemporary rumors that Father Allah was assassinated by the Nation of Islam, rumors that nearly incited a civil war between the Nation of Islam and the Five Percenters.[72] A report filed by an unidentified FBI agent in the New York office proposes that Allah, Charles Kenyatta (leader of the Mau Maus), and Anthony Reed, Jr., were all shot by a small group of extortionists associated with an organization known as the Fair Play Committee. Supposedly, Reed was hired by the Committee to shoot Kenyatta and Allah because they were working for the mayor, and then Reed was killed because he "knew too much."[73] These theories, however, were never substantiated. Five Percenters themselves are divided in their theories concerning Father Allah's death. Whereas some believe his death was ordered by the CIA, legendary MC Rakim Allah believes the rumors of Nation of Islam involvement. Culture Freedom (of the hip-hop crew Poor Righteous Teachers) simply offers, "there are a lot of things that the physical eye didn't bear witness to."[74] Clarence 13X's biographer Beloved Allah believes that those closest to Clarence 13X—Five Percenters—are the most likely suspects: "like Jesus, [Father Allah] could even have been betrayed from amongst one of his own; those who are closest to you can hurt you the most. Allah always said that the only one that can ever hurt me is a Five Percenter."[75]

Since Father Allah's death there has been no titular leader of the Five Percent

Nation. Allah's right-hand man Justice (also known as Jesus) would seem to have been Allah's obvious successor. Gottehrer suggests, however, that Justice did not have the strength of character to carry on Allah's mission, noting, "Justice was, at heart, timid . . . he wasn't the man to take charge of five hundred tough street kids."[76] Beloved Allah maintains that Father Allah never intended to appoint a successor, even though he had positioned several of his "first born," his earliest disciples, to take over after his eventual death: "Allah had told his Five Percenters before he left them that his death would born [i.e., give birth to] the Nation of Gods and Earths. That they did not need a leader because they were all leaders of themselves and their family, and when black people have leaders the devil can easily execute them to derail the movement."[77] Rapper Lakim Shabazz agrees with this theory: "there's a big fear to put one man in charge. . . . I feel that Father Allah taught us we are all leaders unto ourselves."[78]

Within five years of Father Allah's death, hip-hop culture was forming in New York City's African American and Latino neighborhoods; Five Percenters quickly became part of the new cultural movement. The pairing of rap and the Five Percent Nation was perhaps inevitable. The Five Percent Nation, essentially a youth movement, found resonance in hip-hop, another youth-oriented culture. Furthermore, both matured in New York City, taking root first in Brooklyn, Harlem, and the Bronx. Pioneering hip-hop DJ Kool Herc remembers Five Percenters taking part in hip-hop parties as early as the mid-1970s. Recalling the heavy gang presence at early hip-hop parties, Kool Herc says, "a lot of Five Percenters . . . used to come to my party. . . . you might call them 'peace guards,' and they used to hold me down [promise me protection]: 'Yo Herc, don't worry about it.' So we was just havin' a good time."[79] In other words, even in the earliest days of hip-hop, the Five Percenters were regarded as an integral part of the hip-hop scene, recognized for their collective ability to keep gatherings peaceful. Rap first gained national attention in 1979, and by 1987 the first MC to openly claim membership in the Five Percent Nation—Rakim Allah—had appeared on the commercial rap scene. The year 1987 also saw the emergence of MCs and crews faithful to the Nation of Islam, revitalized under Louis Farrakhan's leadership. Public Enemy, the rap collective featuring lead MC Chuck D, "trickster" Flavor Flav, and a back-up militia crew, all faithful to the Nation of Islam, produced its first album, *Yo! Bum Rush the Show,* in 1987. Public Enemy, seminal for so many reasons, is largely responsible for bringing the Nation of Islam and Louis Farrakhan to the attention of American youth. Chuck D has made no mystery of his mission: "I try to bring the youth into a level where they'll be interested to even begin to get into what the minister's speaking and the teachings of Elijah Muhammad, and the reason for self sufficiency in America, and the curiosity to learn more about themselves."[80]

The schism between the Nation of Islam and the Five Percent Nation has been bridged under the leadership of Minister Louis Farrakhan, whom Five Percenters greatly respect.[81] Furthermore, the rise of conscious rap in general and Five Percenter rap in particular must be in part credited to Farrakhan, who has recognized the significant role youth will play in the future of his organization. One of Farrakhan's key steps was appointing Prince Akeem, an MC, to the position of minister of youth. Recognizing that "our voice is for today's time,"[82] Prince Akeem has done much to establish connections between the Nation of Islam and the hip-hop community. Minister Farrakhan has himself taken great interest in hip-hop's role in youth culture, and was invited to give the keynote speech at a recent hip-hop summit organized and sponsored by one of rap's leading moguls, Russell Simmons.[83] Billed as the first annual Hip-Hop Summit, the gathering took place at the New York City Hilton Hotel over the weekend of 12–13 June 2001. Throughout his address, Farrakhan encouraged MCs to provide leadership and asked those present, "will you accept your responsibility as a leader, and as a teacher, and lead and guide the youth?"[84] Supported by Farrakhan's claim that "one rap song is worth more than a thousand of my speeches,"[85] rappers associated with both the Five Percent Nation and the Nation of Islam are thus positioned as missionaries, key players in the Black Muslim goal to "civilize the uncivilized."

# 2

# The Five Percenter "Way of Life"

The Five Percent Nation may be unknown to most Americans, yet within hip-hop culture, Five Percenters have long been an active presence. Any "old-school hip-hop head" (long-time fan of hip-hop music and culture) will speak knowingly of the "Gods" and may even have passing familiarity with basic Five Percenter doctrines, yet the details of Five Percenter theology—an idiosyncratic mix of black nationalist rhetoric, Kemetic (ancient Egyptian) symbolism, Gnosticism, Masonic mysticism, and esoteric numerology—are not widely understood. In this chapter I examine Five Percenter theology in depth, taking into account the lessons Clarence 13X inherited from his forerunners and brought with him from the Nation of Islam, as well as the new lessons Father Allah devised for his new Nation. Because Five Percenters believe that what they practice is not a religion but a "way of life," the second half of this chapter considers the impact of Five Percenter theology on daily life. The chapter concludes with a consideration of the Nation's most effective methods for bringing their message to the masses, including hip-hop music and culture.

Readers should be aware that as an outsider, an "etic" observer, my perspective is limited, subject to the availability of sources, and influenced no doubt by my own theological upbringing and the specific consultants whose views inform this book. Throughout this and subsequent chapters I quote liberally from consultants, Five Percenters who generously shared their experiences and opinions with me. I am deeply grateful to these consultants for enriching my understanding of their way of life. Quotations from my consultants should be read as authoritative personal opinions and not as representative of an entire body of thought; as I will explain in the following pages, Five Percenter theology is a highly individualized matter.

I also draw extensively from Five Percenter lessons, which I have gathered from a number of printed and on-line sources. As far as I know, the lessons have not been compiled in a single place and published for study.[1] In the early stages of this project, I envisioned including the complete lessons as an appendix. One of my consultants strongly suggested, however, that doing so would be a disservice both to the Five Percent Nation and to my readers. In the Five Percent Nation the lessons are not considered secret rites; they are tools. In their proper cultural context, the tools are handed down as part of an enculturation process that includes mentoring by older Gods and Earths. If not accompanied by the cultural knowledge of how to interpret them, the lessons are simply words ripe for misunderstanding. In my consultant's opinion, printing the lessons in full would rob readers of the opportunity to encounter them within their cultural context and could also open the Nation to an even greater number of harmful attacks. To honor my consultant's advice, in the following discussion (and in the chapters that follow) I quote complete lessons only when necessary to clarify specific theological points.

## Lessons

Clarence 13X and his followers may have split from the Nation of Islam for theological reasons, yet doctrinal differences between the two groups are few. Initiates in the Nation of Islam—known as "Lost-Founds"—learn doctrine through a series of lessons that use a question-and-answer format, like a catechism. Initiates must know both questions and answers by rote and be able to explain each lesson in order to complete a stage.[2] The series begins with the "Student Enrollment Lesson," ten questions and answers concerning the population of various ethnic groups, the measurements of the earth, and the origins of mankind; completion of this stage earns the student his X. (The letter X replaces the initiate's last name, considered to be his slave name. X is used because it mathematically represents the unknown: in this case, the unknown original family name of the initiate. In the Nation of Islam's early days, an initiate could choose to retain his or her X through future stages, or petition Elijah Muhammad for a new, "original" name.) Initiates then move on to "Actual Facts," eighteen questions and answers concerning the features and measurements of the earth. "Actual Facts" are followed by "English Lesson no. C1," a series of thirty-six questions detailing Master Fard Muhammad's mission. Finally, initiates move to the two-part "Lost-Found Moslem Lessons." Part one consists of fourteen questions, and part two of forty questions; together they concentrate on geography, the history of the races, and the coming Armageddon.[3]

Five Percenters use many of the same lessons in a different order, with additional lessons of their own devising (see figure 2.1 for a comparison). They begin with two lessons not included in the Nation of Islam's instruction: the "Science of Supreme Mathematics," and the "Supreme Alphabet."[4] Initiates then move on to the same "Student Enrollment Lesson" used in the Nation of

| Nation of Islam Lessons | Five Percent Nation Lessons |
|---|---|
| Student Enrollment Lesson | Supreme Mathematics |
| Actual Facts | Supreme Alphabet |
| English Lesson No. C1 | Student Enrollment Lesson |
| Lost-Found Lessons (parts 1 and 2) | English Lesson No. C1 |
| | Lost-Found Lessons (parts 1 and 2) |
| | Actual Facts |
| | Solar Facts |

**Figure 2.1. Nation of Islam and Five Percent Nation lessons**

Islam, followed by "English Lesson no. C1" and the "Lost-Found Lessons." The "Lost-Found Lessons" are followed by two final lessons: "Actual Facts" (also borrowed from the Nation of Islam) and "Solar Facts" (original with the Five Percent Nation). Five Percenters thus learn the same history, geography, origin theories, and eschatology as the Nation of Islam, but the re-ordering of lessons and the addition of new lessons suggest different spiritual priorities in the Five Percent Nation. Specifically, by beginning their training with the "Science of Supreme Mathematics" and the "Supreme Alphabet" and ending with "Solar Facts," Five Percenters underscore the significance of science and numbers in their theology.

Clarence 13X and his right-hand man, Justice, began the Five Percent Nation's emphasis on numbers with their invention of the Science of Supreme Mathematics and of its counterpart, the Supreme Alphabet. At some point in the history of the Nation of Gods and Earths, symbolic significance was attached to specific numbers (see figure 2.2).[5] According to Beloved Allah, Father Allah and Justice devised the Supreme Mathematics and Supreme Alphabet in order to teach the youth "how to break down and form profound relationships between significant experiences within life," including "the meaning of their names, age (degree), why life was so hard and cold for the blackman and other significant facts of life."[6] As a result, Five Percenters believe that the Science of Supreme Mathematics is the key to understanding man's relationship to the universe. Indeed, the ultimate way to prove that something does not make sense in Five Percenter logic is to proclaim—as does Lord Jamar in Brand Nubian's song "Ain't No Mystery"—"Mathematically that just don't go."

Once Gods and Earths (Five Percenter men and women) have committed the numbers and their meanings to memory, they use the numbers to creatively "show and prove" facts and ideas. For example, in an interview with social scientist Yusef Nuruddin, Five Percenter Sincere Allah gives the following explanation of Degree Five of the Student Enrollment Lesson:

The Five Percenter "Way of Life"

```
1 = Knowledge
2 = Wisdom
3 = Understanding
4 = Culture or Freedom
5 = Power or Refinement
6 = Equality
7 = God
8 = Build-Destroy
9 = Born
0 = Cipher
```

**Figure 2.2. Science of Supreme Mathematics**

Then the fifth degree says, "What is the area in square miles of the planet earth?" The area in square miles of the planet earth is 196,940,000 square miles. Now, the way I see that right, only showing and proving right, like, you give me a piece of paper I could show you, like, years in it. In the 196,940,000 square miles, you've got the year 1960 in there; you've got the year 1964 and 1969. Now, the way I see it is when Allah—Knowledge was born by equality, born back to the culture, to the cipher [this is the numerological analysis according to the Supreme Mathematics; knowledge = 1, equality = 6, born = 9, culture = 4, cipher = 0, i.e., 1960 = knowledge–born–equality–cipher] only showing and proving that year 1964 when Almighty God Allah (Clarence 13X) when he left the temple, you know, in 1964 he showed and proved that the black man was God.[7]

What Sincere Allah does here in casual conversation with his interviewer is standard practice in Five Percenter circles (or "ciphers"). He methodically applies the meanings he has learned from the Science of Supreme Mathematics to the fifth Student Enrollment lesson. For outsiders, the lesson has no obvious bearing on Clarence 13X's life, but for Five Percenters, numbers reveal hidden relationships between all levels of existence.

Every stage of Five Percenter training emphasizes the relationship between numbers and cosmology. Initiates learn by rote the distance between the earth and the sun, the circumference of the earth, and the amount of water and land on the earth (among many other measurements). Each initiate should be able to "show and prove" these scientific facts through the manipulation of numbers. The lessons known as "Solar Facts," which simply state the distances of the planets from the sun (see figure 2.3), are particularly ripe for manipulation. Like all lessons, "Solar Facts" are merely a starting point for the revelation of higher truths, as a Five Percenter scholar named Divine Ruler Equality Allah illustrates on the Five Percent Nation's Website.[8] He begins by finding the internal sums of

Mercury is 36,000,000 miles from the Sun.

Venus is 67,000,000 miles from the Sun.

Earth is 93,000,000 miles from the Sun.

Mars is 142,000,000 miles from the Sun.

Jupiter is 483,000,000 miles from the Sun.

Saturn is 886,000,000 miles from the Sun.

Uranus is 1,783,000,000 miles from the Sun.

Neptune is 2,793,000,000 miles from the Sun.

Pluto (Platoon) is 3,680,000,000 miles from the Sun.

**Figure 2.3. Solar Facts**

each planet's distance from the sun: for instance, Mercury's distance from the sun is 36,000,000 miles, and when the digits are added they produce 9 (born). Similarly, Venus's distance from the sun produces 4 (culture or freedom); Earth's distance from the sun produces 3 (understanding); Mars's distance from the sun produces 7 (God); Jupiter's distance from the sun produces 6 (equality); Saturn's distance from the sun produces 4 (culture or freedom); Uranus's distance from the sun produces 1 (knowledge); Neptune's distance from the sun produces 3 (understanding); and Pluto's distance from the sun produces 8 (build–destroy). He then adds these internal sums again ($9 + 4 + 3 + 7 + 6 + 4 + 1 + 3 + 8 = 45; 4 + 5 = 9$) and produces 9 (born). This final internal sum of 9 holds symbolic significance for Divine Ruler Equality Allah because, as he points out, "this is also equivalent to the Sum of the Mathematics" ($1 + 2 + 3 + 4 + 5 + 6 + 7 + 8 + 9 = 45; 4 + 5 = 9$). Divine Ruler Equality Allah's point here is that the Science of Supreme Mathematics must be a valid system because it is perfectly aligned with the workings of the universe. He goes on to justify why there is life only on Earth by explaining that the Earth is the only planet to have a distance from the sun that "borns" (produces) the same number as its relative position from the sun. That is, Earth is the third planet from the sun, and its distance from the sun reveals understanding, or three, through internal sums.

Icons of the Nation of Gods and Earths capitalize on the relationship between numerology and cosmology. The Universal Flag of the Nation of Gods and Earths, for example, features a number 7, as well as the sun, the moon, and a star: here, the number 7 indicates both God and man, while the combination of the sun, moon, and star represents the basic building block of the nation, the family unit of man, woman, and child (see figure 2.4).[9] Thus the harmony of celestial bodies is mirrored in the harmony of the family.

Figure 2.4. Universal Flag of the Five Percent Nation

The flag and its meaning are ready symbols for use in lyrics. Poor Righteous Teachers make use of this symbol in "Strictly Ghetto": "The sun, the seven, the moon, and the star / Supremely shows and proves who we are." A more complete treatment is found in King Sun's song "Universal Flag," which "breaks down" the flag's symbolic significance, devoting a verse each to the sun (man), moon (woman), and star (child). "Universal Flag" ends with a rousing didactic challenge: "are you able to show and prove on this flag that you bear?"

In keeping with Clarence 13X's emphasis on mathematical truths, the Five Percent Nation draws both its name and its identity from mathematical percentages found in Lost-Found Lesson no. 2, questions 14 through 16:

14. Who are the 85 percent? The uncivilized people; poison animal eaters; slaves from mental death and power; people who do not know who the Living God is, or their origin in this world and who worship that direction but are hard to lead in the right direction.

15. Who are the 10 percent? The rich slave-makers of the poor, who teach the poor lies to believe: that the Almighty, True and Living God is a spook and cannot be seen by the physical eye; otherwise known as the bloodsuckers of the poor.

16. Who are the 5 percent? They are the poor righteous teachers who do not believe in the teachings of the 10 percent and are all-wise and know who the Living God is and teach that the Living God is the Son of Man, the Supreme Being, or the Black Man of Asia, and teach Freedom, Justice and Equality to all the human family of the planet Earth; otherwise known as civilized people, also as Muslims and Muslim Sons.[10]

Five Percenters are thus those who have knowledge of self and are charged with sharing that knowledge with the 85 percent. In their own words, Five Percenters must "civilize the uncivilized."

For Gods and Earths, numbers not only unlock the mysterious scientific workings of the universe, but also provide a way to understand the "true" meanings of words. The Science of Supreme Mathematics is typically used in conjunction with an alphabetic system known as the Supreme Alphabet, in which every letter of the alphabet is assigned a mystical meaning, or sometimes several (see figure 2.5). The meaning of individual words can therefore be determined by treating words as acronyms and "adding" together the meaning of each letter to find the "true" meaning of the word. As Nuruddin demonstrates, "Five Percenters illustrate that the black man is divine by unfolding the secret meaning of the word 'man': My Almighty Name. This human/divine relationship is further corroborated by unveiling the name of Allah which means *Arm Leg Leg Arm Head*."[11] In other words, in "breaking down" the word "Allah" to mean "*Arm Leg Leg Arm Head*," Allah is given human form, described by making a transit of the body. Describing Allah in human form is consistent with the Five Percenter belief that each black man is divine. As examples from Five Percenter rap lyrics will illustrate in chapter 3, Five Percenters do not limit themselves only to the original meanings ascribed to each letter but instead creatively apply the spirit of the system to find meaning.

Although the Science of Supreme Mathematics and the Supreme Alphabet are new systems, Clarence 13X's interest in numerology finds a precedent in an ancient Muslim interest in cosmology and numerology.[12] The Supreme Alphabet takes as its model the spiritual science *Hurufa-i-jay-Hurufa-Ab-jay,* an Arabic science of interpreting mystical meanings from each letter of the Arabic alphabet; the Five Percent Nation's version simply uses the Roman alphabet.[13] Since the late 1970s, the Nation of Islam has also shown interest in numerology, although it does not seem to have been influenced by the Five Percent Nation's brand of

| A | Allah | B | Be; Born |
|---|---|---|---|
| C | Cee or understanding | D | Divine |
| E | Equality | F | Father |
| G | God | H | He; Her |
| I | I or Islam | J | Justice |
| K | King; Kingdom | L | Love, Hell, or Right |
| M | Master | N | Now; Nation; or End |
| O | Cipher | P | Power |
| Q | Queen | R | Ruler |
| S | Self; Savior | T | Truth; Square |
| U | You or Universe | V | Victory |
| W | Wise or Wisdom | X | Unknown |
| Y | Why | Z | Zig-Zag-Zig |

**Figure 2.5. The Supreme Alphabet**

numerology. In 1975, Rashad Khalifa, an American Sufi mystic, used his computer to uncover a mathematical code in the Qur'an and claimed that it contains hidden messages based on the number 19. His findings encouraged leading Nation of Islam theologians to uncover hidden Qur'anic meanings for themselves. Mother Tynetta Muhammad, one of the Nation of Islam's leading theologians, adopted Khalifa's revelation that the number 19 is the key to the Qur'an. According to Mattias Gardell, the Nation of Islam has also adopted an Arabic practice of assigning numerical values to letters, known as the Abjad scheme.[14] Unlike the system in the Supreme Alphabet, which assigns numbers to letters according to their position in the alphabet, the Abjad scheme assigns numbers to letters according to symbolic values.[15] But whereas the Nation of Islam uses numbers to uncover hidden Qur'anic mysteries, Five Percenters call on the power of numbers in their everyday lives. For the Five Percent Nation numbers are a flexible way to find and create meaning; numerology is used creatively to "show and prove" ideas that otherwise would be matters of faith.

### The Five Percenter "Way of Life"

Five Percenters take care to distinguish between Islam as a science or "way of life" and Islam as a religion, and maintain that they are, above all, scientists, investigating Islam in a mathematical manner. Indeed, the Nation of Islam refers to Five Percenters as "philosophers" or "scientists," evidence of the Five Percenter emphasis on metaphysics and esoterica.[16] Using the spirit of the Supreme Alphabet, Five Percenters "break down" the word "Islam" to mean "I Self Lord Am Master," emphasizing the divine essence of each black man. In an article entitled "Why We Are Not Muslims," Sincere Allah Merciful God explains that Islam as a religion is based on the idea of submission to Allah—the word "Islam" itself means "submission"—but for Five Percenters submission to Allah has no meaning since each (black) man is Allah incarnate. As Sincere Allah Merciful God puts it, "God is not a Muslim. God does not submit."[17] In other words, instead of seeing Islam as a set of practices intended to give reverence to a Supreme Being, Five Percenters see Islam as a flexible way of life, a mode of encountering the world in their own self-deified orbit.

   Furthermore, Five Percenters argue that whereas religions have clear moments of beginning, the Islamic "way of life" does not. As taught by Elijah Muhammad, the original state of the universe was a triple blackness of space, water, and divinity.[18] If blackness is original, blackness has no birth record. Rap MC Wise Intelligent explains,

People consider us a religion. This does not have anything to do with religion. This has nothing to do with something which was started up in the past. This has no said birth record. That blackness that was there at the beginning that created all things in the universe was that of Islam. That's what we're dealing with. When you're saying Islam you're saying I-Self-Lord-Am-Master, or an Independent Source of Life and Matter. For that's showing and proving the ability to create.[19]

Wise Intelligent's statement attests to a foundational belief shared by both the Nation of Islam and the Five Percent Nation: that Islam—equated with blackness—is the natural state of the Original Man, that is, the black man. "Lost-Founds" have found the "natural" way of life—Islam—lost to them through the centuries. Adherence to Islam is thus not a conversion for the black man, but a return to his original self.

Five Percenters take pride in their ability to "show and prove" the naturalness of their way of life, instead of allowing useless rules to determine their daily practices. As Islamic scholar Yusef Nuruddin points out, "because Five Percenters view Islam as just a natural 'way of life' rather than a religion, they 'break down' the term *Sunni Muslim* to mean 'Soon to be Muslim,' (i.e., not yet Muslim and still hung up in the useless performance of a lot of rituals)."[20] One of my consultants explained this in a similar way: "what makes the Nation of Gods and Earths so great is its absence of structure. There have been people who try to add more structure, but it never works, it's not supposed to, and it couldn't."[21] Unlike members of the Nation of Islam, Five Percenters tend to ignore the five pillars of mainstream (Sunni) Islamic faith: declaring there is no God but Allah, daily prayer, fasting, giving alms to the poor, and making the *hajj* to Mecca.[22] Five Percenters value their freedom from strict rules, and their belief that each black man is a God allows for a looser moral code than is allowed in other Black Muslim sects. In the words of Lord Jamar of the rap group Brand Nubian, "See, in the Five Percent Nation, each man is the sole controller of his own universe. If you're the god of your universe, you set up your own laws."[23] As members of the 5 percent who know and understand the identity of the true God, they believe they have self-knowledge hidden from the rest of the 95 percent, rendering their individual decisions beyond reproach.[24]

Much of Five Percent doctrine hinges on the identity of God, or Allah. Five Percenters believe that each black man is divine and is in fact a god. They stress, however, the connections between divinity and humanity. As mentioned above, Gods "break down" the meaning of the word "Allah" to indicate that the black man is indeed divine: "*A*rm *L*eg *L*eg *A*rm *H*ead." Throughout history Allah has taken a variety of incarnations. According to the Nation of Islam, W. D. Fard was the latest incarnation, but the Five Percent Nation counters that Clarence 13X was also Allah in the flesh. The essential idea of Allah incarnate begins, then, not with the Five Percent Nation, but with the Nation of Islam. In a 1959 interview with African American journalist Louis Lomax, Elijah Muhammad was asked about this idea:

> *Mr. Lomax:* Now if I have understood your teachings correctly, you teach that all of the members of Islam are God, and that one among you is supreme, and that one is Allah. Now have I understood you correctly?
> *Mr. Elijah Muhammed:* That's right.[25]

Five Percenters stress two fundamentals when "showing and proving" that the black man is God. First, in both the Nation of Islam and the Five Percent Nation it is believed that all humanity is descended from the black race. According to their theology it is genetically impossible for a race of beings to progressively add color to their skin, but it is possible, through inbreeding with inferior races, to lighten skin color. The Nation of Islam holds that black skin is the progenitor of all other skin colors, and is therefore the purest; all other variations are corrupted and thus cannot realize divinity. According to one of my consultants, however, the Nation of Gods and Earths approaches this doctrine with more flexibility:

> lighter skin is not a hindrance, or weaker according to NGE theology. . . . the eight rays of the Sun each contain two elements, one yellow and one black, signifying the "16 shades" of the original man, from black, "dark skinned," to "[yellow]." . . . So the darkest pur[e]st "African" Blackman is not necessarily closer to being God, just like the lightest "mixed" Blackman is not necessarily further from being God. But as far as a whiteman being God, that's starting from a complete contradiction in terms.[26]

Second, both the Nation of Islam and the Five Percent Nation believe that God is not a spirit (a "spook"), but is a man. Elijah Muhammad spends the first chapter of his *Message to the Blackman in America* discussing the identity of God and uses both the Bible and the Qur'an to prove that God is not a spirit. Five Percenters further categorize anyone who teaches the masses that the Living God is a "spook" as part of the 10 percent, the "bloodsuckers" of the poor.

Because each black man is a God in his own right, each man has the ability to make his own decisions about clothing, use of drugs and alcohol, consumption of particular foods, and roles in relationships. Nevertheless, many Five Percenters do advocate healthy living: most eschew pork and some are strict vegetarians. Clarence 13X continued the Islamic ban on eating pork on the grounds that the pig is "one-third dog, one-third rat, and one-third cat," and no one in his right mind would eat any one of these animals.[27] Five Percenters recognize that heart disease, diabetes, high blood pressure, and other ailments rampant in the black

community are greatly affected by food choice.[28] Wise Intelligent articulates this **33**
idea:

> You have to understand, you being what you eat, when you eat the food
> becomes a part of your way of thinking. Eating foods that are not fit for a living
> man, that will cause the brain to gain fat, and when you get fat on the brain,
> you get lies on the mind, and when you get lies on the mind you get poison
> in the body, and when you get poison in the body you are dead.[29]

Earths (women) are therefore encouraged to select and prepare wholesome, nutritious foods for their Gods (men) and seeds (children).

Furthermore, unlike the Nation of Islam and other Black Muslim groups such as the Ansaaru Allah Community—another black Islamic sect active primarily in the United States, especially in New York City—the Five Percent Nation follows no strict dress code.[30] Indeed, as rap MC Lakim Shabazz suggests, the lack of a dress code indicates a major difference between the Five Percent Nation and the Nation of Islam: "The only difference between the Five Percent Nation and the brothers who follow Farrakhan is that they have a dress code. They are always dressed nicely with a suit and tie, where the Five Percent Nation, we figure you can wear any garment you want as long as you're dressed."[31]

Such free individualism inevitably leads to charges of hypocrisy and inconsistency. Wise Intelligent himself points out that not all self-proclaimed Five Percenters are true believers: "In the 5% you have your hypocrites. You have your brothers who are not 5%ers, but jive pretenders. They are fronting [pretending] like they are Gods, but they are not Gods they are god damn fools."[32] Wise Intelligent is not the only Five Percenter MC to charge his brethren with hypocrisy. In an interview with journalist Charlie Ahearn, rapper King Sun accused all Five Percenter MCs (excepting himself) of being "phony," but singled out Big Daddy Kane for a specific allegation: "like Big Daddy Kane is supposed to be Five Percent—his name is King Asiatic Allah. But he made a record, *Pimping Ain't Easy*. Doesn't sound very righteous, does it?"[33]

Five Percenters value the foundational role of the family, and maintain the patriarchal family model set forth by Elijah Muhammad for the Nation of Islam. Gods (men) should provide for their families financially and emotionally and are responsible for teaching their mates, called Earths, the "knowledge of self." The family unit of man, woman, and children is often spoken of in a celestial metaphor of sun, moon, and stars; just as the moon receives its light from the sun, so, too, the Earth receives the light of knowledge from her God. According to one Earth, the relationship between a man and a woman "is that of equality," illustrated metaphorically in the solar system:

> There exists a homeostasis between the Sun and the Earth, a natural systematic
> relationship governed by the laws of mathematics. The Sun can exist without

*The Five Percenter "Way of Life"*

the Earth, however she complements his greatness and radiance by taking that light and turning it into life. . . . He provides her with that environment that is conducive to the growth and development of life on her [planet] as she submits herself to him and endlessly revolves around him, bearing witness that he is the foundation for her existence.[34]

While Gods are free to choose their own paths in life, the role of Earths is somewhat more restricted. A woman's body should be at least three-fourths covered with clothing, just as the earth is three-fourths covered by water. Like orthodox Muslim women, Earths often wear head coverings.[35] The main goal for an Earth is reproduction, because through reproduction a woman symbolizes the life-giving forces of the earth.[36]

A family unit of "sun, moon, and stars" is theoretically the goal, yet Earths in the inner city often find themselves with multiple stars fathered by multiple suns. In her study of the role of females in gangs, Anne Campbell traced one young girl, Sun Africa, from her involvement with a minor gang called the Puma Crew through her subsequent initiation into the Five Percent Nation. Sun Africa rejoices in her role as an Earth and submits willingly to her God. By age seventeen she has dropped out of high school, is seven months pregnant, and is living with a new God, his first Earth, and his Earth's children.[37] Gottehrer, too, was struck by the high rate of teenage pregnancy in the early days of the Nation: "I couldn't get used to the young Five Percenters, the girls who had children while they themselves were still children of thirteen or fourteen."[38] By mainstream American standards, Sun Africa's situation (and that of other Five Percenter girls) would be seen as another sad tale of an unwed teenage mother. Yet from a Five Percenter worldview, Sun Africa is fulfilling her intended role in the universe, which is a cause for rejoicing. Furthermore, Five Percenters are at best ambivalent about "marriage under the government." Sources close to Father Allah in the early days of the Nation maintain that he did not recognize state-sanctioned marriages, and the relevancy of marriage under the government continues to be debated.[39]

For many Gods and Earths, the Five Percenter "way of life" is severely tested on a daily basis by the high incarceration rates among Five Percenters. Like the Nation of Islam, the Five Percent Nation recruits heavily among prison populations. The Five Percent Nation's homepage includes links to letters and essays written by Five Percenter inmates, contacts for prisoner outreach, and reproductions of penal codes concerning prisoner civil rights. Because most law enforcement agencies still consider the Five Percent Nation to be a gang, state corrections systems routinely deny Five Percenter prisoners access to Five Percenter literature and materials. One God in the "injustice," Lord Natural Self Allah, included the following testimonial in an essay titled "The Five Percent Dilemma" now posted to the Nation's Website:

In 1996, the New York State Department of Correctional Services began confis-
cating 5%'er literature and emblems under the guise that the 5% were an
unauthorized organization i.e., gang. This stigma began in the southeastern
states of the country, more specifically North and South Carolina, and has now
spread to Ohio, New Jersey, Massachusetts, and Georgia. South Carolina and
New Jersey have gone so far as to create "indoctrination programs" where
known 5%'ers and other "gang members" are placed in a special unit where
they remain locked in cells for 23 hours per day with one hour of recreation
(most often chained and shackled), no contact visits, and limited telephone
[calls] and showers until they renounce their affiliation as being 5%'ers.[40]

Five Percenter inmates in New York State have only recently been granted the
right to worship as they please.[41]

## "Each One, Teach One"

To instruct new believers, Five Percenters rely primarily on the pedagogical technique of "each one, teach one," passing each lesson down to younger members
through oral teaching, and more recently through photocopies.[42] The Nation has
also taken advantage of various printed media to spread its ideology. In 1987,
*The WORD,* a short-lived, bimonthly newspaper limited primarily to the boroughs
of New York City, made its debut. On the last page of every issue, the following
list, entitled "What We Teach," appeared:

1. We teach that Black People are the Original People of the Planet Earth.
2. We teach that Black People are the Mothers and Fathers of Civilization.
3. We teach that the Science of Supreme Mathematics is the key to understanding man's relationship to the universe.
4. We teach Islam as a natural way of life: not a religion.
5. We teach that education should be fashioned to enable us to be self-sufficient
   as a people.
6. We teach that each one should teach one according to their knowledge.
7. We teach that the Blackman is God and his proper name is Allah.
8. We teach that our children are our link to the future and they must be nur-
   tured: respected, loved, protected, and educated.
9. We teach that the unified Black Family is the vital building block of the
   Nation.[43]

In recent years, the Nation has found new, effective ways to spread doctrine
widely. "What We Teach" is now available on the World Wide Web, another
media source appropriated by the Five Percent Nation for proselytizing. The Five
Percent Nation's homepage includes links to "What We Teach," as well as to
the following list of goals entitled "What We Will Achieve":[44]

1. National Consciousness: National Consciousness is the consciousness of our origin in this world, which is divine. As a nation of people we are the first in existence and all other peoples derived from us. National Consciousness is the awareness of the unique history and culture of Black people and the unequaled contributions we have made to world civilization, by being the fathers and mothers of civilization. National Consciousness is the awareness that we are all one people regardless to our geographical origins and that we must work and struggle as one if we are to liberate ourselves from the domination of outside forces and bring into existence a Universal Government of Love, Peace, and Happiness for all the people of the planet.

2. Community Control: Community Control of the educational, economic, political, media, and health institutions on our community. Our demand for Community Control flows naturally out of our science of life, which teaches that we are the Supreme Being in person and the sole controllers of our own destiny; thus we must have same control on the collective level that we strive to attain on the individual level. It is prerequisite to our survival that we take control of the life sustaining goods and services that every community needs in order to maintain and advance itself and advance civilization. Only when we have achieved complete Community Control will we be able to prove to the world the greatness and majesty of our Divine Culture, which is Freedom.

3. Peace. Peace is the absence of confusion (chaos) and the absence of confusion is Order. Law and Order is the very foundation upon which our Science of Life rests. Supreme Mathematics is the Law and Order of the Universe, this is the Science of Islam, which is Peace. Peace is Supreme Understanding between people for the benefit of the whole. We will achieve Peace, in ourselves, in our communities, in our nation and in the world. This is our ultimate goal.[45]

In addition to "What We Teach" and "What We Will Achieve," twelve key concepts known as "The Twelve Jewels" appear frequently in Five Percenter teachings, including their music.[46] In order, the "Twelve Jewels" are Knowledge, Wisdom, Understanding, Freedom, Justice, Equality, Food, Clothing, Shelter, Love, Peace, and Happiness.[47] The Five Percent Nation has produced no document that gathers its doctrine in a single place, but "What We Teach," "What We Will Achieve," "The Twelve Jewels," and the lessons learned during indoctrination together outline the essential teachings and goals of the Five Percent Nation. These lessons all appear regularly in Five Percenter lyrics, as will be discussed in more detail in chapter 3.

Originally a movement confined to the boroughs of New York City, today the Five Percent Nation is a national and increasingly international phenomenon, thanks to the wide availability of Five Percenter doctrine.[48] Rap music has played an important role in spreading this doctrine. As Gardell rightly suggests, "the hip-hop movement's role in popularizing the message of black militant Islam cannot be overestimated. What reggae was to the expansion of the Rastafarian movement in the 1970s, so hip-hop is to the spread of black Islam in the 1980s and 1990s."[49] The Five Percent Nation's Website gives a good deal of space to "God Hop"—rap produced and performed by Gods and Earths—illustrating the importance rap holds for the Nation.[50] Five Percenter MCs and DJs include such major figures as Rakim Allah, the Wu-Tang Clan, Poor Righteous Teachers, Brand Nubian, Capone and Noreaga, Queen Latifah (a former member), Guru (of Gang-starr), DJ Pete Rock, Mobb Deep, Doodlebug (and perhaps also Ladybug Mecca) of Digable Planets, Leaders of the New School (featuring Busta Rhymes), and Black Thought of The Roots.[51] Many of these artists perform regularly on world tours, thus influencing hip-hop music and culture in other nations. The Five Percent Nation continues to grow, adding members throughout the United States and abroad. And where the Five Percent Nation takes root, God Hop is sure to follow.

Rap is a perfect medium for spreading the Nation's doctrine. Rap not only captures the attention of an international audience, but also capitalizes on the Nation's emphasis on verbal ability. As the following chapters will show, God Hop musicians have many tools at their disposal. They quote and paraphrase Five Percenter lessons in lyrics; craft infectious grooves in order to capture the attention of their intended audience; make use of particular digital sound samples in order to create multiple levels of meaning; and give careful attention to album organization and packaging. Together these tools help Five Percenter musicians spread their message of redemption, a task eloquently outlined by Wise Intelligent of the rap group Poor Righteous Teachers: "Rap is [a] gardening tool. Get the brains right and exact so we can drop the seed. Drop that seed, fertilize it, and it's bound to grow to infinity."[52]

# God Hop's Tools

# 3 Lyrics

In chapter 2, I stated that "old-school hip-hop heads"—fans of hip-hop music whose knowledge of hip-hop culture and rap music extends even to the early days of rap in the mid-1970s—typically have at least a passing familiarity with basic Five Percenter doctrine. Old-school fans are likely to remember that the common phrase of the 1990s, "What up, G?" originally meant not "What up, gangsta?" as is commonly assumed, but "What up, God?" a greeting that circulated first among Five Percenters and later in hip-hop culture at large. Likewise, the affirmations "word" and "word is bond," common to hip-hop argot of the 1980s and 1990s, derive from Five Percenter lessons. As Five Percenter MCs became increasingly visible (and commercially audible) in the late 1980s, Five Percenter rhetoric gained a foothold in rap lyrics. Phrases such as "dropping science," meaning sharing knowledge or instructing, became commonplace not only in the lyrics of Five Percenter MCs, but in rap lyrics in general.

Even so, much of the language of Five Percenter rap lyrics resists easy comprehension. Five Percenter lyrics are often shrouded in hazy metaphors and arcane references to Five Percenter beliefs and black nationalist history and philosophy. Indeed, mystical obscurity has come to be expected from certain Five Percenter MCs, such as Ghostface Killah of the Wu-Tang Clan. As music journalist Jonathan "Gotti" Bonanno remarked of Ghostface, "Ghost's eccentric choice of nouns, verbs and numerous obscure references to food and [Five Percenter] terminology, seems like the ranting of a lunatic."[1] Bonanno goes on to make clear that there is indeed a method to Ghost's seeming madness. And like Ghostface, other Five Percenter MCs quote, paraphrase, trope, gloss, and allude to Five Percenter lessons and doctrines for a purpose, a purpose which echoes throughout Five Percenter songs: to "civilize the uncivilized."

In this chapter, I examine Five Percenter rap lyrics, the first and most immediate and accessible tool available to Five Percenter rap musicians. My discussion considers lyrics from two perspectives. First, I analyze how lyrics reveal the inner workings of the Five Percent Nation's theology. Within their lyrics, Five

Percenter MCs bring their doctrine to the public's ears by presenting themselves as authoritative teachers; offering personal testimonials; and quoting, paraphrasing, and interpreting Five Percenter lessons and other teachings. Second, I consider how Five Percenters use lyrics to reach outside their immediate community in order to construct and reinforce alliances with other closely related political, social, and cultural communities and traditions, such as the Nation of Islam, al-Islam (the world community of Islam), and traditions of black nationalism and protest. Together these lyrical strategies allow Five Percenter musicians to both reach out to the "uncivilized" masses and share communal messages with listeners already familiar with Five Percenter teachings.

### Teaching, Preaching, and Reaching Out

Five Percenter MCs strive first and foremost to proclaim and fulfill their role as teachers. They see teaching, or "civilizing," as part of their duty, a duty first proclaimed by Elijah Muhammad in *Message to the Blackman in America:* "The duty of the civilized man is to teach civilization to the uncivilized."[2] This theme appears prominently in songs by Poor Righteous Teachers and Brand Nubian, who search for ever more inventive ways both to proclaim their vocation and to expand on the idea of "civilizing the uncivilized." Wise Intelligent of Poor Righteous Teachers often plainly identifies his purpose: "The duty of the civilized is to civilize the uncivilized" ("Gods, Earths and 85ers"); "I educate you through the teacher in me" ("Word Iz Life"); "Yes, I am the teacher that be teachin' " ("Strictly Ghetto"); and "I'm the teacher teachin' those that lack what I be teachin' " ("Holy Intellect"). Elsewhere he expresses the same theme in more poetic terms. In "Gods, Earths and 85ers," for example, Wise Intelligent identifies Poor Righteous Teachers as "truth suppliers, for Gods, Earths, and 85ers," and in "We Dat Nice" he claims to "shine the light that knowledge ignites." The latter song also yields the following extended self-definition:

> We ain't just rappers, we changers of black situation
> Teaching this Nation the way to conquer damnation
> My occupation, to stimulate your elevation
> To motivate and navigate the revelation.

Wise Intelligent takes an aggressive turn in "Conscious Style": "So in the head of ignorance, I rip some conscious clip / Niggas is small, my task is educate y'all." And later in the same song: "I be schoolin' your ass, 'cause being truth is a task."

In Brand Nubian's "Dance to My Ministry," Lord Jamar creates a metaphorical classroom and presents himself as both minister and teacher of "truth" and "black facts" as he echoes Elijah Muhammad in verse 2: "Cause manifestin' is the duty of the civilized / From the dumb you bring forth the wise / So they can open their eyes to their being." In other words, Lord Jamar's duty is to lead his listeners to self-knowledge. He accomplishes this duty by breaking through the barriers that separate his "students" from the "truth": "Seminar I give is for you to live / Not try to keep your mind captive." The ultimate goal, then, is to "awaken" the unconscious "true self" of black men and women, as we hear from Lord Jamar in "Wake Up": "I keep to striving to do my duty to awaken."

In "Drop the Bomb," Grand Puba (of Brand Nubian) describes a key teaching method of the Five Percent Nation, as stated in tenet 6 of "What We Teach": "I come to reach one / Each one teach one, so here I come to the drum." Through the process of "each one, teach one," Five Percenter MCs also hope to inspire a new generation of teachers. "Gods, Earths and 85ers" shows Wise Intelligent exhorting new teachers: "Wake up all you teachers time to teach a new way / Grass roots, pass truth into the ears of black youths." In "Conscious Style" Wise Intelligent also chastises his colleagues for losing sight of their purpose: "Yo, where the teachers went, with all that pro-black shit?"

Five Percenter MCs recognize that effective teaching begins with practicing what they preach. Wise Intelligent is especially quick to promote his own right-eousness: "Watch me talk the talk and walk the walk right now" ("Gods, Earths and 85ers"). He also speaks for his group. In "Strictly Ghetto" he raps, "Teaching positively 'cause we're teaching what we practice," and in "Holy Intellect" he echoes the idea while paraphrasing the well-known hymn "Amazing Grace": "PRT, Poor Righteous Teachers teachin' from the heart / I was lost but now I'm found and all are being taught."

Five Percenter MCs also teach through personal testimony, sharing their own experiences of conversion or enlightenment. GZA's "B.I.B.L.E. (Basic Instructions Before Leaving Earth)" is such a narrative. The first verse begins with the telling line "Knowledge this wisdom, this goes back when I was twelve." ("Knowledge" here is used not as a noun but as an imperative, as in "know this," "acknowl-edge," or "listen.") We know, then, that this story begins in GZA's youth. He describes a church-filled childhood and his own disillusionment with church doc-trine. Yet persistent truth-seeking brings him to "knowledge of self" ("I studied till my eyes was swollen / and only arose when / I found out that we were the chosen"), and he reveals the goal of this rap to be sharing that knowledge: "No hocus pocus 'cause I focus on the facts / . . . too much knowledge, it might break up the rhyme / I did it anyway just to wake up the mind." In verse 2, GZA refutes specific points of Christian doctrine and replaces them with Five Percenter doctrine: "Why should you die to go to heaven? / The earth is already in space"; and "The white image of Christ, is really Caesar Borgia and uhh / the second son of Pope Alexander the Sixth of Rome."

Poor Righteous Teachers use a similar strategy but tell a different story in "Ghetto We Love." They, too, describe disillusionment with the Christian church ("Then they give us church, a trick to try to ease this / Thought I'd check it out, had to learn about Jesus / Told them he was black and they called me a hater / Then he's on a church wall, yeah like a slave trader"), but most of their narrative dwells on their experiences growing up in the ghetto ("Rats in my front room, roaches in the back / Junkies in the alley running sale for the crack"). The purpose of these lyrics is to establish their authenticity. They know whereof they speak and therefore have the right to comment on ghetto life: "It was ill on the real, I be still buggin' off it / in the ways I was walking, so today I can talk."[3] Having established their street credibility, they can move on to their ultimate purpose of "dropping knowledge," whether or not their audience is interested in their message: "We're out perfectin' these skills I be talkin' / 'Nuff to teach the facts, but the brothers in the back / Can't see what I'm sayin' cause the blunt smoke's fogging."[4]

## Lessons

Having established their authority as teachers, Five Percenter MCs then must decide what knowledge to include in their lyrics. Many turn to their Five Percenter training for inspiration, quoting or paraphrasing lessons within their new songs. Allusions to Lost-Found Lesson no. 2, questions 14 through 16, are especially common (see chapter 2 for these Lost-Found Lessons). The Wu-Tang Clan, for example, opens *Wu-Tang Forever* with "Wu-Revolution," the end of which presents a detailed, spoken (not rapped) embellishment of these particular Lost-Found Lessons:

It was a hundred percent of us that came on the slave ships.
Eighty-five percent of our people was uncivilized, poison animal eaters;
they're slaves of the mental death and powers.
They don't know who the true living God is, nor their origins in the world.
So they worship what they know not,
and they're easily led in the wrong direction,
far fewer men than right. Now you got the ten percent,
who are rich slave makers of the poor,
who teach the poor lies to make the people believe
that the Almighty true and living God is a spook in the sky,
and you can't see him with the physical eyes.
They're also known as blood suckers of the poor.
And then you got the five percent, who are the poor righteous teachers who
    do not believe in the teachings of the ten percent,
who is all wise and know the true and living God and teach that the true
    and living God is the Supreme Being, Black man from Asia.

The members of Brand Nubian use a similar technique in their "Meaning of the 5%," a recording of a Louis Farrakhan speech[5] set to a groove sampled from Marvin Gaye's "T Is for Trouble." The speech develops a concept of Five Percenter identity in another neat paraphrase of these Lost-Found Lessons:

> The poor have been made into slaves by those who teach lies. They don't teach the law of cause and effect. They make the people believe when they see it rain that a spook is producing it. But the rain is real; how then can the cause be unreal? You are witnessing conditions in the world that are produced by real men, but you don't see the cause of the effect of your own suffering because the bloodsuckers of the poor make you think that God is some mystery God. Well, the Honorable Elijah Muhammad said to us that there is five percent who are the poor, righteous teachers, who don't believe the teaching of lies of the ten percent. But this five percent are all-wise and know who the true and living God is, and they teach that the true and living God is the son of man, the Supreme Being, the Black Man of Asia. They're also known as civilized people, Muslims, and Muslim sons. Here is a small percentage of people who know God, and when they know God they have a duty. And that duty is to teach what you know to those who do not know.

In these two songs, Lost-Found Lesson no. 2, questions 14–16 are repeated almost word for word, emphasizing the centrality of these questions in Five Percent doctrine. In other examples, however, rappers use these lessons as a point of departure for a personalized narrative. Lakim Shabazz's exegesis of these same lessons, for example, emphasizes his self-appointed role as a teacher:

> Ten percent of us can help but don't feel a need
> They love greed, and this really bothers me
> Eighty-five percent of us are totally ignorant
> Walking around with the nigger mentality
> Five percent of us are ready to die for the cause
> Of course, the source is Elijah
> Knowledge of self is what you need to stop the war
> If you don't get it, I'm held responsible
> Rhymes I make are designed to reach the youth,
> I gotta teach, that's why I speak the truth
> Some waste time dwelling on the past
> It's time they know, that we're the lost tribe of Shabazz.

This passage shows that Lakim holds himself personally responsible for the education of the youth, as do many Five Percenter rappers. Big Daddy Kane also links these Lost-Found Lessons with a personal duty to teach in the last lines of "Mortal Combat": "I teach freedom, justice, equality, / peace to the brothers and sisters that follow me / Pity poisoned minds of the people are ours / slaves from mental death and power."

Other Lost-Found Lessons also serve as a basis for personal exegesis. (See table 3.1 for a list of other lesson paraphrases and their sources.) Brand Nubian, for example, paraphrases Lost-Found Lesson no. 2, question 11 in "Ain't No Mystery": "Now would you set up home, and wait for a Mystery God / to bring you food, clothing, and shelter? / Emphatically no! Mathematically that just don't go." The group taps into the Lost-Found Lessons again in "I'm Black and I'm Proud" and "Ragtime" with Lord Jamar's claim that his brain weighs seven and one-half ounces, a "fact" taught in Lost-Found Lesson no. 2, question 32. Lakim Shabazz draws on the Lost-Found Lessons as he claims in "The Lost Tribe of Shabazz" that his "rhymes weigh six sextillion tons / heavy as the earth," a figure found both in Lost-Found Lesson no. 2, question 6 and Actual Facts no. 15, and again when he explains in "Brothers in Action," "Columbus discovered the poor part of the planet Earth / We didn't care; we preserved the best part for ourself," which is drawn from Lost-Found Lesson no. 1, question 3.

The very title of Poor Righteous Teachers' "Word Iz Life" refers to Lost-Found Lesson no. 1, question 11, and the lyrics of this song are filled with lessons. Within four quick measures (mm. 43–46) Wise Intelligent works with three lessons: "One thousand thirty seven one-third miles per hour / I put your planet in continuous revolution / Penetrate, draw mist from a lake, create / rain, snow, sleet, hail and earthquakes, snowflakes." The first two lines of this excerpt come from both Actual Facts no. 17 and Lost-Found Lesson no. 2, question 7, while the second two paraphrase Lost-Found Lesson no. 2, question 8.

Also common are the phrases "word life" and "word is bond," contractions of Lost-Found Lesson no. 1, question 11. "Word life" works in these songs as an affirmation of truth-telling, as for example in Mobb Deep's "Still Shinin' ": "The Mobb got it locked with the master keys / Word life combination to the safe it's on." Sadat X proves the veracity of his verbiage in "Ragtime" as he asserts, "Keep on, yes my word is bond / Speakin' that knowledge like Farrakhan." King Sun, on the other hand, chooses to present this lesson as a didactic question in "Pure Energy": "Have you not heard that your word is bond?"[6]

The Student Enrollment Lessons are also popular sources for lyrics. Versions of the answer to Student Enrollment Lesson no. 1, "The original man is the Asiatic Black man; the Maker; the Owner; the Cream of the planet Earth, Father of Civilization, God of the Universe," appear in Brand Nubian's "Wake Up" and "Drop the Bomb" and the Wu-Tang Clan's "Wu-Revolution." Original godhood is also of central importance to Lord Jamar in "Ragtime"; he encourages his listeners to "take our steps and retrace back / to a time when black was defined as / Original, god-like, supreme, divine." C. L. Smooth recalls the same lesson when he calls for "peace, justice, and freedom for the Original man / architect

**Table 3.1. Lesson Paraphrases and Sources**

| Song title | Lyric | Lesson | Source |
|---|---|---|---|
| "Ain't No Mystery" (Brand Nubian) | "Now would you set up home, and wait for a Mystery God / to bring you Food, Clothing, and Shelter? / Emphatically no! Mathematically that just don't go." | "Will you sit at home and wait for that mystery God to bring you food? Emphatically No!" | Lost-Found Lesson no. 2, question 11 |
| "Anger in the Nation" (Pete Rock and C. L. Smooth) | "Peace, justice, and freedom for the Original man / architect of the Motherland" | "Who is the Original man? The original man is the Asiatic Black man; the Maker; the Owner; the Cream of the planet Earth—Father of Civilization, God of the Universe | Student Enrollment Lesson no. 1 |
| "A Better Tomorrow" (Wu-Tang Clan) | "Can a Devil Fool a Muslim nowadays?" | "25. Can the Devil fool a Muslim? 26. Not nowadays." | English Lesson No. C1, 25–26 |
| | "A voice cries from the wilderness of the north." | "What is the population of the Colored people in the wilderness of North America, and all over the planet Earth? . . ." | Student Enrollment Lesson, nos. 3–4 |
| "Brothers in Action" (Lakim Shabazz) | "Columbus discovered the poor part of the planet Earth / We didn't care; we preserved the best part for ourself / to build and add on" | "Why did we let half-original man, Columbus, discover the Poor Part of the planet earth? Because the original man is the God and Owner of the Earth, and knows every square inch of it, and has chosen for himself the Best Part. He did not care about the Poor Part. Columbus was a half-original man was born in Italy, which is southeast Europe. His full name was Christopher Columbus and the place he discovered was North America." | Lost-Found Lesson no. 1, question 3 |
| | "Using 23 million miles of useful land / to show and prove I'm the original man" | "How much of the useful land is used by the original man? The Original man uses 23,000,000 square miles." | Student Enrollment Lesson no. 7 |

**Table 3.1.** *(continued)*

| Song title | Lyric | Lesson | Source |
|---|---|---|---|
| "Butt-Naked Booty Bless" (Poor Righteous Teachers) | "Teaching is the Duty of the Civilized man / Teaching truth to the youth that be thirstin' for the knowledge" | "What is the Duty of a civilized person? To teach the uncivilized people—who are savage—civilization (righteousness, the knowledge of himself, the science of everything in life: love, peace and happiness)." | Lost-Found Lesson, no. 2, question 18 |
| "Children R the Future" (Big Daddy Kane) | "The children be building, each boy and girl / cause you are the cream of the planet earth." | "Who is the Original man? The original man is the Asiatic Black man; the Maker; the Owner; the Cream of the planet Earth, Father of Civilization, God of the Universe" | Student Enrollment Lesson no. 1 |
| "Dial 7 (Axioms of Creamy Spies)" (Digable Planets) | "Hey, we can make life better together, not divided / Universal, original, creamy" | "Who is the Original man? The original man is the Asiatic Black man; the Maker; the Owner; the Cream of the planet Earth—Father of Civilization, God of the Universe" | Student Enrollment Lesson no. 1 |
| "Drop the Bomb" (Brand Nubian) | "By the course of Allah / the true and living cream of the planet earth God of the universe" | "Who is the Original man? The original man is the Asiatic Black man; the Maker; the Owner; the Cream of the planet Earth—Father of Civilization, God of the Universe" | Student Enrollment Lesson no. 1 |
| | "The first soul, black like coal / That's how old, there's no set birth record" | "What is the birth record of the said Nation of Islam? The said Nation of Islam has no birth record. It has no beginning nor ending." | Student Enrollment Lesson no. 9 |
| "I'm Black and I'm Proud" (Brand Nubian) | "Our immediate stance when we came to the game / was completely advanced so no one sounds the same / 7 and one-half ounces of brain" | "Tell us the mental and physical power of a real devil? The mental power of a real devil is nothing in comparison with the original man. He only has six ounces of brain, while the original man has seven and one-half ounces of brain which are original. The devil has six ounces of brain; they are grafted brains." | Lost-Found Lesson no. 2, question 32 |

| Song (Artist) | Lyric | Nation of Gods and Earths Lesson | Source |
|---|---|---|---|
| "The Gods are Taking Heads" (King Sun) | "We have a duty and our duty is to teach and civilize" | "What is the Duty of a civilized person? To teach the uncivilized people—who are savage—civilization (righteousness, the knowledge of himself, the science of everything in life-love, peace and happiness)." | Lost-Found Lesson, no. 2, question 18 |
| "Gods, Earths and 85ers" (Poor Righteous Teachers) | "The duty of the civilized is to civilize the uncivilized" | "What is the Duty of a civilized person? To teach the uncivilized people—who are savage—civilization (righteousness, the knowledge of himself, the science of everything in life-love, peace and happiness)." | Lost-Found Lesson, no. 2, question 18 |
| "The Lost Tribe of Shabazz" (Lakim Shabazz) | "My rhymes weigh six sextillion tons / Heavy as the earth, a lyrical function" | "What is the total weight of our planet? 6-sextillion tons (a unit followed by twenty-one ciphers)." | Lost-Found Lesson no. 2, question 6 |
| | | "The Earth weighs six sextillion tons (a unit followed by 21 ciphers)." | Actual Facts no. 15 |
| | "The original man uses 23 million square miles of the planet earth / constantly buildin'" | "How much of the useful land is used by the original man? The Original man uses 23,000,000 square miles." | Student Enrollment Lesson no. 7 |
| "Pit of Snakes" (Gravediggaz) | "What makes rain and hail, snow and earthquakes?" | "What makes rain, hail, snow and earthquakes? …" | Lost-Found Lesson no. 2, question 8 |
| "Pure Energy" (King Sun) | "Have you not heard that your word shall be bond?" | "Have you not learned that your word shall be Bond regardless of whom or what? Yes. My word is Bond and Bond is life, and I will give my life before my word shall fail." | Lost-Found Lesson no. 1, question 11 |
| | "Keep on, yes my word is bond / Speakin' that knowledge like Farrakhan" | "Have you not learned that your word shall be Bond regardless of whom or what? Yes. My word is Bond and Bond is life, and I will give my life before my word shall fail." | Lost-Found Lesson no. 1, question 11 |
| "Ragtime" (Brand Nubian) | "I do this with my seven and one-half ounces of brain / which I contain, to manifest thought." | "Tell us the mental and physical power of a real devil? The mental power of a real devil is nothing in comparison with the original man. He only has six ounces of brain, while the original man has seven and one-half ounces of brain which are original." | Lost-Found Lesson no. 2, question 32 |

**Table 3.1.** (*continued*)

| Song title | Lyric | Lesson | Source |
|---|---|---|---|
| "Ragtime" (Brand Nubian), cont. | "Take our steps and retrace back / to a time when black was defined as / Original, god-like, supreme, divine." | "Who is the Original man? The original man is the Asiatic Black man; the Maker; the Owner; the Cream of the planet Earth, Father of Civilization, God of the Universe" | Student Enrollment Lesson no. 1 |
| "Wake Up" (Brand Nubian) | "The maker, the owner, the cream of the planet Earth / Father of civilization, God of the universe" | "Who is the Original man? The original man is the Asiatic Black man; the Maker; the Owner; the Cream of the planet Earth, Father of Civilization, God of the Universe" | Student Enrollment Lesson no. 1 |
| | "Manifesting thought with my infinite styles / making sure this travels only 23 million miles." | "How much of the useful land is used by the original man? The Original man uses 23,000,000 square miles." | Student Enrollment Lesson no. 7 |
| | "Can a devil fool a Muslim? (No, not nowaday bro) / Do you mean to say the devil fooled us 400 years ago? / Y equals self, a trader made an interpretation saying that / we'd receive more gold for our labor in this nation / Did we receive more gold? Now-cipher" | "25. Can the Devil fool a Muslim? 26. Not nowadays. 27. Do you mean to say that the Devil fooled them three hundred seventy-nine years ago? 28. Yes, the trader made an interpretation that they receive gold for their labor, more than they were earning in their own country. 29. Then did they receive gold? 30. No. The Trader disappeared and there was no one that could speak their language." | English Lesson No. C1, 25–30 |
| "Word iz Life" (Poor Righteous Teachers) | Title | "Have you not learned that your word shall be Bond regardless of whom or what? Yes. My word is Bond and Bond is life, and I will give my life before my word shall fail." | Lost-Found Lesson no. 1, question 11 |
| | "One thousand thirty seven one-third miles per hour / I put your planet in continuous revolution" | "How fast does our Planet travel per hour? 1,037 1/3 miles per hour." | Lost-Found Lesson no. 2, question 7 |

| "Wu Revolution" (Wu-Tang Clan) | | |
|---|---|---|
| "Penetrate, draw mist from a lake / create rain, snow, sleet, hail and earthquakes, snowflakes" | "The Earth travels at the rate of 1,037 1/3 miles per hour." "What makes rain, hail, snow and earthquakes? ... The Sun draws this water up into the Earth's rotation, which is called gravitation, in a fine mist that the naked eye can hardly detect. But as this mist ascends higher, and increasing with other mists of water in different currents of the atmosphere, until when she becomes heavier than gravitation. Then she distills back to the Earth in the form of drops of water or drops of ice . . ." | Actual Facts no. 17 Lost-Found Lesson no. 2, question 8 |
| "The planet earth belongs to God / Every square inch of it that he chose for himself is the best part" | "Why did we let half-original man, Columbus, discover the Poor Part of the planet earth? Because the original man is the God and Owner of the Earth, and knows every square inch of it, and has chosen for himself the Best Part." | Lost-Found Lessons 1, question 3 |
| "The universe is not completed without the sun, moon, and stars" | " . . . The Universe is everything: Sun, Moon, and Stars." | Lost-Found Lesson 1, question 9 |
| "So all you . . . thinkin' you gonna survive out here without your black woman, you're wrong / They have attraction powers on the planet" | "What makes rain, hail, snow and earthquakes? . . . The Sun and moon, having Attracting Power on our Planet . . ." | Lost-Found Lesson 2, question 8 |
| "We are original man, the Asiatic black man / the maker, the owner, the cream of the planet Earth / Father of civilization and God of the universe" | "Who is the Original man? The original man is the Asiatic Black man; the Maker; the Owner; the Cream of the planet Earth, Father of Civilization, God of the Universe" | Student Enrollment Lesson no. 1 |

**Table 3.1.** *(continued)*

| Song title | Lyric | Lesson | Source |
|---|---|---|---|
| "Wu Revolution" (Wu-Tang Clan), cont. | "The population was seventeen million / with the two million Indians making a total of nineteen million / four billion, 400 million all over the planet earth." | "What is the population of the Colored people in the wilderness of North America, and all over the planet Earth? The population of the Original nation in the wilderness of North America is 17,000,000. With the 2,000,000 Indians makes it 19,000,000. All over the planet Earth is 4,400,000,000." | Student Enrollment Lesson no. 3 |
| | "At one time it was told to me that man came from monkeys / That we was swinging from trees / I hardly can believe that unless I'm dumb, deaf, and blind." | "21. Did I hear you say that some of the seventeen million do not know that they are Muslims? 22. YES, SIR! 23. I hardly believe that unless they are blind, deaf and dumb." | English Lesson No. C1, 21–23 |

of the Motherland" in "Anger in the Nation." Wise Intelligent also claims god-hood in "Miss Ghetto" as he asserts, "the black man is god, the twelfth jewel is thirteen."[7] And I Self Devine of the Micranots alludes to his status as "original man" in "Culture": "This is original, indigenous / this is all that we know that we have: culture." Big Daddy Kane taps into the same Student Enrollment Lesson in "Children R the Future" as he encourages children to pursue education: "yes the children be building, each boy and girl / 'cause you are the cream of the planet earth." Later in the same song Big Daddy Kane extends his metaphor to emphasize the importance children hold for our collective future: "young brothers and sisters considered the cream / that must rise to the top and fulfill the dream."

Student Enrollment Lesson no. 1 also inspires the metaphorical underpinning of Digable Planets' "Dial 7 (Axioms of Creamy Spies)." Metaphors of "cream" and "creamy," both referring to "the cream of the planet earth" and thus to members of the black diaspora, run throughout the song. The first lines of Sara Webb's sung introduction initiate this metaphor ("We are the creamy spies, the cream always rises up") and the last lines of the introduction call for unity among "creamy spies": "Hey, we can make life better together, not divided / Universal, original, creamy." Chace Infinite of Self Scientific also makes use of this metaphor in "The Long Run" as he explains, "may take a minute for the cream to rise to the top / But Allah as my witness y'all we can't be stopped." (In hip-hop parlance, a "minute" usually designates not the equivalent of sixty seconds but a longer, indefinite period of time. This line could therefore be paraphrased, "even if it takes a while for the black nation to rise to the top, Allah will make sure we succeed.")

Student Enrollment Lesson no. 3, which dwells on the populations of the planet, finds its way into the Wu-Tang Clan's "Wu-Revolution": "The population was seventeen million / with the two million Indians making a total of nineteen million / 4 billion, 400 million all over the planet earth." Masta Killah begins his verse in the Wu-Tang Clan's "A Better Tomorrow" with the poetic line "A voice cries from the wilderness of the north." The wilderness to which he refers is the wilderness of North America as described in Student Enrollment Lessons nos. 3–4. Brand Nubian ("Wake Up") and Lakim Shabazz ("The Lost Tribe of Shabazz" and "Brothers in Action") paraphrase Student Enrollment Lesson no. 7, which deals with how much useful land the original man uses. And Brand Nubian uses Student Enrollment Lesson no. 9 to back up a claim of racial superiority in "Drop the Bomb": "The first soul, black like coal / That's how old, there's no set birth record."

English Lesson no. C1, a series of questions and statements that outlines W. D. Fard's mission, also inspires song lyrics. The most extended quotation from these lessons appears in Brand Nubian's paraphrase of lessons 25–30 in "Wake Up":

Can a devil fool a Muslim? (No, not nowaday bro).
Do you mean to say the devil fooled us 400 years ago?
Y equals self, a trader made an interpretation
saying that we'd receive more gold for our labor in this nation.
Did we receive more gold? Now-cipher.[8]

By contrast, instead of quoting one of these questions intact, the Wu-Tang Clan uses an answer from English Lesson no. C1, question 23 to follow up a statement of their own devising in "Wu-Revolution": "At one time it was told to me that man came from monkeys / That we was swinging from trees / I hardly can believe that unless I'm dumb, deaf, and blind." In "A Better Tomorrow," also by the Wu-Tang Clan, RZA draws from English Lesson no. C1, question 25 when he asks, "Can a devil fool a Muslim nowadays?"

### THE SCIENCE OF SUPREME MATHEMATICS

In chapter 2, I introduced the foundational role numbers play in Five Percenter training. Five Percenters begin their indoctrination by mastering the Science of Supreme Mathematics, that is, by learning to manipulate and "break down" the meaning of any given number (see figure 2.2). "Breaking down" a number's meaning requires not only rote memorization of the primary meanings associated with the numbers, but also a flexible, creative ability to recognize and decipher relationships between numbers and the rest of the world.

In most numerology systems, each number after nine is simply a combination of the first nine numbers through division, addition, or multiplication of the internal sums of the digits. Although Five Percenters do sometimes create meaning by figuring internal sums, typically they are less concerned with adding numbers then with "adding" meanings. In other words, instead of using the number 16 to produce 7 through the internal sum $1 + 6$, and thus the meaning "God," Five Percenters are more likely to speak of 16 as the added meaning of each number: 16 thus signifies "knowledge-equality." Grand Puba provides an example of this type of number play in "Soul Controller": "Knowledge Cipher [10], divided by Power [5] Equals Wisdom [2] / But you know we have to start with Knowledge first."

Numbers appear in a variety of guises in God Hop lyrics. In some cases, references to numbers are primarily informative. When communicating with each other about dates and other numbers associated with timekeeping, for instance, Five Percenters typically use the meanings of numbers instead of the numbers themselves. Brand Nubian's "Wake Up," for example, contains the line "I wrote this on the day of wisdom power," probably referring to the 25th of the month.[9] And in "Brothers in Action," Lakim Shabazz explains to his guest MC Tashin Allah, "Tashin my brother, this is the knowledge born born cipher year," that is, 1990, giving the date of the album. Similarly, one's age is spoken of not with numbers, but with their meanings: a twenty-nine-year-old woman is considered a woman of wisdom-born years. References to calendar dates depend on both the Science of Supreme Mathematics and on the Supreme Alphabet (to be discussed below). An update to the Five Percent homepage, for example, indicated that it had last been updated on Allah Power Rule, Knowledge Understanding, year 40, or April 13, 2004.[10]

Numbers also often appear as direct references to the scientific weights and measures of the universe Five Percenters are required to memorize during their training: the speed of the earth's rotation is mentioned in "Word Iz Life" by Poor Righteous Teachers ("One hundred thirty seven one-third miles per hour / I put your planet in continuous revolution"); Wise Intelligent raps of the earth's speed around the sun in "They Turned Gangsta" ("Sixty-six thousand seven hundred five and a half miles per hour / Submit while you circle the sun"); and the weight of the earth comes up in "We Dat Nice" ("Six sextillion tons earth / I levitate hold the universe and press weight"), also by Poor Righteous Teachers.

Numbers can also be used for their associative or symbolic values. In "7XL," Scaramanga Shallah draws on mathematics as he describes the power of his collaboration with the members of Brand Nubian: "God wisdom cipher, 720 build two circles." Not only is 720 the sum of the degrees of two complete circles, its meaning also emphasizes the wisdom to be gained when Gods "build" together, or converse, in a cipher, a circle of fellowship. Indeed, the very title of Scaramanga Shallah's "7XL" depends on the meaning of 7: God. The title affirms an "extra-large" or affluent lifestyle for Gods, and specifically for Scaramanga and his guest MCs Sadat X and Grand Puba of Brand Nubian. The title's meaning is further clarified in the chorus: for these Gods, living well includes cash, checks, clientele, expensive beer (namely, Guinness), richly customized automobiles, and plenty of leisure time.

Sadat X also makes use of 7 (God) in Brand Nubian's "Allah u Akbar" as he explains how he rises at 7 A.M. each morning to hone his craft: "The only way I'd fall off is if I got fat and lazy / and I won't 'cause I work real hard / wake up in the morning at the hour of God and make beats."[11] Rakim Allah, too, uses the God number, but in a way that aligns the MC with popular culture as well as with Five Percenter doctrine: he identifies himself as 007 in his song "In the Ghetto," and thus not only marks himself as God through number symbolism but also metaphorically as British secret agent and action hero James Bond.

In his song "Mystery (Who Is God)," Rakim highlights individual points in his narrative by mentioning an appropriate number. Throughout "Mystery," Rakim contemplates the origins of the universe, and in verse 2 he refers to the number 9 and clearly gives its meaning—"the complete number 9 which means born or existed"—further emphasizing the foundational role numbers play in the universe. The placement of this song on the album could also be related to

Supreme Mathematics and to this particular textual line. "Mystery" is the thirteenth track on the disc, but it is the ninth ("born") song. The role of mathematics in album organization will be discussed in greater detail in chapter 6.

Grand Puba's "Lickshot" contains perhaps the most obscure reference to the Science of Supreme Mathematics: Grand Puba finishes the song with the line "knowledge knowledge." The number associated with this meaning is 11. With this greeting, however, Grand Puba wishes us not a double dose of knowledge but "peace," the eleventh of the twelve jewels.[12] Killarmy's "Wake Up" further illustrates the flexibility of the Science of Supreme Mathematics. In the last line of verse 1, guest MC Madman of Sunz of Man raps, "my culture nickel put holes in your face like dimples," referring to his gun, his .45 (culture, nickel). Madman does not limit himself only to meanings associated with the Science of Supreme Mathematics but feels free to use "nickel" in place of "power" or even "refinement" for the number 5. Even though the substitution does little to clarify the sentence for the "uncivilized," its imagery is difficult to miss, especially given the extensive violence and war imagery throughout the rest of the song.

Five Percenter MCs also use the Science of Supreme Mathematics to create narratives based on all the numbers in succession, as in Brand Nubian's "Allah and Justice." The members of Brand Nubian fashion the four sections of their song around an explication of the numbers 1 through 10; the numbers serve as the basis of a symbolic narrative of faith (see chapter 5 for a discussion of this song's origin). Each verse is heard simultaneously with the chorus "Peace to Allah and Justice," a reference to and praise of Clarence 13X (Allah) and Justice, the "creators" of the Science of Supreme Mathematics. Each member of the crew explicates three numbers, while the number ten, a combination of the numbers for knowledge and cipher, which refer to the science itself, is given a joint interpretation. Recording a song constructed around all ten numbers of the Science of Supreme Mathematics is perhaps the highest form of praise Brand Nubian can offer the founders of their faith:

> [Chorus]
> Peace to Allah and Justice . . .
>
> [Verse 1: Lord Jamar]
> The **knowledge** is the foundation  [knowledge = 1]
> The **wisdom** is the way  [wisdom = 2]
> The **understanding** shows you  [understanding = 3]
> That you are on your way
>
> [Verse 2: Lord Sincere]
> The **culture** is our God  [culture = 4]
> The **power** is the truth  [power = 5]
> **Equality** only shows you  [equality = 6]
> That you have planted your roots

[Verse 3: Sadat X]
**God** came to teach us     [God = 7]
Of the righteous way
How to **build** and be **born**     [build = 8; born = 9]
On this glorious day

[all three]
The **knowledge** of the **cipher**     [knowledge-cipher = 10]
Is to enlighten you
To let you know
That God is right inside you.

The members of Brand Nubian again make reference to the entire Science of Supreme Mathematics in "Wake Up." The numbers here come at the end of verse 1 and are given slightly out of order: wisdom comes before knowledge, but once understanding is added to knowledge and wisdom, the correct order of the numbers is restored. The group refrain at the end of each line, "murderer," sustains the thoughts of the preceding lines, a complaint against both the 10 percent and self-destruction.

| | |
|---|---|
| And put our **wisdom** before us (murderer) | [2] |
| That makes it **wisdom knowledge** (murderer) | [2, 1] |
| So we need **knowledge wisdom** to bring forth | [1,2] |
| the **understanding** (murderer) | [3] |
| **Culture freedom** (murderer) | [4] |
| **Power refinement** (murderer) | [5] |
| **Equality god build destroy born**'s our **cipher** (murderer) . . . | [6, 7, 8, 9, 0] |

Rakim's "Mystery (Who Is God)," a three-verse tour de force that investigates the birth of the world and the divinity of black men, also explicates all numbers of the Science of Supreme Mathematics, thus grounding his cosmological investigation in Five Percenter doctrine. Verse 2 prepares us for such a narrative. With the lines "He dealt with measurements, his language was mathematics / His theoretical wisdom of the numerical system," Rakim reveals the very language of the Creator to be mathematics, and his wisdom to be based on the numbers Five Percenters cherish. Furthermore, beginning in the last line of verse 2 and extending into verse 3, Rakim, like Brand Nubian, methodically includes the meaning of each number in turn:

(from verse 2)
Like the planets your **cipher** remains perfectly round

(verse 3)
From unconsciousness, to consciousness
My **knowledge** in his **wisdom** his response is this
A **understanding**, which is the best part
He picked the third planet where new forms of life would start

He pursued show and prove every move in order
Back to the source he let off his resources in the water
Climb his climax, where the climate is at, high degrees
See he start to breathe deep in the darkest seas
And the plan is, to lay in the clays to form land
And expand, usin' the same clays to born man
In his own image our origin begins in the East
**Culture** rise to breed, with the **powers** of peace
Deal in **equality** nature's policy is to be **God**
**Build or destroy** positively **born** life like Allah
And each one was given everlasting perfection
If each one keep living in the same direction
And life was life, and love was love
We went according by the laws of the worlds above
They showed us physically, we could reach infinity
But mentally, through the century we lost our identity
Life start and ending, we got trife[13] and started sinnin'
Lost touch with the beginning now **ciphers** stop spinnin'
And what was once easy became confused and hard
Which brings us back, to the mystic question: who is God?[14]

In other examples, Rakim, Big Daddy Kane, and Grand Puba refer to the entire system metonymically by noting its cycle from knowledge (1) to born (9) and back again. Rakim makes use of this cycle in his classic "In the Ghetto" ("from knowledge to born back to knowledge precise") and Big Daddy Kane proves his stamina by comparing himself to this cycle in "Mortal Combat" ("As I go on, from night to morn / Beginning to end, from knowledge to born"). Grand Puba, on the other hand, refers to this system to emphasize his lyrical prowess over other MCs: "My knowledge is born, so you brothers better move on / you bought your wack style from Trader Horn" ("Lickshot"). Lord Jamar also taps into the first four numbers of the Supreme Mathematics at the end of his verse in "Ragtime":

You got to know Knowledge of Self's the foundation
Know wisdom's the way to let it out 'cause
Understanding is the manifestation and
Culture Freedom, the final turnout, 'cause it's Ragtime!

Grand Puba and Sadat X join Lord Jamar for these lines and their participation is closer to chanting or singing than rapping, suggesting that with the exception of the final three words, these lines may come from a song common to Five Percenter worship.

Finally, some MCs merely mention mathematics, expecting that their audience will understand the reference. Rakim, for example, claims to have "stacks of mathematics to feed you Asiatics" ("The 18th Letter"). Other MCs are more explicit about the role mathematics plays in their lives. The importance of numbers cannot be mistaken in Prodigy's verse of Mobb Deep's "Still Shinin' ": "fuck the myths, the science of numbers is how I live / if we ain't getting mathematics somethin' got to give." Similarly, Aceyalone claims to "talk the math, speaking like a genuine" ("I Got to Have It Too").

Given the Five Percent Nation's interest in numerology and the multiple references to numbers in their lyrics, one might expect to find some significant numerological connections between music and text in these examples. But these musicians, at least, do not seem interested in adapting their numerology to the level of musical composition. Arguments for numerical relationships can certainly be made. Rakim's "Mystery," for example, an examination of the nature of God, has 115 measures, the internal sum of which is 7, the God number. And the seventh line of verse 1 of Poor Righteous Teachers' "Holy Intellect" has three references to the number 7: "God," "Allah," and "seven." Aside from the word "seven" itself, "God" and "Allah" also make reference to 7 through the Science of Supreme Mathematics. Lakim Shabazz's "The Lost Tribe of Shabazz" shows a different interest in numbers. The chorus of this song contains a single line— "Our people will survive America"—but the phrase is heard a different number of times with each statement of the chorus: it is heard once the first time, twice the second, four times the third, and eight times the fourth, a mathematical series (1, 2, 4, 8) built on powers of two. The verses of this song also have different lengths—sixteen, twenty, and twenty-four measures respectively—creating a mathematical proportion of 4:5:6. (As will be discussed in more detail in chapter 4, rap songs are typically constructed in variations of verse-chorus form.) Such numerical patterns appear to be intentional, yet their significance is unclear. With these few exceptions, numbers do not seem to play an important role in the compositional process and are limited to verbal references. There is some evidence, however, that Five Percenter rap musicians have the Science of Supreme Mathematics in mind when constructing both songs and albums, as will be discussed in chapter 6.

### THE SUPREME ALPHABET

MCs treat the Supreme Alphabet in a similarly flexible manner. To find the hidden meanings in particular words, the words are treated as acronyms; each letter is investigated in accordance with the Supreme Alphabet (see figure 2.5). The meanings of the letters are then added together to find the meaning of the entire word. Expanded acronyms and extensive word play based on this procedure are common themes in Five Percenter lyrics. "Allah" makes an appearance in Brand Nubian's "Dance to My Ministry": "Black Man Supreme, knowledge machine / The Alpha and Omega, the *A*rm-a-*L*eg-a-*L*eg-a-*A*rm-a-*H*ead." "Islam" is perhaps the word most often "broken down" in Five Percenter lyrics. Most often "Islam" becomes "*I* *S*elf *L*ord *A*m *M*aster" (see, for example, Brand Nubian's "Drop the

Bomb," and Poor Righteous Teachers' "Pure Poverty" and "Rock Dis Funky Joint"), but Islam can also reveal "*I Sincerely Love Allah's Mathematic*" ("Drop the Bomb"), "*I Self Lord And my Methods*" (Poor Righteous Teachers' "Word from the Wise"), and "*I Self Lord And my Musical way of building*" ("Word from the Wise"). Other examples include "*Proper Education Always Creates Energy*" and "*Proper Education Allah's Correction Eternalize*" for "peace" (Poor Righteous Teachers' "Self-Styled Wisdom" and Lord Jamar in Brand Nubian's "Sincerely" respectively); "*Basic Instructions Before Leaving Earth*" for "Bible" (GZA's "B.I.B.L.E."); and *He Allah Justice Islam* (Sadat X in Scaramanga's "7XL") for *haji*, a term designating one who has undertaken the sacred pilgrimage—the *hajj*—to Mecca. These many examples are but a few illustrations of the Supreme Alphabet's inherent flexibility.

Spelling, like finding meaning, is often a creative endeavor. To produce different versions of *haji*, for example, Brand Nubian substitutes a soft G for J, producing phrases such as "*He Allah God Islam*" ("Wake Up") and "*Helpful to Another God In need*" ("Drop the Bomb"). The members of Brand Nubian spell the word "job" in at least two ways: "*Justice Cipher Bond*" and "*Justice Cipher Born*" ("Drop the Bomb" and "I'm Black and I'm Proud" respectively). And they spell an emphatic no with "*Now Cipher*" in both "Pass the Gat" and "Wake Up." Gatekeeper of the Gravediggaz uses this same spelling method, producing "*God Cipher Love Divine*" for "gold" ("The Night the Earth Cried"). The use of "cipher" in place of the letter "O" in these last examples illustrates just how closely the Supreme Alphabet and the Science of Supreme Mathematics are linked. The letter "O" in the Supreme Alphabet has a designated meaning of "cipher," the meaning also assigned to the number 0. In these examples, then, Sadat X, Lord Jamar, and Gatekeeper use the meaning of both "O" and zero to spell "job," "no," and "gold" respectively.

Within the Supreme Alphabet, each letter is also assigned a number according to its place in the alphabet, which offers yet another tool to MCs. Rakim's "Mystery," for example, is from his album *The 18th Letter,* a reference to the Supreme Alphabet. Rakim frequently uses "the eighteenth letter" to refer to himself: "R" is the eighteenth letter of the alphabet and the first letter of his name. Five Percenters also sometimes spell words with numbers that refer to letters of the alphabet, a technique known as gematria. So when Wise Intelligent raps "Intelligent, twenty-three, nine, nineteen, five" in "Gods, Earths and 85ers," he is not simply reeling off a series of numbers but is spelling his name; the twenty-third, ninth, nineteenth, and fifth letters are WISE. In "Allies," a collaboration with the Fugees, Wise Intelligent wishes "peace" as he raps "sixteen, five, one, three, five coincide, greet Wise," and in "Allah u Akbar" Lord Jamar indicates his battle-preparedness by indicating that his "gun" is ready: "my seven, twenty-one, fourteen's ready / and my scope with the laser beam steady."

In addition to quoting from and paraphrasing their catechism-styled lessons, MCs also allude to teachings and beliefs that go beyond those lessons. Lyrics that address the nature and identity of God, the knowledge of self, and gender and family roles fall into this category.

### THE IDENTITY OF GOD

As mentioned in chapter 2, investigating and understanding the nature of God are crucial to Five Percenter theology. Lost-Found Lesson no. 2, questions 10–11 introduce the topic of a "Mystery God":

10. Who is that mystery God? Answer: There is not a mystery God. The Son of man has searched mystery God for trillions of years and was unable to find a mystery God. So they have agreed that the only God is the Son of man. So they lose no time searching for that that does not exist.
11. Will you sit at home and wait for that mystery God to bring you food? Answer: Emphatically No!

Investigations into the nature of God extend beyond the Five Percent Nation's lessons. Elijah Muhammad also discusses the nature of God at great length in his *Message to the Blackman in America,* giving particular attention to refuting the possibility that God could be a "spook" in the sky and promoting the Gnostic idea that each black man is a god. This long-standing discussion now extends into God Hop lyrics.

In "Ain't No Mystery," Brand Nubian proclaims that the 10 percent have kept the identity of God a secret in order to keep the black man enslaved. But Brand Nubian also emphasizes the Five Percenter idea that the black man is God:

> See me and my people been lost for over 400 years
> And done tried this mystery God and all we got was
> Hard times, hunger and nakedness from the snake that hissed
> Beaten and killed by the ones who said
> Look to the sky for your piece of the pie
> They didn't wanna tell you that God was yourself.

In "The Night the Earth Cried," RZA addresses this teaching through a tragic rhetorical question: "how many more black Gods gotta die / before we realize there's no god in the sky?" Wise Intelligent of Poor Righteous Teachers resorts to particularly clever word play when emphasizing this point. In "Conscious Style" Wise Intelligent claims, "God degree, you see, God's the size of me," intimating not that God is small, but that God takes a human form, specifically his own.

Lyrics

And in "Gods, Earths and 85ers," he insists, "the duty of the civilized is to civilize the uncivilized / And make the world recognize / That God is Wise, and Wise is God to the death." The Almighty truly has the attribute of Wisdom, but through his word play, Wise Intelligent also indicates his own divinity: Wise (Intelligent) is God.

In "Mystery," Rakim attempts to explain the identity of God by examining the miracle of creation. He calls on the Qur'an and the Bible to prove the godliness of black men and uses tropes from the Science of Supreme Mathematics and cosmology to round out his logic.

> Which brings us back, to the mystic question, who is God?
> Sixty-six trillion years since his face was shown
> When the seventh angel appears, the mystery will be known
> Check Revelations and Genesis, St. Luke and John
> It even tells us we are gods in the Holy Qur'an
> Wisdom, Strength, and Beauty, one of the meanings of God
> G.O.D. you and me, Gomars Oz Dubar,
> Knowledge, Wisdom, Understanding, Sun, Moon, and Star
> Man, Woman, and Child, and so is Allah.

Knowledge, wisdom, and understanding are 1, 2, and 3, respectively; when knowledge and wisdom are combined, understanding is the product. In the same way, the sun and the moon represent man and woman; when they are combined, they produce the star, a child. The completion of both cycles shows the perfection of creation. As the circle of man, woman, and child is complete, so is Allah complete. Rakim further refers to the number 7, which represents both God and man.

### KNOWLEDGE OF SELF

One of the themes inherent in Five Percenter teachings is "knowledge of self." Those who lack knowledge of self live as "savages" and need to be brought to self-knowledge through the teachings of Elijah Muhammad. (See Lost-Found Lesson no. 1, question 2, and Lost-Found Lesson no. 2, question 18.) Big Daddy Kane identifies this as his duty in "Children R the Future": "Take my hand child and let me show you how / 'cause I'm here to help those who need knowledge of self." Lakim Shabazz refers to self-knowledge as the "science of self" and explains how he will pass on this knowledge in "Black Is Back": "I'll drill the science of self inside the head of it / I'll build a strong foundation." In the chorus of "Inner City Boundaries" Freestyle Fellowship emphasize the freeing power self-knowledge brings: "Once we have the knowledge of self as a people then we could be free / and no devil could ever enter the boundaries." The members of Brand Nubian collectively assert, "You got to know knowledge of self's the foundation" at the end of Lord Jamar's verse in "Ragtime," and Aceyalone in-

### FAMILY AND GENDER ROLES

Other songs make reference to the importance of the family and to women as Earths. Whereas Sara Webb makes use of the celestial sun, moon, and star metaphor in "Dial 7," Lord Jamar refers exclusively to his patriarchal role as sun in "Sincerely" as he raps to his Earth: "Now I'm the sun and I know you're my reflection / Let me give you love and my protection." Women take their position as Earths in Wu-Tang's "Impossible," Poor Righteous Teachers' "Miss Ghetto," Ghostface Killah's "Motherless Child," and Killarmy's "Wake Up," to name just a few. Seeds, or children, also play an important role in these songs. I Self Devine of the Micranots boasts in "Culture" that "kings and queens conceive seeds" to their music. Grand Puba raises the subject of seeds in Brand Nubian's "Sincerely" in order to praise strong single mothers: "Some raise seeds all alone with no father in the home / but they still find the strength to continue on." Furthermore, seeds form an integral part of the choruses of two songs. In "A Better Tomorrow," the Wu-Tang Clan reminds its listeners to be good examples for children:

> You can't party your life away, drink your life away
> smoke your life away, fuck your life away
> dream your life away, scheme your life away
> 'cause your seeds grow up the same way.

Chace Infinite of Self Scientific, on the other hand, makes his future plans evident in the chorus of "The Long Run": "When it's all said, when it's all done / I'm just trying to have seeds and live in the long run."

Busta Rhymes's collaboration with Erykah Badu, "One," explores the family unit in even greater detail.[15] Busta's first verse emphasizes his respect for his Earth, his willingness to protect her, and his dedication to family unity.

> One understanding amongst me and my woman so that we can't fall
> And keep moving forward based on actual facts
> Yes y'all my beautiful Mother Earth, respect her to the max.

Whereas Erykah Badu makes clear that she (or her persona) wants a career of her own ("Now don't you let my ambition make you feel like competition / we should both play a role in our whole living condition"), in her role as Earth she also humbly submits to her God's teachings ("you showed degrees"). Yet although she submits to her God, this Earth also demands help around the house: "As my sunlight I bear witness to you being the foundation / you can come home and watch the babies too." Nevertheless, as the chorus makes clear, a family's essential goal should be unification:

As one, one family.
As one, one little kiss now.
As one, one entirety.
As one, so let us all uplift now.

## CONSTRUCTING SPIRITUAL, POLITICAL, AND CULTURAL ALLIANCES

The examples discussed in the preceding pages may give the impression that all God Hop songs are saturated with doctrine, yet in many songs the references to Five Percenter theology are brief and isolated, key words that provide color and detail for a variety of themes. Nevertheless, using even a handful of key words within a song can both establish the MC's identity as a Five Percenter and reinforce ties between Five Percenter teachings and those of their spiritual, political, and cultural allies. In so doing, Five Percenters reach beyond their own immediate community to become part of long-lived, well-established communities and traditions.

### THE COMMUNITY OF AL-ISLAM

Five Percenter rappers establish their spiritual allegiances by using key words or phrases associated with the Five Percent Nation, the Nation of Islam, or the community of al-Islam, and by citing tenets of belief held in common with either the Nation of Islam or al-Islam. The most common momentary references to Five Percenter doctrine and rhetoric come in the form of self-naming, that is, identifying oneself or others as God(s), Asiatic(s), or Blackman(men) from Asia; speaking of women as Earths, children as seeds, and the family unit in the metaphor of sun, moon, and stars; and identifying oneself as a member of the Five Percent Nation. Butterfly of Digable Planets directly claims his allegiance in "Dial 7": "The Five Percent Nation is my representation," and AZ describes the role of the Five Percent Nation in his childhood in "Life's a Bitch": "We were beginners in the hood as Five Percenters / but somethin' must've got in us 'cause all of us turned to sinners." Rakim and Big Daddy Kane both refer to the black man's "Asiatic" origins. In "The 18th Letter," Rakim offers "stacks of mathematics to feed you Asiatics." Big Daddy Kane, on the other hand, identifies himself as Asiatic both with his name ("King Asiatic") and by calling himself "the Asiatic chosen one" in "Mortal Combat."

Calling oneself or others God(s) is also commonplace in God Hop lyrics. Many MCs simply drop "God" nonchalantly into their phrasing, but a few of the more creative examples deserve mention. Big Daddy Kane, for example, gives a new spin to an old adage as he chastises a weak competitor in "Mortal Combat": "boy, you get your ass kicked / for frontin' like you hittin' hard / when your arms are too short to box with God." Likewise, Lord Jamar freshens an old colloquialism as he boasts of his crew's abilities in "Allah u Akbar": "We're bound to win, 'cause God don't like ugly." And vocalist Sara Webb spins elaborate metaphors in Digable Planets' "Dial 7," claiming "we are God's sequels" and "we are God pieces." Tekitha's chorus in Wu-Tang's "Impossible"—"You can never defeat the Gods"—takes advantage of a subtle double meaning. The chorus suggests a nihilistic worldview, a reaction to the chaos and senseless suffering described throughout the song and the inability of victims to rise above their circumstances (or "defeat the gods"), but also promotes the God-filled Wu-Tang Clan's superiority, warning away competitors.

References to the Nation of Islam are also frequent. Mobb Deep, for example, reveal their familiarity with the history of the Nation of Islam as Prodigy rhymes in "Still Shinin' ": "My infamous Mobb get on they job / the truth gets revealed like with W. Fard." Big Daddy Kane closes "Mortal Combat" with a shout-out to the Nation of Islam: "I say peace to the Nation of Islam." Indeed, Minister Farrakhan and his mission receive frequent praise in these songs. From Lakim Shabazz, for example: "Peace released upon Minister Farrakhan / for preachin' and teachin' the truth to the deaf and blind" ("Black Is Back"). Lord Jamar shows respect for Minister Farrakhan's authority when he claims, "my word is bond / Speakin' that knowledge like Farrakhan" ("Ragtime"). Grand Puba refers to the Nation of Islam's successful drug rehabilitation programs in "Lickshot": "I build with the Gods to get the addicts off the nods," and C. L. Smooth equates his own strength with that of the military arm of the Nation of Islam in "Anger in the Nation": "I want to drop the bomb but remain calm / strong like the power of the Fruits of Islam."

"Black Is Back" by Lakim Shabazz and "Inner City Boundaries" by Freestyle Fellowship both refer to the newspaper founded and run by Minister Farrakhan, *The Final Call.* In so doing, both songs play with a double entendre. When Lakim Shabazz claims, "this rhyme was designed for the *Final Call,*" he means both that the content of his rhyme is in keeping with the teachings of Minister Farrakhan's newspaper, and also that he adheres to the Nation's eschatology: his rhyme is meant to save the uncivilized from the universal destruction the Nation expects at any moment. Aceyalone weaves the same double meaning through his virtuosic verse in "Inner City Boundaries": "I see, I saw, I'm the future, the past, I'm me, I'm y'all / I'm the enemy, friend, and the law / The beginner, the end-all, *The Final Call.*"

The Nation of Islam's doctrine that the white man is a devil has also found its way into God Hop lyrics. Some songs promote cultural self-protection against the devil's civilization, as we hear in the chorus of "Inner City Boundaries": "Once we have the knowledge of self as a people then we could be free / and no devil could ever enter the boundaries." Other songs blame the devil and his civilization (that is, western society) for modern social ills. In "A Better Tomorrow," Inspectah Deck reminds his listeners that "Devils resort to tricknowledge," and Method

Man explains that "Envy, greed, lust, and hate separate / through the devil mind-state blood kin cannot relate." RZA holds himself personally responsible in "Impossible" for the destruction of the devil: "My occupation, to stop the inauguration of Satan / Some claim that it was Reagan, so I come to slay men." (RZA here draws on the Nation of Islam's numerological system, which teaches that former president Reagan carried the "mark of the beast" within his name. Each part of his name—Ronald Wilson Reagan—has six letters, thus producing 666 when combined.)[16] Within the Armageddon-soaked imagery typical of Killarmy tracks, guest MC Hell Razah (of Sunz of Man) gives his vision of the future: "Devils disappear like they went through the Bermuda triangle / erupting on Ryzarector tracks like volcanoes."[17] And Masta Killah reminds his collaborators in "5 Stars" that their duty is to "awaken a nation of sleeping giants who are clients to the devil civilization."[18]

While Five Percenters make their allegiance to the Five Percent Nation and the Nation of Islam evident, they also align themselves with al-Islam through references to Allah and the Qur'an. In "Affirmative Action," Foxy Brown notes (somewhat strangely), "The Gods, they praise Allah with visions of Gandhi," and RZA maintains in "Impossible" that "Allah's heard and seen everywhere." In "The 18th Letter" Rakim calls the mind—especially his own—"one of Allah's best designs," and stakes his verbal reputation on his knowledge of holy scriptures: "I know the Scripture but nowadays ain't it vicious / date back: I go beyond, check the holy Qur'an." The members of Freestyle Fellowship collectively praise Allah for revealing to them "knowledge of self" in the chorus of "Inner City Boundaries": "I stand in the center around all these sounds I see / Blessin' Allah that I found the key." Also in "Inner City Boundaries," guest MC Daddy-O notes Allah's guiding presence in his life: "I'm livin' kinda lovely, only Allah above me." Finally, Chace Infinite of Self Scientific calls on Allah to witness his dedication to a strong black future in "The Long Run": "may take a minute for the cream to rise to the top / but Allah as my witness y'all we can't be stopped."

Some songs also mention locations important to orthodox Islam, the Nation of Islam, and the Five Percent Nation, specifically Mecca and Medina in Saudi Arabia and "Mecca" (Harlem) and "Medina" (Brooklyn) in New York City. Cormega, for example, mentions in "Affirmative Action" that his people come from Medina, likely referring to Brooklyn and not the Middle Eastern city. Cormega and his colleagues of The Firm hail from Queens, making it highly likely that he would have friends in Brooklyn, the neighboring borough. But other references are not as clear. Rakim names both Mecca and Medina in his song "In the Ghetto": "reaching for the city of Mecca, visit Medina." Given that he calls Mecca a city, he likely means Mecca, Saudi Arabia, but the meaning of Medina is ambiguous. Likewise in the chorus of "The 18th Letter," Rakim raps, "bring a praise from Mecca, make a phrase for the better." Mecca here could be Harlem, the birthplace of the Five Percent Nation, or Mecca, the birthplace of al-Islam. Such ambiguity gives voice to the ambivalent position of Five Percenters, who see themselves both as Muslims and as something apart from al-Islam.

MCs also frequently refer to Islamic dietary restrictions, specifically to the avoidance of pork. In Brand Nubian's "Pass the Gat," Lord Jamar remarks of his own arrival, "Here comes the God who don't eat pig lard," and in Brand Nubian's "Ragtime," Sadat X claims that he "never ate the pig, can't deal with the swine." Referring to another MC's flow in "What Cool Breezes Do," Butterfly of Digable Planets remarks over a break, "If they call it phat we just ignore it like it's pork."[19]

### BLACK NATIONALISM AND AFRO-CENTRICITY

As I have argued elsewhere, much of Five Percenter rhetoric falls squarely within black nationalist traditions.[20] Like many black nationalists, Five Percenters seek to establish both cultural and historical ties to Africa and the African diaspora in order to form a sense of identity. A frequent corollary to black nationalism is Pan-Africanism, the belief that the fate and future of all black people are somehow linked. In his exhaustive study of Pan-Africanism, Imanuel Geiss identifies several themes, two of which are especially prominent in Five Percenter rap: believing with what Geiss calls "quasi-religious fervor" that the modern world will fall and African civilization will rise; and referring to the history of Egypt in order to prove that Africans and those of African descent are capable of producing highly sophisticated civilizations.[21] Both themes appear in Five Percenter rap. The members of Brand Nubian, for example, predict in "I'm Black and I'm Proud" that, although their people were slaves, they will someday rule the earth ("Afflicted with the curse of the slave / Predicted to inherit the earth in the last days"). And references to Egyptian culture and civilization frequently appear in Five Percenter lyrics. Poor Righteous Teachers and KRS-One jointly proclaim the connections between the scientific leanings of the Five Percent Nation and ancient Egyptian culture in "Conscious Style": "I remember yesterday when y'all was Gods and Earths / Egyptians and metaphysicists on the verge of giving birth / To understanding, and planting seeds that grow." Here Egypt is used as a metaphor for knowledge and culture; Gods and Earths who have "knowledge of self" and "civilize the uncivilized" have access to ancient culture and wisdom. In other lyrics, Egyptian icons are invoked for their symbolic meaning. Brand Nubian uses an Egyptian hieroglyph, the ankh, in "Dance to My Ministry": "Come into my laboratory, I'ma take you on a tour / An ankh is the key and the key is knowledge / Unlocks my lab's door." The ankh, an ideogram for life, here unlocks mysteries of knowledge otherwise hidden from the 85 percent. Lord Jamar's "laboratory" is a classroom where knowledge of the ancient self is taught. The ankh symbolizes life, but for Lord Jamar the ankh is the key to a new mental life: "knowledge of self."

One outgrowth of Pan-Africanism is race pride. As African Americans learn more about their past and about the exemplary lives of members of the diaspora, they take pride in their heritage and in the color of their skin. Often in tandem with race pride is racial solidarity, the belief that the race will not prosper unless all work together physically, spiritually, and economically. The teachings of Elijah Muhammad and the Five Percent Nation justify race pride both theologically and quasi-scientifically. The Nation's justification for race pride comes from its strong belief that black people were the earth's original people and the mothers and fathers of civilization, beliefs they share with the Nation of Islam. Elijah Muhammad claimed that blacks are the "descendants of the Asian black nation and of the tribe of Shabazz" and explained the significance of the tribe of Shabazz and how it came to inhabit the earth.

> You might ask, who is this tribe of Shabazz? Originally, they were the tribe that came with the earth (or this part) 60 trillion years ago when a great explosion on our planet divided it into two parts. One we call earth and the other moon. This was done by one of our scientists, God; who wanted the people to speak one language, one dialect for all, but was unable to bring this about. He decided to kill us by destroying our planet, but still He failed. . . . We, the tribe of Shabazz, says Allah (God), were the first to discover the best part of our planet to live on. The rich Nile Valley of Egypt and the present seat of the Holy City, Mecca, Arabia.[22]

Rapper Lakim Shabazz bases his entire persona on this origin theory. He took the name of the tribe, Shabazz, as his last name to symbolize his connection with the original tribe and titled his second album *The Lost Tribe of Shabazz* (1990). Brand Nubian refers to both the tribe of Shabazz and the belief that the tribe was the original men in "Dance to My Ministry": "It's the Tribe, the God Tribe of Shabazz / First on the planet Earth, but definite to be the last." In "Wu-Revolution," the members of the Wu-Tang Clan celebrate their origins and further identify the original man as the Asiatic Blackman: "We are Original Man, the Asiatic Blackman / The maker, the owner, the cream of the planet earth / Father of civilization and God of the universe."

The Five Percent Nation also draws its race pride from social developments concurrent with its birth in the 1960s. Echoing James Brown's cry, members of the Five Percent Nation once again shout "I'm black and I'm proud" in the 1990s.[23] In their song "I'm Black and I'm Proud," an anthem alluding both to the 1960s and to the teachings of the Five Percent Nation, Brand Nubian clearly identifies the origin myth preached by Elijah Muhammad as the source of its pride:

Now did you know it was you who was first
to walk the earth, gave birth to the universe . . .
The maker, the owner, the cream of the earth,
Proud to be Black because the Black man's first.

Reference to the black pride of the 1960s is strengthened by sampling James Brown's song of the same name; indeed, the chorus is taken directly from James Brown's hit: "Say it loud . . . I'm black and I'm proud!" Brand Nubian calls on its audience to shout out, but their respondents are sampled from James Brown's recording, creating a solid, sonic tie between generations of black pride.

Once racial pride has been established, black nationalist leaders often exhort their people to solidarity and self-sufficiency. For Elijah Muhammad, the solution to lack of unity is knowledge of self: "gaining the knowledge of self makes us unite into a great unity."[24] Brand Nubian concludes that unity is a solution to all racial and social ills. In "Wake Up" the group claims, "You see the answer to me is black unity / Unification, to help our bad situation." Even the title of the album on which this song appears, *One For All*, shows its interest in unification. And as Wise Intelligent complains in "Word from the Wise,"

> If I was to say "yo black stop selling crack,"
> No, I don't think a single soul will listen.
> But if I was to riff, bum rush, and start dissin'
> I'd get their total comprehension.
> Cause all dem wants to see is violence and negativity
> When the problem is lack of unity.

Also like other black nationalists, many Five Percenters seek social reform and frequently use doctrine to buttress themes of social protest in their lyrics. Their calls for reform often target aspects of American politics (or "politrix") that affect African Americans and other minorities. Freedom, equality, and racism are all popular topics, as Lakim Shabazz illustrates in "The Lost Tribe of Shabazz":

> It's really sad,
> I know some people think that one day
> we'll be treated as equals.
> The land of the freedom, or so they say so.
> They tell you you're free, yeah, but free to do what though?
> Off our arms and legs they took the chains, big deal!
> They still left 'em around our brains.

The current state of urban environments also incites comment, as in Brand Nubian's "Wake Up":

> Drugs in our community (That ain't right)
> Can't even get a job (That ain't right)
> Poisoning our babies (That ain't right)
> Lying who is God (That ain't right).

Brand Nubian's "Drop the Bomb" offers similar views: "Take a look around at the black man, see us / Illiteracy rules, they showin' cartoons in school / they're way understaffed, and I don't understand the math."

Black-on-black violence also inspires words of protest from Five Percenters. In "I'm Black and I'm Proud," Brand Nubian asserts, "Do the knowledge, black, look at the way that we act / Smoking crack or each other with the gat / The only race of people who kill self like that."[25] Here Brand Nubian speaks directly to black Americans. Indeed, instead of merely protesting against white America, Five Percenter MCs often use their poetic platform to encourage proactive involvement within the African American community. Knowledge of self is the ultimate goal and lack of information is no excuse for inaction. Lord Jamar makes this point in "Drop the Bomb": "I have no tolerance for black ignorance."

Some MCs take an anti-materialist stance, a trope common to conscious rap in general and especially to Islamic rap. Poor Righteous Teachers preach anti-materialism in "Gods, Earths and 85ers" with the lines "Learn that time is the same on Casio or Rolex / Knowledge James, chapter two, verses one through six / but try not to judge a man by the price of his kicks."[26] Here Wise Intelligent points his audience to a New Testament passage from the epistle of James, a passage that cautions believers not to get caught up in class distinctions and to regard men of all classes as equals. The verses read,

> My brothers, as believers in our glorious Lord Jesus Christ, don't show favoritism. Suppose a man comes into your meeting wearing a gold ring and fine clothes, and a poor man in shabby clothes also comes in. If you show special attention to the man wearing fine clothes and say, "Here's a good seat for you," but say to the poor man, "You stand there" or "Sit on the floor by my feet," have you not discriminated among yourselves and become judges with evil thoughts? Listen, my dear brothers: Has God not chosen those who are poor in the eyes of the world to be rich in faith and to inherit the kingdom he promised those who love him? But you have insulted the poor. Is it not the rich who are exploiting you? Are they not the ones who are dragging you into court? (New International Version)[27]

Wise Intelligent expands on the biblical message in the following line by encouraging his listeners not to judge others by their wealth, here indicated through the price of "kicks," or shoes. He also compares watch brands to make his point. The value of Casio and Rolex watches may be different, but both keep time.[28] Stronger yet is Wise Intelligent's advice to the youth in "Conscious Style" to pay no heed to MCs who speak incessantly of their own wealth: "Black youth don't follow them, because they don't know shit / they sellin' you death on that pursuit for Benz and Lexus."

Rappers associated with the Nation of Islam and the Five Percent Nation are uniquely positioned to spread their spiritual message through music and are

encouraged to do so by leaders they respect, such as Minister Louis Farrakhan.
Considering themselves Black Muslim missionaries, Five Percenter rappers use their musical platforms to minister to African American youth who would otherwise have no way to learn "knowledge of self." Yet when direct messages of faith are couched in the heavily coded language of their lessons, the Five Percenter message may still get lost in the ears of the uninitiated. Lakim Shabazz admits as much in an interview with journalist and filmmaker Charlie Ahearn: "they'll be, like, 'that beat sounds fresh.' They don't really take heed of the lyrics. But some people will hear '1st in Existence' [one of his songs] and it's going to slap them in the face no matter what they be doing. I'm letting the people know that we are the original people of this earth."[29] Five Percenter musicians clearly recognize the challenges involved with spreading their "gospel," but nevertheless show consistent concern for the moral and spiritual health of the masses, as many of these God Hop songs illustrate.

Fans familiar with Five Percenter doctrine listen eagerly and carefully for words of wisdom from their favorite Gods and Earths. One fan (and journalist), Wakeel Allah, recalled Rakim's musical efforts:

> I thought about how the god has become a drum major for the Five Percent Nation of Islam. I thought about how he remained true to himself, as well as our Nation by being consistent. I mean, the Gods and Earths could always depend on Rakim, and he never let us down. Not to judge or discredit anyone, but there have been and still are many MC's that claim to have Islam, or be god, but appear to continuously contradict the very principles that we stand on. But when all things appear to be bleak for the righteous in Hip-Hop, the god Rakim reappears again and he is still standing on his square. He's still representing Islam. I mean, there is no questioning the god's integrity. We all respect him and revere him as the "god in Hip-Hop."[30]

While praising Rakim, Wakeel Allah also suggests that not all Gods and Earths consistently represent their nation, a charge upheld by other Five Percenters such as Wise Intelligent.

Indeed, not all songs by Five Percenter musicians show the same commitment to teaching truth to the masses. Many of their lyrics are clearly violent, or at least less than "righteous," and seem to reinforce charges of hypocrisy within the rap community. One recent attack came from The Goodie Mob, who begin their song "The Nigger Experience" (from *Still Standing*, 1998) with the lines: "I thought you said you was the G.O.D. / sound like another nigga to me." Yet we must remember that Gods and Earths take as their due the right to "define their own orbit," to make individual lifestyle decisions.

Furthermore, as one of my consultants suggests, using Five Percenter language does not necessarily indicate a desire to teach:

I would say that "proselytizing" is not always really the main thing, like a conscious agenda. See, a lot of times when you hear the math on records it's just part of the way the MC communicates regularly, and might not necessarily be proselytizing, just being fresh [stylish]. And especially in [New York], there are neighborhoods where learning the Lessons was what you did as just part of growing up, so for a lot of people these words are just part of the English that they speak on a regular basis.[31]

Nevertheless, even songs with only brief references to Five Percenter theology can serve a purpose in the overall plan of "civilizing the uncivilized," whether or not MCs intend to proselytize. Brief references in the midst of otherwise standard rap fare not only serve as momentary nods to those already initiated, but can also attract the attention of curious youth, who can then turn to other songs or other materials for more information.[32]

In the end, it is important to remember that lyrics are only one tool in spreading "knowledge of self." Five Percenter musicians make the most of all hip-hop tools. *How* the lyrics are delivered is just as important as lyrical content; musical style, intertextuality, and other non-musical cues complete the proselytizing efforts. To examine the interaction of God Hop lyrics and music, I now turn to flow, layering, rupture, and groove.

# 4 Flow, Layering, Rupture, and Groove

Lyrics illustrate Five Percent doctrine at work, but they must be delivered with force, style, and appropriate musical packaging in order to effectively reach an audience. As hip-hop scholar Tricia Rose has argued, "simply to recite or to read the lyrics to a rap song is not to understand them; they are also inflected with the syncopated rhythms and sampled sounds of the music. The music, its rhythmic patterns, and the idiosyncratic articulation by the rapper are essential to the song's meanings."[1] In this chapter, I examine how both the delivery of lyrics and the underlying musical tracks contribute to the message of God Hop. I do so using three concepts first articulated by Tricia Rose and now common to hip-hop scholarship: flow, layering, and rupture. Rose distinguishes between flow, layering, and rupture, but she also stresses their interaction: "[hip-hop's lyrical, musical, and visual works] create and sustain rhythmic motion, continuity, and circularity via flow; accumulate, reinforce, and embellish this continuity through layering; and manage threats to these narratives by building in ruptures that highlight the continuity as it momentarily challenges it."[2] Her analysis reveals particular concern with the socio-cultural ramifications of flow, layering, and rupture: for her, the sum of these concepts forms "a blueprint for social resistance and affirmation."[3] I would argue, however, that flow, layering, and rupture in rap music have aesthetic as well as social value. Together they create a song's groove, and in so doing establish a participatory musical community within which the Five Percenter message can be effectively heard.

## Flow

In hip-hop parlance, flow is the musical application of the MC's skills to a poetic line. Each MC hones an individual flow style—what Rose calls an "idiosyncratic articulation"—consisting of phrasing, rhyme scheme, rhythmic play, timbre, and accents. Gifted MCs can impose a variety of desired effects upon a given poetic form. Consider, for example, the following lines from Poor Righteous Teachers' "Ghetto We Love":

> Then they give us church, a trick to try to ease this,
> thought I'd check it out, had to learn about Jesus.
> Told them he was black and they called me a hater,
> then he's on a church wall, yeah like a slave trader.

These four lines make up two rhyming couplets, with the rhyme in each couplet limited to end rhyme, a typical phrase structure in rap poetry. Yet as I will illustrate below, Wise Intelligent's flow—his musical delivery of these lines—greatly transforms the poetic form suggested by their written form.

Patterning is an important measure of flow and is best illustrated by comparing measures in vertical stacks. Therefore, instead of using standard musical notation, in figure 4.1 I have charted Wise Intelligent's flow in a "flow map," using beat-class analysis as a basis to mark the rhythmic fall of each syllable.[4] Each horizontal line of figure 4.1 represents a single measure of music in 4/4 time; each beat is marked at the top of the figure, as are sixteenth-note divisions (asterisks mark the placement of the "back beat," the halfway point of each beat, while dashes mark the second and fourth sixteenth notes of each beat). The syllables of Wise Intelligent's text, on the right side of figure 4.1, correspond to each x on the left side of the figure.

```
      1 –  *  –  2 –  *  –  3 –  *  –  4 –  *  –
m 88                          x  x  x  x                     Then they give us
m 89  x      x x x x x x   x      x x x x   church, a trick to try to ease this, thought I'd check it
m 90  x    x x x x x   x   x      x x x x   out, had to learn about Jesus.  Told them he was
m 91  x    x x x   x x x x   x x x x x x   black and they called me a hater, then he's on a chu
m 92  x      x x x x   x x             wall, yeah like a slave trader.
```

**Figure 4.1. Poor Righteous Teachers, "Ghetto We Love," mm. 88-92.**

As Figure 4.1 illustrates, Wise Intelligent creates his own form from these lines, a form built around regular patterning. First, he finishes each line of poetry not within beat 4 of each measure, but within beat 3, leaving beat 4 open to begin the next line of text before the new measure of music begins. In so doing, he also places the rhyming words of each line—"ease this," "Jesus," "hater," and "trader"—on beat 3 of their respective measures and allows himself a breath, a sixteenth-or eighth-note rest before beginning the next line. Furthermore, he accents the syllables that fall on the first sixteenth notes of beats 1 and 3 of every measure (italics indicate accented text and beats). Between his textual accents and the snare drum hits on the backbeats (beats 2 and 4), every beat is clearly delineated. His flow in this example is also marked by speed: the high number of syllables in these lines demands quick delivery and Wise must use consistent sixteenth-note divisions in order to fit his couplets within the four measures. In short, Wise Intelligent's flow transforms his text from mundane rhyming couplets to rapidly delivered, rhythmic syllables that both help define the meter and fill up the meter's subdivisions.

As Adam Krims has pointed out, flow styles mark both geographic and personal styles, and also help define generic boundaries. Rap fans recognize MCs by their rhyme patterns, syncopations, textual accents, triplets, timbre, and poetic enjambment. Describing flow is therefore an essential element of rap analysis.[5] Krims admits that fans recognize many flow styles, but for purposes of his discussion he distinguishes three types: "sung" flow, "percussion effusive" flow, and "speech effusive" flow, each of which is marked by a characteristic rhyme scheme, patterns of beat accentuation, and timbral delivery.[6] According to Krims, sung style features rhythmic repetition, on-beat accents, regular on-beat pauses, and strict couplet groupings. The effusive flows, on the other hand, "spill over the rhythmic boundaries of the meter, the couplet, and, for that matter, of duple and quadruple groupings in general."[7] Whereas sung flow tends to be squarely placed within the given duple meter, effusive flows work against duple division and produce polyrhythms and subdivisions. In the passage shown in figure 4.1, Wise Intelligent's delivery may therefore be referred to as a kind of effusive flow.

Krims's terms are merely his way of dividing what are known more generally in rap circles as "old school" flow (Krims's "sung" flow) and "new school" flow (Krims's effusive flows). The transition between "old school" and "new school" flow happened gradually around 1990, and since most of the songs analyzed for this study date from 1990 or later, it makes sense that their MCs would make use of modern, faster, percussive, syncopated, or speech-like styles.[8] Whereas the term "flow" is used in the rap community, Krims's terms for flow styles are not. Hip-hop publications tend instead to use adjectival descriptions of flow; distinct categories have not been fixed. In a single issue of the *Source*, for example, Project Pat (of the Three 6 Mafia) has a flow style described as "leisurely" and "choppy"; unsigned artist Saigon has a "clear, forceful flow"; and Aceyalone has a "mind-blowing," "multilayered," "bouncy," and "Dirty-Dirt-type flow."[9] Krims's categories may not be as vivid as these journalistic flow descriptions, but they are a useful starting point, a simplified way to understand basic differences in flow styles.

Understanding and mapping flow styles also helps us to visualize the moments when MCs effectively break flow patterns to emphasize a key word or concept. Lakim Shabazz's exegesis of Lost-Found Lesson no. 2, questions 14–16 in "The Lost Tribe of Shabazz," for example, makes the most of a varied flow pattern, particularly in the passage describing the 10 percent (see figure 4.2). His strongest indictment is of the 10 percent's greed (m. 30), and this he highlights with poetic enjambment, space, and dotted rhythms. Instead of splitting the text of measures 29–30 into two equal phrases (after "need"), he deliberately places "greed" on the downbeat—a heavily accented beat—of measure 30. Furthermore, the lines surrounding measure 30 fill up the sixteenth-note space, but after "greed" falls on the downbeat of measure 30, Lakim rests until the final sixteenth note of the second beat, leaving time for his message to sink in. The syncopated figures for the text "this really bothers me," illustrated in the flow map of figure 4.2 by closely packed Xs in measure 30, aptly depict his agitation.

```
      1 –  *  –  2 –  *  –  3 –  *  –  4 –  *  –
m 29  x x  x  x  x x  x  x  x x  x  x     x  x     Ten percent of us can help but don't feel a need/th
m 30  x                x  x   xx    x   xx          greed, and this really bothers me./
m 31  x x  x  x  x x  x  x  x x  x  x  x  x          Eighty-five percent of us are totally ignorant/
m 32  x      x  x  x      x  x  x  x  x     x  x  x   Walkin' around with the nigger mentality/
```

**Figure 4.2. Lakim Shabazz, "The Lost Tribe of Shabazz," mm. 29–32.**
Courtesy of Tufamerica.Inc. Used with permission.

Even these few examples illustrate a point raised by Robert Walser (echoing Tricia Rose) in his seminal article on the music of Public Enemy: "the music is not an accompaniment to textual delivery; rather, voice and instrumental tracks are placed in a more dynamic relationship in hip hop, as the rapper interacts with the rest of the music."[10] In short, there must be a medium to deliver the message. Or, to paraphrase Walser, without the groove under the flow, the lyrics are simply poetic utterances with little rhetorical power.[11] To understand the rhetorical power of these songs, then, we must also look to the musical layers under the text and the overall groove that music and text together produce.[12]

## Layering and Form

The way in which rap music is produced demands specific attention to musical layers. DJs and producers lay down (create) tracks one line at a time, thereby building texture not in vertical stacks, but in horizontal layers. Each layer is then coaxed into appropriate interaction with the other tracks. When arranging tracks, producers pay attention not only to timbral variation, but also to the overall form of the song.[13] Indeed, each section of a song has a signature sound created through the manipulation of musical layering.[14] Therefore, as a prelude to describing specific approaches to musical layering, the following paragraphs provide a brief description of the typical form of a rap song.[15]

Modern rap (that is, rap of the 1990s and beyond) relies heavily on verse/chorus form, a form common to American popular music of many genres. But this form has not always dominated rap composition. Many early rap songs simply strung together enough verses to account for each MC of a crew, as in

the Sugarhill Gang's "Rapper's Delight." It has been argued that modern rap's
dependence on catchy "hooks" (choruses) reflects rap's crossover into mainstream popular music.[16] According to this argument, hip-hop musicians began to
include R&B-style melodic choruses to appeal to a wider audience as a response
to naysayers who found no melodic value in rap. Music critic Nelson George
suggests that the commercial value of the melodic hook increased after prose-
cution for sampling heated up in the early 1990s, noting that after the through-
composed, complexly interwoven sample-based production of groups such as
Public Enemy, rap production turned to "often simpleminded loops of beats and
vocal hooks from familiar songs."[17] George's critique shares the familiar criticism
that hooks signify the act of "selling out," turning away from "pure" hip-hop
aesthetic values. Verse/chorus form may currently dominate rap production, but
the form itself occupies contested terrain in the hip-hop community, a community
deeply concerned with issues of authenticity.

Songs which do fall into verse/chorus form often begin with a brief introduction, typically of four, eight, twelve, or sixteen measures.[18] The first verse or
the first chorus follows the introduction. Verses are nearly always rapped and
verse lengths typically range from sixteen to thirty-six measures.[19] Likewise, choruses (or refrains) are usually four to eight measures long, but need not be
standardized, even within a single song. Choruses may be rapped, sung, or instrumental, but they share repeated musical or textual material with each statement, thereby unifying the song through repetition.[20] Verses and choruses alternate throughout the songs, and most songs end with either a final chorus or a
coda.[21] Finally, codas—called "outros" in hip-hop speak, since they lead out
from the song in the same way that "intros" lead in to the song—share musical
tracks from the song and are typically places for the MC to speak, not rap, over
the music, often to give "shout-outs" to friends and compatriots.

In order to illustrate the centrality of layering in rap's formal construction, I
have charted the following examples onto a new form of transcription, a "groove
continuum." The groove continuum separates the many sounds of a single rap
composition into two large groupings—melodic layers and percussive layers—in
order to tease out the interplay between groove and melodic ornamentation, a
figure/ground relationship common to black musical genres.[22] Melodic layers tend
to be those pitched instruments and timbres not included in a rhythm section of
a live band: reeds, brass, and strings, for example. I also include some sung
vocals within melodic layers in order to differentiate their function from that of
rapped sections of a song. The percussive layers of my groove continuum chart
the activity of instruments typically considered part of a rhythm section: drums
of all sorts (such as the typical rap complement of kick drum, snare drum, and
hi-hat) and bass line, produced either by keyboard or guitar. But keyboards and
guitar occupy liminal space: at times these instruments act like part of a rhythm

section and keep time, while at other moments they carry a song's only melodies, revealing an inherent flexibility in hip-hop musicality and necessitating an individual approach to each song rather than a fixed methodology. The ultimate purpose of my groove continuum therefore is not only to graphically illustrate individual timbral moments but also to demonstrate the forward-moving nature of layering techniques and the interplay between layering and song form. In other words, both melodic and percussive layers contribute to a song's groove, a continuously unfolding, participatory musical experience.

Consider figure 4.3, a groove continuum analysis of Digable Planets' tour de force "Dial 7 (Axioms of Creamy Spies)." The graph itself should be read from left to right. Under the measure numbers four lines follow the composition layer by layer: the top two lines track the activity of melodic and percussive layers by measure, and the bottom two lines track the formal divisions of the text. (Note that this groove continuum does not graph every musical event of "Dial 7" but attends specifically to the interplay of musical layers.) "Dial 7" is built from four primary melodies—labeled 1, 2, 3, and 4 and written for synthesized sax, voice, keyboard, and keyboard respectively—and two percussive patterns—labeled 1a and 1b because they are similar.[23] The key below the graph explains and notates what each number in the graph represents.

The graph helps to illuminate several points. First, the layers I have classified as melodic confine themselves to non-verse sections of the song. In other words, during the verses Digable Planets carefully pare down the texture to only a percussive groove in order to clear textural space for the rapped text. Conversely, the group seems to prefer a thicker bass sound (percussion pattern 1a) for the majority of the song, including the verses, excepting the second half of Doodlebug's verse. The second percussion pattern, essentially the same as the first but without the added depth of keyboard bass, is otherwise held in reserve for transitional moments just before and after verses. The looped sax riff is also confined to Sara Webb's sung choruses and the final four measures of the song. The Planets also vary their melodic layering, introducing a secondary synthesizer melody nearly halfway into the song (m. 45), lightly sprinkling their composition with the looped sax riff, and freely mixing all four melodic layers in different combinations throughout the song. Clearly, Digable Planets valued the interplay of musical layers and formal structure in the "composition" of "Dial 7."

Whereas the groove continuum for "Dial 7" illustrates the interaction of layering changes and form, Freestyle Fellowship's "Innercity Boundaries" emphasizes the continuity of layers over an extended musical structure (see figure 4.4). Here the percussive groove of hi-hat, snare, and cymbal remains consistent throughout the song (with the exception of occasional fills and embellishments) while variable bass, vibraphone, and sax melodies weave over and through the percussive layer. I include the bass and vibes in the melodic layer in this example

Measures

1 2 3 4 5 6 7 8 9 0 1 2 3 4 5 6 7 8 9 0 1 2 3 4 5 6 7 8 9 0 1 2 3 4 5 6 7 8 9 0 1 2 3 4 5 6 7 8 9 0

melodic |------------------|------------------2------------||----------------2/3--------||-----------------|-----------2/3/4--------|
perc.    |---------------------------------------1a-----------------------x----1a-----------------------||----------------1b----------1a------|
verse    |----------------------------------------------------------------Butterfly-------------------------||--------||
chorus   |----------------|

70                    80                   90                  100                110

1 2 3 4 5 6 7 8 9 0 1 2 3 4 5 6 7 8 9 0 1 2 3 4 5 6 7 8 9 0 1 2 3 4 5 6 7 8 9 0 1 2

melodic |----------||--------------2/3/4------------|-----------------------|------------||1b||-----------------------|-----3/4---||---|
perc.   |----1b--|x|----1a----||-1b||---1a--|------1a--------|x|------1b----||1a||1b||--------1a--------|
verse   |---|                                      |----Doodlebug--------|
chorus  |----------------|

**Key**

X: break

**Melodic Layers:**

1. looped 1-measure synthesized sax riff

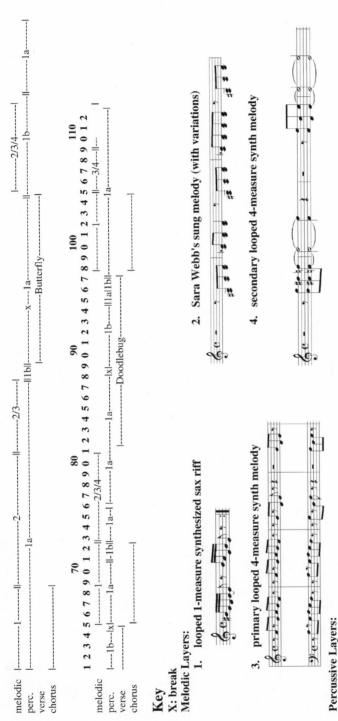

2. Sara Webb's sung melody (with variations)

3. primary looped 4-measure synth melody

4. secondary looped 4-measure synth melody

**Percussive Layers:**

1a. looped 4-measure pattern: hihat + snare + bass (keyboard doubles bass)

1b. same as percussive pattern 1, but no keyboard

**Figure 4.3. "Dial 7 (Axioms of Creamy Spies)" Groove Continuum**

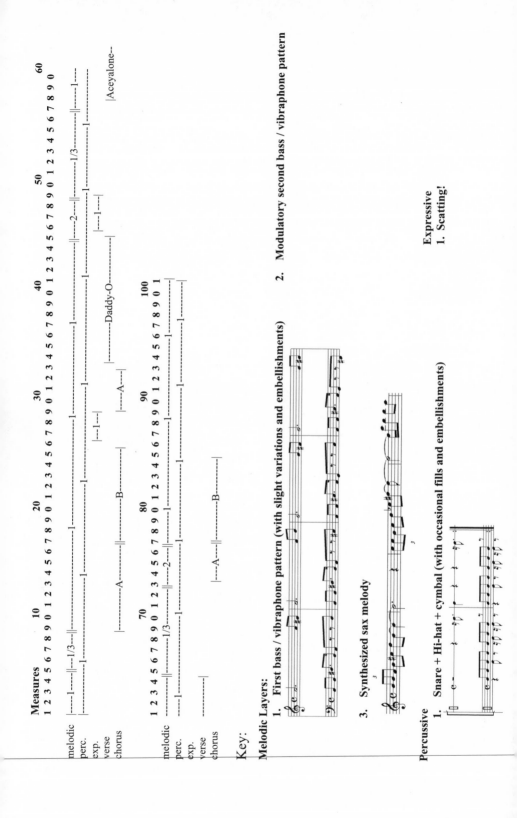

because of their prominent melodic patterns and soloistic treatment as they vary slightly with occasional embellishments throughout the song. Unlike most hip-hop songs, in which performers rhyme over pre-recorded music, "Innercity Boundaries" uses a live band. The embellishments and variations are therefore more frequent and flexible than usual. But again, the producer—Daddy-O, formerly of Stetsasonic—reserves certain instrumental layers for key structural moments: the sax riff, for example, marks only the second half of the introduction (mm. 5–8) and the instrumental breaks before and after Aceyalone's verse (mm. 49–56 and 65–72). And whereas a primary bass and vibraphone duet pattern play for most of the song, a modulatory secondary bass and vibraphone duet take over in transitional moments: during the harmonically unstable scatting just after Daddy-O's verse (mm. 45–48) and again against the final statement of chorus A (mm. 73–76) as a Freestyle Fellowship member expressively expands the original melody of chorus A, neatly imitating a saxophone in the process.[24]

## Rupture

Both "Dial 7" and "Innercity Boundaries" illustrate the interlocking nature of form and layering: on a large scale, layering produces a continuous groove, an unfolding and repetitive musical structure over which MCs deliver their flow of words. But just as layering helps delineate form, so, too, do moments of discontinuity, moments when effective producers and DJs manipulate musical layers to interrupt—or rupture, as Rose would have it—the musical groove and continuity for a variety of expressive and formal purposes. Rose's discussion of rupture points especially to rhythm:

> the flow and motion of the initial bass or drum line in rap music is abruptly ruptured by scratching (a process that highlights as it breaks the flow of the rhythm), or the rhythmic flow is interrupted by other musical passages. Rappers stutter and alternatively race through passages, always moving within the beat or in response to it, often using the music as a partner in rhyme.[25]

Here Rose distinguishes between three forms of rupture: the rhythmic rupture produced by scratching; the rhythmic rupture that occurs when musical patterns interrupt each other (perhaps a description of sampling); and the rupture produced when MCs change their flow patterns over the musical tracks. Given the percussive and polyrhythmic nature of rap, it is not surprising that Rose focuses primarily on rhythmic rupture. But her treatment of rupture downplays melodic layers, subtly agreeing with (and perpetuating) the canard that rap has no melody worth discussing. Therefore, instead of describing rupture as a predominantly rhythmic process, I prefer to see rupture as textural change, as manipulation (whether subtle or abrupt) of both melodic and percussive layers. Seen in this way, rupture can emphasize formal design, outlining, for example, the boundaries between verses and choruses. Rupture can also highlight structural repetition, helping to delineate four-and eight-bar phrasing. And finally, rupture in the form of textural changes can be used for expressive purposes in order to stress specific moments of text.

### PERCUSSIVE RUPTURES

For percussive ruptures to be effective, the discrete drum layers must be recognizable and their functions understood. Rap percussion instruments typically include a hi-hat or ride cymbal, often relegated to the function of outlining straight or swung eighths; a snare drum, typically given the backbeats; and a kick (bass) drum, often heard in one-, two-, or four-measure patterns. Thus, each of these instruments—whether acoustic or produced with drum machines—not only performs a different timekeeping function, but also occupies distinct timbral space. Indeed, every layer of rap music relies heavily on differentiated timbral spaces, what Olly Wilson calls the "heterogeneous sound ideal," a key element of black diasporic and African American music-making.[26] Producers attend to even the smallest details when manipulating percussive layers, and their compositional choices are broad. The most common strategy used to rupture percussive layers is dropping one or more drum layers out of the musical texture to mark formal and structural divisions or expressive details of the text. Rupture can also take the form of complete musical breaks under the text. Less frequently, producers rupture not textures but specific rhythms. Detailed examples of all three techniques follow.

In order to mark formal divisions of the text, the bass drum pattern of Poor Righteous Teachers' "Conscious Style" changes significantly between the introduction and verse 1 and between the last line of each verse and the following chorus. The snare drum pattern also adjusts in these measures: it is absent at the ends of the introduction and the first two verses, and only sounds on beat 2 of the last measure of verse 3. For the rest of the song, however (with a few exceptions to be discussed below), the snare and bass drum fall into a two-measure pattern, as in example 4.1.

Rakim's "The Mystery (Who Is God)" reveals a similar strategy. Naughty Shorts, the producer, varies the percussive textures to mark the formal divisions between the introductory chorus and verse 1, the second chorus and verse 2, and the third chorus and verse 3. In the last two measures before verse 1 (mm. 14–15), Naughty Shorts strips the texture down to only synthesized horn and kick drum, adding hi-hat in the second measure. He then elongates the pattern into four measures between the third chorus and verse 3: measures 63–64 have only kick drum and synthesized horn, measure 65 adds the hi-hat on beats 1

Example 4.1. "Conscious Style," typical 2-measure percussion pattern

and 3, and measure 66 repeats the pattern found in measure 15. Between the second chorus and verse 2, however, he keeps the kick drum intact and gives the hi-hat a new rhythmic pattern; only the snare drum is absent.[27]

Subtle changes in percussive textures can also mark elements of large-scale and small-scale structural repetition. Poor Righteous Teachers' "Conscious Style," for example, shows changes in percussive texture at similar points in each verse. Whereas the hi-hat articulates each eighth note for the majority of the song, it drops out in the sixteenth measure of each verse for either the entire line (verses 1 and 2) or a single beat (beat 4 in verse 3). The kick drum and snare drum patterns are also altered in the same measure of each verse: in the first two verses the kick is absent on beats 2 and 3 while the snare hits only on beat 4, and in the third verse no percussion sounds on beat 4 (compare these exceptions to example 4.1).

Poor Righteous Teachers use a different approach in "Word Iz Life." For most of the song, the drums fulfill typical rap drum roles: the snare hits the backbeats, the hi-hat outlines every eighth, and the kick drum provides structure with the two-measure pattern seen in example 4.2. At regular intervals throughout the song, however, this percussion pattern is disrupted. The first measure of verse 1 (m. 9) has no kick drum, no snare on beat 2, and no hi-hat until beat 4. In other words, until beat 4 we are left with only melodic instruments (bass guitar, lead guitar, and synthesizer) and voice. Exactly eight measures later (m. 16), the same pattern occurs; however, whereas measure 9 is the first measure of the two-measure kick drum pattern outlined above, measure 16 is the second measure of this pattern. Measure 16, then, completes a cycle of four kick drum statements. Verse 2 uses the same reduced texture with two small differences:

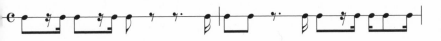

Example 4.2. "Word iz life" bass drum pattern

this time the first measure of the pattern is the second measure of the verse (m. 38), and the second measure with this texture occurs only five measures later (m. 42). Here both affected measures are the second measure of the kick drum pattern.

The kick drum pattern is again a determining structural element in Poor Righteous Teachers' "We Dat Nice." Father Shaheed uses a four-measure pattern, and throughout the song, percussive textures change primarily within the fourth measure of the pattern (see example 4.3). Although the verses are of different lengths (25, 25, and 21 measures respectively), they all end with measure 4 of this pattern, and within each verse, a variety of subtleties mark the fourth measure of this pattern. In measure 18 (the twelfth measure of verse 1, and hence the last measure of the third four-measure kick pattern in the verse), the kick drum is silent for the second half of the measure and the snare hits not the back beats, but beats 2 and 3. In measures 26, 54, and 86 (all of which are, again, measure 4 of the kick pattern), however, the kick pattern is intact, and the snare hits beats 2, 3, and 4. Changes of percussive texture in this song are thus linked at the levels of both the verse and the four-bar phrase.[28]

DJ Khalil of Self Scientific uses a similar strategy in "The Long Run" but organizes his four-bar phrases around the hi-hat, the percussive layer that is entrusted with timekeeping in the vast majority of rap songs. There is, in fact, no kick drum in "The Long Run": all drumming is left to the snare, which takes a typical backbeat pattern, and the hi-hat, which elaborates slightly on the common eight-to-the-bar timekeeping pattern. The first three measures of the hi-hat pattern are identical; the only change in this pattern comes in the second half of beat 4 of the fourth measure (see example 4.4). Just as the majority of changes in percussive textures in "We Dat Nice" come in measure 4 of the kick drum pattern, in "The Long Run" most textural changes happen in measure 4 of the hi-hat pattern. The hi-hat's pattern shifts in the final measure of each verse and each statement of the chorus, coinciding with both with the fourth measure of the hi-hat's pattern and with the end of formal sections. DJ Khalil varies the percussive textures in a variety of ways, although he seems to prefer emptying the first two or three beats of a measure and retaining beat 4's activity as a pick-up to the next measure. More isolated moments of change happen for expressive purposes: in measures 14, 38, 40, and 44 Khalil makes room for Chace

Example 4.3. "We Dat Nice," bass drum pattern

**Example 4.4. "The Long Run," percussion**

Infinite as the MC names himself (m. 38), speaks of the power of his rhymes (mm. 38 and 40), and explains his purpose: "living my life hoping that the youth remember us" (m. 44).

DJ Khalil's preference for four-bar patterning and subtle text accentuation reflects his obvious concern for structure. His attention to even momentary effects results in compelling and effective musical structures, artfully ruptured here and there to give life to Chace Infinite's rhymes. And Khalil is just one example of a meticulous producer at work. Indeed, as this section illustrates, close inspection of rap's percussive ruptures reveals a wealth of constantly shifting, obviously intentional details programmed by producers who understand the impact of their every musical decision.

### COMPLETE RUPTURES: BREAKS IN THE MUSICAL TEXTURE
Complete breaks in the musical texture, just like changes in percussive layers, often serve as markers of key formal or structural divisions.[29] The only complete breaks of musical texture in Poor Righteous Teachers' "We Dat Nice," for example, occur within measure 4 of the song's four-measure kick drum pattern, emphasizing the song's four-bar phrasing. Two of these breaks, those in measures 14 and 78, occur within the eighth measure of their respective verses, but the third break (m. 89) occurs in the last full measure of verse 3, helping to delineate the song's form. Likewise, in "Gods, Earths and 85ers" breaks occur either as divisional markers (as at the beginning of verse 1, the end of verse 1, and the end of verse 2), or as an element of structural repetition within the fourth measure of the song's four-measure kick drum pattern (as in mm. 16, 47, and 83). "Miss Ghetto" shows a similar interest in aligning breaks with formal and structural elements. Two breaks separate verses from choruses (mm. 36 and 60, the last lines of verses 1 and 2 respectively), but these and the remaining three breaks come in the fourth measure of the kick drum's four-measure pattern. On the other hand, breaks and other percussion changes in Poor Righteous Teachers' "Holy Intellect" have little to do with the kick drum pattern, since the drum pattern here is only one measure long. Instead, breaks tend to occur at similar places in each verse: at the fourth measure of verses 1, 2, and 4.

"Allies," the joint effort of Poor Righteous Teachers and the Fugees, features three breaks, one in Culture Freedom's verse and two in Pras's verse. But in this song, breaks are not aligned with percussion patterns, as the drums are relatively skittish and often deviate from their primary one-measure patterns. Instead, breaks in "Allies" come in the first measure of a four-measure synthesizer and sax riff (see example 4.5). Because these melodic lines are so spare, all that is necessary to produce a break in the first measure of the pattern is to leave out percussion between beats 1 and 4, which is indeed what happens in all three breaks. Pras further emphasizes the breaks in his verse by delaying his triplet-driven flow (indicated by brackets) until after the downbeats of measures 49 and 53 (see figure 4.5; underlined text falls within the break), each of which coincides with the first measure of the four-measure pattern. Pras's words thus fall between beats 1 and 4, making the most of the measure's momentary break.

**Example 4.5. Synth and Sax riff from "Allies"**

```
        1 – * – 2 – * – 3 – * – 4 – * –
m 49        x x x     x    x x x     x     x x   Catch the midnight train to Georgia as my
m 50    [ x x x ]  [ x x x ]  [ x x x ]  x        tongue does a dropkick like Sgt. Slaughter
m 51    [ x x x ]  x       x  [ x x x ]  [ x x x ] New world order, you lions who trying to
m 52    x    x x x  x    x  x  [ x x x ]  x        Roar, I'll silence your lambs like Jodie Foster
m 53        x  x x     x    x    x x x     x       There's no need to feel sentimental . . .
```

**Figure 4.5. "Allies," flow and breaks, mm. 49–53 (brackets indicate triplets).**

A similar break caused by textural change comes in measure 64 of Eric B. and Rakim's "In the Ghetto." Eric B. constructed the song over three samples: 24 Carat Black's "Ghetto: Misfortunes Wealth" (from *Misfortune's Wealth*, 1973); Donny Hathaway's "The Ghetto" (from *Live*, 1971); and Bill Withers's "Kissin' My Love" (from *Still Bill*, 1971). The drum line from "In the Ghetto" comes from "Kissin' My Love," but over the sampled drum layer Eric B. foregrounds a jangly hi-hat line playing heavily swung eighth notes. For measures 61 through 64 Eric B. takes away the added hi-hat for the first time, and this reduced texture continues for four measures. The only break in this song comes during beat 3 of the fourth measure of this four-measure textural change (m. 64), a brief pause between the bass and keyboard lines that would not be as audible with the hi-hat line (see example 4.6 and figure 4.6).[30]

Example 4.6. "In the Ghetto," bass and keyboard

```
   1 –  *  –  2  –  *  –  3  –  *  –  4  –  *  –
61 x x  x  x  x  x  x  x  x  x  x  x  x  x     Reaching for the city of Mecca, visit Medina/
62    x  x  x  x  x  x  x     x  x  x  x        Visions of Neffertiti, then I seen her/
63 x     x     x  x  x   x x     x     x  x  x  Mind keeps traveling/ I'll be back after I
64 x x  x  x  x  x  x  x x x  x  x  x  x     x  x  stop and think about the brothers and sisters in Africa/
```

Figure 4.6. Rakim's flow from "In the Ghetto" (mm. 61–64)

Breaks in the music can also serve purely expressive purposes; that is, breaks leave a brief window of silence that allows the MC a moment of textual clarity and emphasis. For example, the only break to occur in GZA's "B.I.B.L.E." comes at a textually significant moment. As GZA explains his struggle out of Christianity toward "true knowledge of self," he and the producer for this song, 4th Disciple, silence the music under the text "religion did nothing" (m. 47), thereby not only providing space for textual emphasis, but also illustrating the text "did nothing" by doing nothing.[31] Similarly, both breaks that occur with text in Grand Puba's "Soul Controller" dramatize Grand Puba's text. The first comes in measure 13, after Grand Puba has posed a question to his crew: "You mean to tell me that we're still not a slave / in the land of free and the home of the brave?" Their collective thoughtful response, "mmm," comes at a break. The song's second break with text falls in measure 62 as Grand Puba compares churches to liquor stores, claiming that if churches were good for the black population they would not be on every block. He and DJ Alamo underscore his comparison by placing a break under the statement that church is "no good (no goddamned good), they represent the 10 percent."

Likewise, the only break in the Wu-Tang Clan's "Impossible" comes in the last line of the song. Raekwon, a Wu-Tang member who does not perform in the main body of the song (the three verses are rapped by RZA, U-God, and Ghostface Killah respectively) enters in the coda to present the "moral" of the song. He condemns worldwide violence and especially black-on-black crime, and ends this cautionary tale with the lines " 'cause this is only a story, from the real." The final clause, "from the real," is unaccompanied, producing an unexpected irony in Raekwon's warning. The verses preceding his coda may be only stories, but they are drawn from everyday life events and should not be taken lightly or dismissed as fiction. RZA, the producer, here manipulates musical texture to add depth to the Wu-Tang's anti-violence message.

Big Daddy Kane uses complete breaks in the musical texture for a different expressive purpose in "Mortal Combat." He chooses not to highlight doctrine or a moral center through his breaks, but to put down his lyrical competitors. The break during the final line of his final verse makes way for a shout-out to the Nation of Islam, but the six earlier breaks in his song, falling in measures 30, 52, 60, 68, 96, and 104, each involve elaborate challenges to other MCs, claiming his competitors' rhymes are "old as Pro-Keds" (m. 96), avowing he will play other MCs "like a game of Nintendo" (m. 60), and making general deprecatory accusations such as "rappers are so full of shit they need Ex-Lax" (m. 52). Although the song is not built on repeated patterns of eight measures, the breaks themselves create such a pattern, falling primarily eight measures apart. In this way, Big Daddy Kane, both MC and producer of this song, uses silence as both an expressive and structural element; silence here does not respond to other structural patterns, but creates the pattern.

A few songs, such as Brand Nubian's "Ragtime," take advantage of breaks for both formal and expressive reasons. Two breaks occur in the last measure of each statement of "Ragtime's" chorus, introducing the next MC and separating the verses, but three breaks highlight significant moments. Sadat X's statement in measure 14, "In fact, they failed the test," is a subtle rebuke of his unnamed challengers. And two breaks come in Grand Puba's verse to emphasize boasts of his rhyming abilities (m. 74) and, ironically, his humility (m. 90). Likewise, the single break in the Micranots' "Culture" serves both expressive and formal ends. The break happens on the downbeat of measure 45, the first line of I Self Devine's second verse, thereby clearly delineating the end of the previous chorus and the beginning of the verse, but the text over the break, "pain," is clearly meant to be heard. Breaking here, even for just the downbeat, draws attention to I Self Devine's struggle through the maze of the record industry and his nostalgia for unsullied hip-hop culture.

On the other hand, in Digable Planets' "Dial 7 (Axioms of Creamy Spies)" the reason for the three breaks is somewhat ambiguous. Although the melodic patterns change frequently, the percussion groove provided by the keyboard, bass guitar, hi-hat, and snare remains steady. A four-measure snare and hi-hat pattern provides the underlying phrase structure of the song, and two of the breaks coincide with the fourth measure of this pattern (mm. 64 and 88). But the break in measure 64 comes at the end of Ladybug Mecca's verse and therefore also delineates a formal division. Furthermore, the text of this line, "you subtract the devils that get smoked," reinforces the message of resistance to white oppression throughout the song. The break in measure 34, however, is clearly expressive. Coming in the second measure of the snare/hi-hat pattern and in the middle of Butterfly's verse, this break happens under Butterfly's text "true black man that I am."

As "What Cool Breezes Do" illustrates, Digable Planets use musical breaks eclectically. Two breaks come in Ladybug Mecca's verse, the first as she states her name for the first time (downbeat of m. 13) and the second as Butterfly addresses her by name in beat 4 of measure 19. In measure 58, Butterfly "disses" his competition with a reference to his Muslim dietary restrictions, claming that even if critics find their competition "phat," "we just ignore it like it's pork." But the remaining breaks, in measure 34 and measures 61–62 of "What Cool Breezes Do," have no easy explanation. The groove of this song is continuous: neither melodic nor percussive lines work in cycles larger than a single measure.[32] The break in measure 34 comes at the halfway point of Doodlebug's sixteen-measure verse, and thus could be of structural importance, linking two sections of eight measures, but no other musical layers privilege a division here. On the other hand, the break in measures 61–62 comes in the fifteenth and sixteenth measures of Butterfly's twenty-four-measure verse, suggesting that structure is not the dominant impulse. But Butterfly's verse is a study in textural change. Of the entire song, Butterfly's verse uses call-and-response most extensively as Ladybug Mecca responds to his statements and questions throughout the verse. Furthermore, the fifth through eighth measures of Butterfly's verse feature a drastic textural change: here all melody instruments drop out, leaving only the percussion groove. The full texture then returns for three measures, but a break under measure 58 interrupts what would be a fourth measure for this phrase. Textural variety continues after this break: for two measures the full texture returns, followed by two measures of break in measures 61–62. The Planets round out Butterfly's verse with a return to the song's full texture for his final eight measures. The breaks in Butterfly's verse, then, reinforce a key point: in addition to their structural and expressive uses, breaks generally serve as another textural tool in the hands of a good producer.

### RHYTHMIC CHANGES

Shifting rhythmic patterns is another common rhetorical strategy. Like textural changes, subtle modifications in rhythmic patterns can play key structural or expressive roles, as is true in Poor Righteous Teachers' "We Dat Nice." Like the changes in percussive texture in this song described above, key rhythmic variations are made in the final line of each verse. The default pattern for the snare in this song is accenting backbeats, but in measures 30 and 62 (the last measures of verses 1 and 2 respectively) new, syncopated patterns are introduced (see example 4.7). Additionally, measure 89, the last measure of verse 3, features a

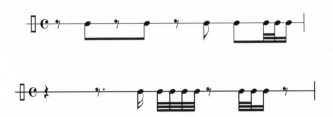

Example 4.7. "We Dat Nice," approximations of snare drum patterns for measures 30 and 62

complete break. In this way, major adjustments in both rhythm and texture mark the end of each verse. These changes are clearly meant to delineate formal divisions, yet the text at these points of rhythmic transformation is key. Each verse ends with the same text, beginning with beat 4 of the previous measure and extending to the downbeat of the following measure: "take / flight, make ice of any MCs you like, I'm dat / nice." In other words, Father Shaheed undergirds Wise Intelligent's boasts of lyrical prowess with complicated rhythmic flexibility, musically "showing and proving" that Wise Intelligent and his crew are capable of creativity and ingenuity.

"We Dat Nice" is a study in frequent rhythmic changes: snare and kick drum patterns change throughout the song, and in most cases these variations occur within the fourth measure of the kick drum pattern. But "Word from the Wise," also by Poor Righteous Teachers, shows yet another approach to rhythmic change. Here rhythmic patterns coincide with melodic textures. A two-measure saxophone riff plays intermittently throughout the song: in the second half of the introduction, throughout the choruses, and during the coda. Both the hi-hat and the kick drum have two primary rhythmic patterns: when the sax plays, the hi-hat, kick, and cymbal play the rhythmic groove seen in example 4.8. When the sax drops out, however, the drums play a different pattern, as seen in example 4.9. Rhythmic modifications here are subtle but also involve a change in timbre; whereas the first pattern includes an open cymbal, the second pattern does not.

In some cases, such as in "Conscious Style," a given rhythm is altered in order to emphasize changes in the MC's flow. In this song, both the otherwise-steady kick drum and snare patterns change throughout guest MC KRS-One's verse, making way for his unusually asymmetrical, almost ametrical, flow. This strategy is likely a deliberate production choice: KRS-One is not only the guest MC, but also the producer of this song, and his production style here makes the most of his guest verses.

Rhythmic changes are also sometimes due to intertextual references, as we see in Brand Nubian's "The Godz Must Be Crazy." The only rhythmic disruption

**Example 4.8. First drum pattern of "Word from the Wise"**

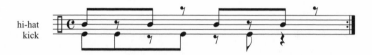

**Example 4.9. Second drum pattern of "Word from the Wise"**

in this song occurs at the text "Punks jump up to get beat down" (m. 76), which happens to be the title of another song on the same album. The full text phrase is "Cee-Cypher-Punks jump up to get beat down," a practical example of using the Supreme Alphabet to create acronyms and new meanings from old words: "Cee-Cypher-Punks" here spells out the word COP, in keeping with Sadat X's verse, which calls for self-defense and decries corruption in American governmental systems. For this single measure, Brand Nubian samples the rhythmic pattern of its own song "Punks Jump Up to Get Beat Down" to draw attention to this line of text.

Rhythmic change can also take the form of the DJ's scratching, the act of moving a record back and forth under the stylus to produce rhythmic or melodic sounds. Although scratching adds rhythmic complexity to percussive layers, there is little variation with respect to where scratching takes place within songs. Scratching is generally limited to choruses, and is sometimes found also in introductions and codas, but a few songs depart from scratching conventions and illustrate other possibilities for this rhythmic layer. The producers of "Soul Controller," "Wake Up (Reprise in the Sunshine)," and "Return" include scratching intermittently throughout the songs for no obvious structural, formal, or expressive purpose. In Rakim's "The 18th Letter," however, scratching partners an eight-measure bass guitar ostinato to delineate Rakim's otherwise unchanging forty-measure verse. Both "Anger in the Nation" and "Culture" feature scratching in the chorus, but the producers of these songs (Pete Rock and Kool Akiem respectively) also use scratching to segue smoothly from the last line of the previous verse into the chorus, thus anticipating the textural change the chorus will bring. Poor Righteous Teachers' "Pure Poverty" features moments of percussive scratching within beat 4 of measures 12 and 58 in addition to scratching throughout the choruses; these two moments of scratching coincide with the fourth measure of both the kick drum and bass guitar patterns and therefore serve structural functions similar to those of other changes in percussive texture. And in "Allies," the only scratching happens in measure 22 for text painting as Wyclef Jean issues the challenge "play it on your turntable, scratch it if you're able." In short, like other layers of rap production, rhythmic changes play a significant role in formal, structural, and expressive design.

### RUPTURING MELODIC LAYERS

Ruptures in melodic layers are made in the same way as their percussive equivalents: through the manipulation of individual musical tracks. Typical melodic ruptures can involve adding new melodic instruments over the current texture, alternating melodic instruments, or lifting all melodic instruments from the musical texture, leaving only voice and percussion. Furthermore, producers use melodic and percussive ruptures for similar purposes: to outline formal and structural design and to highlight expressive moments. GZA's "B.I.B.L.E.," for example, shows attention to both formal and structural details through manipulation of melodic layers. All melody instruments drop out after the downbeat in the measure before verse 2 (m. 56), and all other changes in melodic texture—curiously only found in verse 2—occur only within the second measure of the kick drum's two-measure pattern. Producers also frequently limit certain melodic layers to specific formal sections of the song, as illustrated in both "The Lost Tribe of Shabazz" and "Dance to My Ministry": the former features a pipe or flute only in the introduction, choruses, and coda, and the latter introduces a wordless vocal refrain only in the introduction and choruses.[33] Poor Righteous Teachers' "Holy Intellect" shows a different approach. Wise Intelligent and Culture Freedom begin verse 3 in call-and-response fashion over a sort of stop-time texture: all melodic instruments drop out of the texture here, and only the kick drum keeps time under these four measures.

Melodic changes in these examples seem linked to song form, but in other examples melodic changes merely provide a shifting palette of timbres and harmonies. Nas's "Affirmative Action," for example, strays far from verse/chorus form and instead is simply a strung-together collection of verses from the featured MCs—Nas, AZ, Cormega, and Foxy Brown—between an introduction and a brief instrumental coda.[34] Under the various vocal flows, the production team (Dave Atkinson, Poke, and Tone from Trackmasters) repeats three two-measure synthesized melodies (with a harpsichord timbre) in various repetition schemes (see figure 4.7). Each melodic pattern forms an antecedent/consequent phrase. The

Measures

10 20 30 40 50
1 2 3 4 5 6 7 8 9 0 1 2 3 4 5 6 7 8 9 0 1 2 3 4 5 6 7 8 9 0 1 2 3 4 5 6 7 8 9 0 1 2 3

melodic
verse
    1a   1a  1a 1b 1a 1b  2a 2b 2a 2b 2a 2a 1b 1a 1b 2a 1b 2a 2b 2a 2b 1a 1b 1a 1b 2a 2b 2a 2b 2a 1b 1a 1b 1a 1b

|————————AZ————————||————————Cornega————————||——————Nas————————|

60 70 80 90
4 5 6 7 8 9 0 1 2 3 4 5 6 7 8 9 0 1 2 3 4 5 6 7 8 9 0 1 2 3 4 5 6 7 8 9 0 1

melodic
verse
2a 2b 2a 2b 1a 1b 1a 2b 1a 1b 1a 2b 1a 1b 1a 2b 1a 1b 1a 2b 3a 3b 3a 1b 2a 2b 2a 2b 2a 1b 1a 1b 1a 2b 1a 1b 1a 2b

|————————Foxy Brown————————|

## Key:

**1.** primary melody: synthesized harpsichord over electric bass

  1a              1b

**2.** added trill to harpsichord and same bass line

  2a              2b

**3.** new harpsichord melody with same bass line

  3a              3b

**Figure 4.7. Melodic layers and progression of Nas's "Affirmative Action"**

first measure of all three patterns emphasizes A-flat, while the second measure of each pattern revolves around E-flat, creating a consistent tonic-dominant movement throughout the song. A single two-measure bass pattern provides the harmony for all three melodies. Since the bass's harmonic underpinning is consistent throughout the song, the melodic patterns can be mixed and matched with the appropriate corresponding bass measure. Thus, the second measure of the first melody (1b) follows the first measure of the first melody (1a)—as for example in measures 10–14—but it could just as easily follow the first measure of the second pattern (2a)—as in measures 24–27. And indeed, the production team mixes up melody halves throughout the song to provide variety (see, for example, mm. 70–77).

As figure 4.7 illustrates, melodies 1 and 2 are closely related and clearly dominate the song. The only difference between these melodies is the layering of trilled notes in an upper voice over the arpeggiated melody 1 to form melody 2. The third melody, however, moves away from this arpeggiation for the first time, bringing a new character to the synthesizer, if only for three measures: melody 3 enters only in Foxy's verse (mm. 74–76) and only one and a half statements of this melody are heard. Why the melody changes at this particular point in the song is unclear. Foxy's text in these measures, which concerns a drug sale, does not warrant a new musical sound to attract attention ("flippin' the bigger picture, the bigger nigga with the cheddar / Was mad dripper, he had a fuckin' villa in Manila / We got to flee to Panama, but wait it's half and half") and the measures do not occur at a formally significant moment of the song. Ultimately the melodic variations of this song seem calculated to provide musical interest, to keep the song moving forward as the MCs spin out their drug-sale tale.

But significant changes in a song's melodic layers can also have a more profound effect, such as in the Wu-Tang Clan's "Wu-Revolution," a primer of Five Percent doctrine for the uninitiated (see chapters 2 and 3 for a discussion of these lessons). The song opens as a dialogue between two men, the first (Poppa Wu) "lost" and looking for redemption, and the second (Uncle Pete) comforting. The lyrics below come from the first twenty-one measures of "Wu-Revolution" (each line represents one measure of music). Both voices of the dialogue are in the left-hand column of the example; the second voice is differentiated with italics. These voices are spoken, not rapped.

These things just took over me,
Just took over my whole
body, so I can't even see no
more. I'm calling my black woman a
bitch, I'm calling my peoples all
kinds of things that they not

I'm lost brother, can you help me? Can you
help me brother, please?
*You see what we did, we lost the love*
*I'm talking 'bout the love*
*The love of your own.* But brother, but brother, but brother, check this out. I still don't
understand man, I'm all high off this shit man
*Well, what I'm trying to say my brother*
*Why, why do we kill each*
*other? Look at our children,*
*what kind*
*of a future?* This is the training that's gonna be

| | |
|---|---|
| given to you by the Wu, brothers and sisters. It's time to rise, and take our place so we can in- herit the universe. | [The revolution, the revolution will be televised, televised, televised] |

The bracketed text in the right-hand column beginning in measure 18 is also spoken, but simultaneously rather than in dialogue (later in the song this voice sings). Low in the mix, behind the two initial voices, a woman's voice weaves in and out of the texture, improvising countermelodies over the relatively spare musical tracks, which consist of only snare drum, hi-hat, bass guitar, and the synthesized melodic layers shown in figure 4.8. For the rest of the song Poppa Wu delivers doctrine drawn from Lost-Found Lessons nos. 1 and 2, English Lesson no. C1, and the Student Enrollment Lessons, aided by sung and spoken responses from Uncle Pete and other singers, as well as by patterns of tension and release created by RZA's manipulation of melodic layers.

Three synthesized melodic layers (in addition to the voices) are at work in this song: two keyboard melodies (one with a clear electronic, synthesizer timbre and the other resembling a harpsichord) and a dramatic riff of octave Ds made up of synthesized horns and strings. Figure 4.8 illustrates the complex alternation of these layers. RZA, the song's producer, uses the primary synthesizer melody (labeled "1") most often, and rarely overlaps the horn and string riff (labeled "3"). The synthesizer melody tends to give way to the harpsichord melody, over-lapping its beginning at several points (mm. 19–21, 41–44, 49–51, 67–68, 87, 100, and 107). For the first half of the song the horn and string riff does not segue directly back to the synthesizer melody but instead buffers statements of the harpsichord melody. Yet after setting up these expectations, RZA compresses the lag time between melodies 1 and 3, so that by measure 109—nearly the end of the musical portion of this song—the horn and string ensemble interrupts the harpsichord melody and overlaps the synthesizer melody, bringing the music to a climax as Poppa Wu describes the 85 percent. Throughout this alternating pattern, the song's entire texture slowly thickens: handclaps enter on the back-

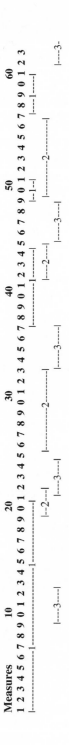

Measures

10 20 30 40 50 60

1 2 3 4 5 6 7 8 9 0 1 2 3 4 5 6 7 8 9 0 1 2 3 4 5 6 7 8 9 0 1 2 3 4 5 6 7 8 9 0 1 2 3 4 5 6 7 8 9 0 1 2 3

70 80 90 100 110

4 5 6 7 8 9 0 1 2 3 4 5 6 7 8 9 0 1 2 3 4 5 6 7 8 9 0 1 2 3 4 5 6 7 8 9 0 1 2 3 4 5 6 7 8 9 0 1 2 3 4 5

## Key:

1.  primary synthesizer melody, 4-measure looped pattern

2.  secondary synthesizer melody, 4-measure looped pattern

3.  synthesized horns and strings, 1-measure looped pattern

(strings)  (horns)

**Figure 4.8. "Wu-Revolution," Instrumental Melodic Layers**

beats and more background singers add their voices one by one. Thus, three separate melodic layers, each occupying a different timbral space, together propel the drama of the song forward and provide the expressive and affective foundation for Poppa Wu's sermon.

"Wu-Revolution" illustrates several of the many tools God Hop producers bring to their musical proselytism. Repetition and shifting melodic textures, both hallmarks of rap's musical style, here provide the continuous groove for Poppa Wu's delivery of lessons all Five Percenters know. Yet RZA, Poppa Wu, and Uncle Pete also reach out to the uninitiated through the dramatic and emotional call-and-response style of traditional African American sermons. The doctrine here may have originated with the Nation of Islam and the Five Percent Nation, but its packaging has an altogether different religious context, a context familiar to the African American audience the Wu-Tang hopes to reach.

## Groove

The doctrine in "Wu-Revolution" could just as easily have been distributed in sermons or pamphlets, yet the music brings a crucial unifying device and rhetorical figure of diasporic black cultural production: repetition. James Snead, one of the many scholars to comment on repetition, speaks of repetition in terms of circulation and flow, of continuous presence: "the thing (the ritual, the dance, the beat) is 'there for you to pick it up when you come back to get it.' "[35] Snead also describes what he calls the "cut," a "seemingly unmotivated break" in the midst of repetition.[36] Although his study appears in a volume on black literature and he speaks generally of music, dance, and language, his descriptions of repetition and cuts could very well serve as an interpretation of rap. Bringing the study of repetition directly to hip-hop, Tricia Rose notes not only the power of repetition, but also the effects of momentary disruptions of repeated patterns: "In hip hop, visual, physical, musical, and lyrical lines are set in motion, broken abruptly with sharp angular breaks, yet they sustain motion and energy through fluidity and flow."[37]

Both Rose and Snead describe the same musical phenomenon without going so far as to name it: groove. As defined by Steven Feld, who, with Charles Keil, opened the way to our understanding of groove, music that grooves is "regular and somewhat sustainable, identifiable and repetitive."[38] Later in the same study, Feld elaborates on his definition, emphasizing the processual, yet cyclic nature of groove: "In the vernacular, a 'groove' refers to an intuitive sense of style as process, a perception of a cycle in motion, a form or organizing pattern being revealed, a recurrent clustering of elements through time."[39] For Feld, repetition is the glue holding together form, content, and groove; without repetition, music ceases to groove. Keil, on the other hand, holds that variations on a groove are just as significant as the repetition itself.[40] Although not intended specifically as descriptions of rap music, the definitions of groove provided by Keil and Feld are highly appropriate to rap. As the musical examples in this chapter illustrate, rap works rhetorically because it grooves. Rap musicians unfold repeated cycles, processes, and patterns over time, occasionally rupturing—or varying—the groove's melodic and percussive layers.

Keil also emphasizes that active participation among musicians, music, and listeners is an essential part of groove.[41] Participation in a musical experience is certainly not limited to musicians, as Christopher Small has reminded us.[42] Feld, too, understands that "getting into the groove" can describe "how a socialized listener anticipates pattern in a style, and feelingfully participates by momentarily tracking and appreciating subtleties vis-à-vis overt regularities."[43] In other words, it is groove that propels God Hop's music and messages into the ready ears of listeners as they participate in the musical experience. Rap audiences socialized to formal, textural, textual, and expressive rap norms will be aware of changes in melodic and percussive textures; will feel expressive and formal breaks; will take note of subtle interactions between music and text, and will respond to affective musical and textual flows. Simply by hearing and responding to a song's groove, fans of God Hop "feelingfully" participate in music intended to introduce them to the Five Percenter way of life.

As these examples of flow, layering, and rupture illustrate, Five Percenter rap musicians use a spectrum of expressive strategies to underpin their messages. But the expressive strategies outlined in this chapter are not specific to God Hop. Flow, layering, rupture, and groove are essential elements of all rap production; God Hop musicians have simply adopted these common practices for specific rhetorical ends. Producers and MCs alike are keenly aware of the rhetorical power their musical choices can have. In a 1999 interview, I Self Devine, MC of the Micranots, spoke deliberately of the coloristic *affect* of compositional choices, the ability of musical programming to ready the ears of a listener:

> Whatever has been built can be destroyed. With that in mind, it is our goal to be able to reprogram people through visual stimulus as well as audio stimulus. You know, colors do affect the way that you think and feel—certain soundwaves, certain vocals, subliminal programming, mental programming and whatnot.[44]

I Self Devine's awareness of the close connection between musical sound and spiritual/social consciousness is commonplace in God Hop, as this chapter reveals.

Counting on their audience's familiarity with rap's genres, styles, forms, and structures, Five Percenter musicians subtly manipulate formal, structural, and expressive details, thus carefully crafting fertile rap soundscapes from haunting melodies, shifting textures, and inviting, infectious grooves in order to capture the attention of their audience and plant seeds of doctrine. Audiences may not understand the specifics of the doctrine in these songs, but that is not necessarily the point of the musical exercise. Musical communication in God Hop is above all intended to invite understanding through active participation. Indeed, Feld's concept of feelingful participation, which he defines as "a form of pleasure that unites the material and mental dimensions of musical experience as fully embodied,"[45] appropriately describes the type of interaction God Hop musicians can expect from their fans. And as Feld understands, feelingful participation produces "a special way of experiencing, knowing, and feeling value, identity, and coherence."[46] By uniting music and message in rap (a practice furthered by sampling and intertextuality, as we shall see in the next chapter), Five Percenter musicians construct a compelling musical voice with which to "civilize the uncivilized."

# Sampling, Borrowing, and Meaning

The practice of sampling, digitally borrowing passages of music from previous recordings for use in a new song, is one of the most discussed and least understood aspects of hip-hop music making. Legal experts debate whether or not copyright laws written long before sampling existed apply to this practice, and whether or not sampling is musical theft.[1] Academics and journalists prefer to ponder sampling through the lenses of contemporary cultural theories, especially post-modernism, intertextuality, and re-contextualization.[2] Other scholars offer evidence that sampling is a form of cultural resistance,[3] or contend that sampling in rap both extends and pays homage to African diasporic music-making practices and oral traditions.[4] Such a wide variety of theories inevitably encourages confusion, often resulting in laundry-list descriptions of sampling. Scholar and cultural critic Michael Eric Dyson, for example, categorizes sampling as a post-modernist, transgressive art form that both pays homage to African American traditions and deprives older African American musicians of remuneration for their years of music-making.[5]

Although these theories all enhance our understanding of sampling, none takes into account the perspective of artists who sample. Artists themselves pay little heed to scholarly theories and grumblings about theft, and instead offer aesthetic justifications for sampling. DJs and producers who sample are well aware of the potential legal nightmares of sampling, yet they continue the practice because it holds musical value for them. DJ Kool Akiem, for example, sees sampling laws as an economic battle that has nothing to do with the creative end of hip-hop composition. He explains his viewpoint on the Micranots' Website:

> The sampling laws are 98% about money. 01% about artist[s] pissed cuz they thought they would get loot from a used sample, come to find some fool they never met gets all the loot. 0.5% about artists who are broke (robbed by labels) who need the income, and the last 0.5% are artist[s] just participating in capitolismoculture. Even legally you caint own a beat, make a beat, I'll play the

same shit to precision, and you couldn't do shit about it. But I would sample [the beat] if it's dope [i.e., good].[6]

In other words, for Kool Akiem the aesthetic pleasure to be derived from sampling holds far more importance than the complex financial loops and legal ramifications now complicating the practice. Furthermore, hip-hop musicians are aware that using live musicians would be easier than sampling, but it would involve less play and aesthetic pleasure, as Hank Shocklee of the Bomb Squad has noted: "It would take less time to bring a band in and have them play this live than it does manipulating it our way [through sampling], but what fun would that be?"[7] Perhaps Stetsasonic said it best in their song "Talkin' All That Jazz" (1988): "A sample is a tactic, a portion of my method, a tool / In fact, it's only of importance when I make it a priority."[8]

The few scholars and journalists who have actually interviewed artists who sample also tend to favor aesthetic observations over cultural and legal theorizing. Scholar Cheryl Keyes, for example, has noted that sampling is above all a form of aesthetic pleasure.[9] Likewise, after dozens of interviews with sample-based producers, Joseph Schloss concludes, "simply put, sampling is not valued because it is convenient or justifiable, but because it is beautiful."[10] David Toop argues that our fascination with the legalities of sampling is misplaced, guiding us instead to examine sampling as a means of composition: "somehow, in the waffle about morality and legality that arose around the subject, the fact that [sampling] was an extraordinary way to compose music was bypassed."[11] Most recently, musicologist David Metzer has included a brief discussion of rap's sampling practices in a chapter on twentieth-century musical borrowing traditions, urging readers to remember that behind digital sampling lies the creative musical tradition of quotation.[12]

As a microcosm of hip-hop music and culture, God Hop provides fertile ground for further study of sampling as a compositional practice. Sampling plays a significant role in God Hop; an overwhelming majority of songs in this study are built upon identifiable samples from music, film and television, speeches and sermons, and various sound effects. In this chapter, I will illustrate how sampling, as yet another "tool" in the hands of capable God Hop artists, can be used to "civilize the uncivilized." I am not concerned here with whether or not sampling is legal and ethical. Neither will I consider the modern, post-modern, deconstructive, reconstructive, or post-structuralist ramifications of sampling. Rather than focus on these arguments, already so prevalent in hip-hop literature, I choose to follow Toop's advice and Metzer's model and examine sampling as a mode of rap composition. I begin by examining the compositional conventions of sample-based rap, a necessary step in order to clearly illustrate that sampling is the result of conscious musical choices. Yet in addition to providing aesthetic pleasure, sampling can also play an important role in constructing a song's rhetorical subtext. For that reason, in the second half of this chapter, I interpret samples within their new contexts, exploring how samples can create a desired atmosphere, trope and interact with a song's lyrics, and facilitate a dialogue between rap's past and present.

Table 5.1 lists by title the God Hop songs that form the basis of my sampling analyses, along with their artists and producers and the sampled sources. It should be noted, however, that the final column of samples and borrowed material is likely incomplete. My information about musical samples comes from two primary sources: compact disc liner notes and a searchable Web database entitled Sample FAQ.[13] Both of these sources are problematic. Since the early 1990s, hip-hop producers have been required by law to identify (and pay for) samples used in their recordings. Some information about samples is therefore available on CD liner notes, but CDs from before 1993 rarely include sampling credits. Furthermore, as Joseph Schloss has argued, because sampling is such a major mode of hip-hop music production, very often samples are used whether or not they are credited.[14] Therefore, post-1993 CDs could very well include unidentified samples. Sample FAQ, a valuable research tool, nevertheless depends on a single, anonymous researcher, likely a DJ or avid fan. Since sample-based producers look to obscure sources (typically vinyl) for their samples, many of the records are now out of print or otherwise difficult to obtain. Thus, I have not been able to verify all of the samples listed in the final column of table 5.1; those samples I have verified are shown in boldface type. Despite these limitations, table 5.1 nevertheless provides more than adequate material with which to illustrate both the formal uses of samples and the resulting intertextual meanings sampling can produce.

It is also worth noting that I differentiate between sampling and quotation. Whereas "quotation" designates any use of borrowed material, whether musical or textual, "sampling" specifically denotes the practice of using digital chunks of previous recordings.[15] The majority of borrowings discussed in this chapter are samples, but in a few cases, either the musical layers or the text is quoted— that is, re-performed—within the new song. Quotation and sampling serve the same ends: both adhere to similar formal conventions and influence the resultant meaning of a song. It is important to differentiate between quotation and sampling, however, because these terms help us identify who makes decisions about borrowing and pinpoint stages of the music-making process in which borrowing takes place: sampling is the realm of the DJ or producer, whereas quotation can be the function of the MC or the DJ.

**Table 5.1. God Hop Samples and Quotations**

| Songs | MC / Group | Producer | Borrowed Material |
|---|---|---|---|
| "5 Stars" | Killarmy (featuring Masta Killa) | 4th Disciple | Quotations of *M.A.S.H.* theme song |
| "The 18th Letter (Always and Forever)" | Rakim | Father Shah for Superman productions | **Sample from Lyn Collins's "Do Your Thing"** |
| "Ain't No Mystery" | Brand Nubian | Brand Nubian | Sample from Wilson Pickett's "Something You Got" |
| "Allah and Justice" | Brand Nubian | Brand Nubian | Sample from Howard Tate's "Look at Granny Run Run" |
| "Allah u Akbar" | Brand Nubian | Brand Nubian | **Muslim call to prayer** |
| "Anger in the Nation" | Pete Rock and C. L. Smooth | Pete Rock; co-produced by C. L. Smooth | **Sample from James Brown's "Funky President"; sample from Sly and the Family Stone's "Sing a Simple Song"; sample from Les McCann's "Talk to the People" (intro)** |
| "A Better Tomorrow" | Wu-Tang Clan | 4th Disciple | Sample from George Benson's "The Changing World" |
| "Black Is Back" | Lakim Shabazz | Produced and mixed by the 45 King | **Sample from James Brown's "Funky Drummer"; sample from Malcolm X's speech "Message to the Grass Roots"** |
| "Brand Nubian" | Brand Nubian | Grand Puba and Dante Ross | **Sample from Cameo's "Rigor Mortis"; sample from J. J. Johnson's "Rosita"** |
| "Buck 'em Down" | Black Moon | DJ Evil Dee (of Tha Beat Minerz) | **Sample from Donald Byrd's "Wind Parade"; sample from Lafayette Afro Rock Band's "Hihache"** |
| "Children R the Future" | Big Daddy Kane | Big Daddy Kane | **Quotation of Whitney Houston's "Greatest Love of All"** |
| "Conscious Style" | Poor Righteous Teachers | KRS-One (for Boogie Down Productions) | Sample from Sluggy Ranks's "Ghetto Youth Bust" |
| "Dance to My Ministry" | Brand Nubian | Grand Puba and Dante Ross | **Sample from Earth, Wind & Fire's "Bad Tune"** |

**Table 5.1.** *(continued)*

| Songs | MC / Group | Producer | Borrowed Material |
|---|---|---|---|
| "Dial 7 (Axioms of Creamy Spies)" | Digable Planets (featuring Sara Webb) | Digable Planets | **Sample from Tavares's "Bad Times"**; sample from Eddie Harris's "Get on up and Dance" |
| "Drop the Bomb" | Brand Nubian | Grand Puba and Dante Ross | **Sample from Kool and the Gang's "Jungle Jazz"** |
| "Ghetto We Love" | Poor Righteous Teachers | Father Shaheed | **Sample from Iron Butterfly's "Her Favorite Style"** |
| "Gods, Earths and 85ers" | Poor Righteous Teachers (featuring Nine) | Father Shaheed | **Sample from Raekwon's "Can It All Be So Simple (Remix)"; sample from Brand Nubian's "Wake Up"** |
| "The Godz Must Be Crazy" | Brand Nubian | Brand Nubian | Sample from The Winstons's "Amen Brother"; **sample from Eddie Harris's "Instant Death"**; samples from several films |
| "I'm Black and I'm Proud" | Brand Nubian | Grand Puba and Alamo (Alamo Worldwide Entertainment) | **Sample from James Brown's "Say It Loud, I'm Black and I'm Proud"** |
| "I Got to Have It Too" | Aceyalone | Fat Jack for Mass Men Productions | **Sample from Ed O. G.'s "I Got to Have It"**; sample from Hamilton Bohannon's "Singing a Song for My Mother" |
| "In the Ghetto" | Eric B. and Rakim | Eric B. | **Sample from 24 Carat Black's "Ghetto: Misfortunes Wealth"**; sample from Donny Hathaway's "The Ghetto"; **sample from Bill Withers's "Kissin' My Love"** |
| "Lickshot" | Grand Puba | Grand Puba and The Stimulated Dummies | Sample from Byrdie Green's "Return of the Prodigal Son"; sample from unidentified comedian |
| "Life's a Bitch" | Nas (featuring AZ) | L.E.S. and Nas | **Sample from The Gap Band's "Yearning for Your Love"**; sample from Grover Washington, Jr.'s "Black Frost" |

| Song | Artist | Producer | Sample |
|---|---|---|---|
| "Meaning of the 5%" | Brand Nubian | Brand Nubian | Sample from Marvin Gaye's "T Stands for Trouble"; sample from a Farrakhan speech |
| "Mortal Combat" | Big Daddy Kane | Big Daddy Kane | Sample from James Brown's "It's a Man's, Man's, Man's World"; sample from James Brown's "Funky Drummer"; sample from James Brown's "Honky Tonk Popcorn"; sample from George McCrae's "I Get Lifted"; sample from Kool Moe Dee's "Let's Go" |
| "Motherless Child" | Ghostface Killah (featuring Raekwon) | RZA | Sample from O. V. Wright's "Motherless Child"; sample from O. V. Wright's "Into Something (Can't Shake Loose)" |
| "The Mystery" | Rakim | Naughty Shorts for Fat Max Recording; Last Platoon | Sample from Charles McPherson's "Good Morning Heartache" |
| "One" | Busta Rhymes (featuring Erykah Badu) | Rockwilder | Sample from Stevie Wonder's "Love Is in Need of Love Today"; sample from Tom Tom Club's "Genius of Love" |
| "Pass the Gat" | Brand Nubian | Brand Nubian | Sample from Eddie Harris's "Superfluous"; sample from Funk Inc's "Kool Is Back" |
| "Pure Poverty" | Poor Righteous Teachers | unknown | Sample from The Fatback Band's "Put Your Love (In My Tender Care)" |
| "Pure Righteousness" | Lakim Shabazz | probably DJ Mark the 45 King | Sample from The Fatback Band's "Put Your Love (In My Tender Care)" |
| "Ragtime" | Brand Nubian | Skeff Anselm | Sample from The Gap Band's "Tommy's Groove" |
| "Rock Dis Funky Joint" | Poor Righteous Teachers | unknown (probably Father Shaheed) | Sample from War's "Slippin' into Darkness"; sample from James Brown's "Funky President" |
| "Self Styled Wisdom" | Poor Righteous Teachers | unknown (probably Father Shaheed) | Sample from War's "Slippin' into Darkness" |
| "Strictly Ghetto" | Poor Righteous Teachers | unknown (probably Father Shaheed) | Sample from Earth, Wind & Fire's "Get Away" |
| "Wake Up (Reprise in the Sunshine)" | Brand Nubian | Grand Puba and Brand Nubian | Sample from Parliament's "Flashlight"; sample from Roy Ayers's "Everybody Loves the Sunshine" |

**Table 5.1. (continued)**

| Songs | MC / Group | Producer | Borrowed Material |
|---|---|---|---|
| "Wake Up (Stimulated Dummies Mix)" | Brand Nubian | Dante Ross | **Sample from Ray, Goodman and Brown's "Another Day"**; sample from the Nite-Liters' "Tanga Boo Gonk" |
| "We Dat Nice" | Poor Righteous Teachers | Father Shaheed | **Sample from Mobb Deep's "Shook Ones Pt. II"; sample from Big Daddy Kane's "Just Rhymin' with Biz"** |
| "What Cool Breezes Do" | Digable Planets | Butterfly | **Sample from Eddie Harris's "Superfluous"**; sample from The Crusaders' "Mystique Blues" |
| "Word from the Wise" | Poor Righteous Teachers | unknown (probably Father Shaheed) | **Sample from James Brown's "The Boss"; sample from Malcolm X speech;** samples from Farrakhan speech(es) |
| "Word Iz Life" | Poor Righteous Teachers | Ezo Brown (for Superman Entertainment) | Sample from the Jungle Brothers' "Jimbrowski"; **sample from LTD's "Don't Stop Loving Me Now"** |
| "Wu-Revolution" | Wu-Tang Clan (featuring Poppa Wu, Uncle Pete) | RZA | Samples from kung fu clips |

Sampling machines are capable of both monophonic and polyphonic extraction; that is, with effective sampling software, a producer can lift an entire musical texture or can simply isolate and use a single instrumental or vocal line. Moreover, producers are not limited to creating a new song from a single sample source. Very often more than one sample (from single or multiple sources) adds to the sonic structure of the new song, as is evident in many of the songs listed in table 5.1. Once samples have been chosen, a producer may then manipulate the sounds in any number of ways. The structure of a sample can be altered through chopping (digitally cutting the sample into smaller pieces), re-ordering the samples, or looping (repeating the sample throughout a song). A sample can also be fed through a synthesizer and given a new timbre.

Until the mid-1980s, sampling practices were limited by storage space: samplers simply could not store more than a few seconds of sound. In the mid-1980s, sampling software gained the ability to retain and loop several measures of music. By the late 1980s, samples of varying lengths could be simultaneously layered, looped, and manipulated, giving rise to elaborate sound collages best exemplified by the Bomb Squad's production work for Public Enemy.[16] The effects could be sonically overwhelming, as Toop describes:

> the actuality of listening to an electronic viral blip-storm of cartoon voices, commercials, bursts of movie and TV dialogue, scratches, funk fragments, power chords, brass stabs, frantic percussion breaks and vaguely familiar two-bar segments from obscure old records could leave you with a hangover. . . . In the end, sampling needed a framework, a context, to enhance the strangeness of its sound world.[17]

The period of densely layered, often chaotic sound collages such as those used by Public Enemy did not last long and gave way to more or less standardized sampling usage. Whether by accident or design, sample-based producers subsequently developed a number of fluid conventions ruling how much should be taken from a source, what sources are appropriate, and how sampled sources should be used.

In the course of interviews with sample-based producers, Schloss developed a list of six "ethical" principles of sample-based hip-hop production, each of which speaks both to the importance of creativity and originality in sampling practices and to a profound sense of an inherited tradition that must be preserved: (1) one *should not* sample material that has been recently used by someone else, a form of imitation pejoratively known as "biting"; (2) one *should* sample only from vinyl records, since vinyl records are an integral part of the DJ tradition; (3) one *should not* sample from hip-hop records: to do so would be to

*Sampling, Borrowing, and Meaning*

shirk one's own responsibility for finding original sources; (4) one *should not* sample records that one respects and could not improve upon; (5) one *should not* sample from compilation recordings such as *Ultimate Breaks and Beats,* since doing so demands neither creativity nor research; and (6) one *should not* sample more than one part of a given record: there is no challenge in combining sounds that have already been combined.[18]

Schloss notes that his consultants did not universally agree on this list of "ethical principles" and also disagreed as to their priority.[19] Furthermore, each of these conventions can be broken for specific rhetorical or musical purposes. For example, Schloss's consultants claim exemption from principle 3 (that one should not sample from hip-hop records) in order to either parody or pay homage to other hip-hop artists with either vocal or instrumental lines. According to Schloss, there are three "pillars" behind this rule: "that sampling may be disrespectful to a great artist, that some music is so good that sampling does not improve it, and that sampling something that was already good is not sufficiently challenging."[20] Or, in the words of DJ Karen Dere, "unless you can add something, or flip it in a totally amazing way, leave it alone."[21] Nevertheless, as the following discussion will show, this "rule" is repeatedly broken, suggesting that there is a striking dichotomy between the "rules" sample-based producers believe should be observed and the conventions that actually shape hip-hop music's style.

Schloss's consultants do not describe how their chosen samples interact with given rap song forms, yet this, too, has its own conventions. Indeed, what and how much of a given song is borrowed has some relationship to where and how a sample (or borrowing) will be used in its new setting. Samples of single layers can be either vocal or instrumental, but producers clearly differentiate between the function of a vocal sample and the function of a single-layer instrumental sample. Vocal samples typically become the chorus of the new song. James Brown's responsorial shout "Say it loud: I'm black and I'm proud," for example, provides the refrain (and the title) for Brand Nubian's "I'm Black and I'm Proud," and a few lines from Byrdie Green's "Prodigal Son" appear as the chorus in Grand Puba's "Lickshot."[22] When not used in a refrain, vocal samples often serve as brief interjections, such as in Pete Rock and C. L. Smooth's "Anger in the Nation." Pete Rock here borrows a single "hey" from James Brown's "Funky President" as an exclamation point for the new song.

The process of sampling and re-using individual instrumental lines follows different compositional conventions. Often these single lines become part of the new song's groove: the borrowed instrumental layer is looped to provide a continuous structure under the vocals. Big Daddy Kane, for example, borrows the famous "Funky Drummer" drum line for "Mortal Combat," looping the drums to create the entire percussive texture for his song. And Killarmy's "5 Stars," built around a quotation of the melodies from the theme song to the television show

*M\*A\*S\*H\**, uses the melodies throughout the song. Producers may also use such samples for specific formal functions, as when Big Daddy Kane borrows the saxophone introduction from James Brown's "It's a Man's, Man's, Man's World" to become the introduction to his own song, "Mortal Combat."

Brand Nubian's "Pass the Gat" and Digable Planets' "What Cool Breezes Do" together offer a particularly striking example of this practice. Both songs take advantage of the same sample, two measures of rich tenor sax from the head (the opening melody) of Eddie Harris's "Superfluous." Although the nature of the two songs could not be more different—Brand Nubian's jam speaks of violent self-defense while the Planets establish a laid-back "do what you feel" theme—the producers of both songs clearly conceive of sample use in a similar way: both songs limit the two-measure, looped sample to statements of their respective choruses. The shared samples in "Pass the Gat" and "What Cool Breezes Do" seem to violate Schloss's "no biting" principle: one should not use a sample recently used by someone else.[23] However, given that the albums on which "Pass the Gat" and "What Cool Breezes Do" appear were both released in 1993, it is unlikely that the producers of either song can be accused of "biting." In this case, use of the same sample in two very different songs is likely coincidence, although using the sample in such a similar way suggests just how entrenched sampling practices have become.[24]

Schloss's set of "ethical principles" also includes a clear restriction against sampling more than one part of a given source, yet the number of songs in this study that borrow multiple layers from a single source suggests that this practice is not unusual. Like other styles of sampling, multiple-layer sampling has its own conventions. (By "multiple-layer sampling" I mean isolating and sampling more than one line from the melodic, percussive, expressive, and textual layers of a given song. See chapter 4 for a discussion of layering in hip-hop music.) Sometimes the entire polyphonic fabric of a brief section of a song is transferred intact to become a key formal moment—such as an introduction—of a new song. Pete Rock, for example, begins his "Anger in the Nation" with nearly thirty seconds from the introduction of Les McCann's "Talk to the People." He samples not only McCann's spoken words, but also the gentle musical accompaniment underneath. More often, however, when producers sample multiple tracks from a given source, they loop the samples to form the musical tapestry of the new song. This is the technique DJ Evil Dee uses to incorporate a sample of Donald Byrd's "Wind Parade" into Black Moon's "Buck 'em Down."[25] Evil Dee builds the basic groove of "Buck 'em Down" from measures 11–12 of "Wind Parade," keeping all layers (including keyboard, chimes, and synthesized harp) of the original song intact, looping the measures throughout the new song, and layering a new kick drum over the sample. At various moments throughout the song (primarily in the choruses), Evil Dee follows the looped groove with measures 13–14 from "Wind

Parade," now introducing strings and horns. Brand Nubian applies a similar technique to "Meaning of the 5%," a great deal of which (including the drums, melody, handclaps, and brief, punctuating sax notes) is borrowed from Marvin Gaye's "T Stands for Trouble." The borrowed layers are then looped throughout the song.[26]

Producers not only borrow multiple lines from a given source, but sometimes also build multiple new songs from the same samples. Poor Righteous Teachers' "Rock Dis Funky Joint" and "Self Styled Wisdom," for example, are built from the same sampling source: War's "Slippin' into Darkness." The producer of these songs (likely Father Shaheed) was obviously attracted by both the polyphonic guitar work and expressive sax interjections that begin about two minutes into War's song. Both sax and guitar samples appear in "Rock Dis Funky Joint" and "Self Styled Wisdom," yet with these songs Father Shaheed illustrates a few of the manifold compositional possibilities samples provide. The core groove of "Rock Dis Funky Joint" is built from the lead guitar and a middle guitar voice from the War song; these voices, however, have been re-programmed into a synthesizer to produce a new timbre. War's saxophone interjections also take a new sound here: the brief sax punctuations have not only been adjusted to a higher pitch, but have also been programmed into a new synthesizer timbre. By contrast, "Self Styled Wisdom" remains close to the source, using both guitars (this time lead and bass guitar) and saxophones in their original timbres. Yet the producer's approach to form is consistent: in both songs the guitars form the essential groove and the sax interjections are limited primarily to introductions, choruses, and codas (also known as "outros").

The conventions of sample use in hip-hop composition have a practical end for both hip-hop musicians and hip-hop fans. Working within these conventions, producers can play with expectations, following or avoiding conventions as it suits their musical or rhetorical needs. Sampling begins with "digging in the crates" (or "digging," for short), the process of searching through old, rare, and usually out-of-print vinyl records to discover obscure, fresh sounds for use in a new composition. Producers speak of choosing their samples for musical reasons; they listen for harmonies, rhythms, and timbres that catch their ear, or respond to an indefinable "vibe" or "feel."[27] DJ Kool Akiem of the Micranots, for example, explained that for him "making beats is a process of discovery, informed only by a pre-existing aesthetic; he is looking for things that sound good together."[28] In another interview, Kool Akiem explained this process in more detail:

> I don't sit down and try to memorize breaks. I don't even look at the artist that I'm sampling in terms of what kind of breaks they have that have been used. Sometimes I don't even remember what breaks I've used. Basically I have a big record collection and I go through it, looking for what's gonna fit into the track that I'm working on. I let the break come to me. I let the idea come out of

thin air. I might start with one track and by the time it's finished it sounds way different from what I started with. Like a painter may have all kinds of paintings underneath what you see.[29]

Kool Akiem consistently describes his sampling as a process of trying things out to see how the sounds will work rather than searching for specific sounds. In a 1999 interview, he described his digging process as follows:

a lot of times, I'm not really looking for a specific sound. . . . I'm not like, "Oh, I need a horn on here." And then go lookin': "I know what horn I want." And go find that horn . . . I mean, occasionally, I guess I'm going for something specific. But usually I'm just randomly throwin' stuff on there, kinda feelin' it out. Tryin' to, you know, "ooh, if I chop it here, it'll sound like that."

Other producers, such as Mr. Supreme, vary their approach according to the demands of a specific project: "sometimes, I'll know exactly what I'm gonna do. I'm gonna use such and such drums with this. Sometimes I'll just grab a stack of records, and come in, sit at the sampler and start putting stuff together."[30]

Years of "digging in the crates" have taught Kool Akiem, Mr. Supreme, and other producers how to find and isolate valuable and aesthetically pleasing musical sounds. We should not discount the possibility, however, that while working within sampling conventions and "looking for things that sound good together," producers also fold samples into their new compositions in ways that produce intertextual meaning, whether intended or accidental. Indeed, my analyses suggest that while carefully attending to form and beauty of sound, producers also choose samples that bring intertextual meaning to their new song, either through providing an appropriate atmosphere for the new song, troping the meaning of the lyrics, or establishing a dialogue between rap's past and present.

## Sampling to Create Atmosphere

Samples are sometimes chosen for the associative atmosphere they bring to a new song. In a brilliant rhetorical move, Brand Nubian opens its album *In God We Trust* with "Allah u Akbar," a song that begins and ends with a sample of the unaccompanied sung, or chanted, Muslim call to prayer for which it is named. "Allah u Akbar" invites listeners to meet the band members and also to hear the message they will share. Although the lyrics do little more than mention Five Percenter doctrine, Brand Nubian solidifies its connection to al-Islam by means of the chosen sample. The call to prayer is also heard between the two verses and during the coda in the company of a snare drum, hi-hat, bass guitar, and other samples, but it is only unaccompanied at the beginning and end of the song. In other words, the unmistakable call to prayer, common to all orthodox

Muslims, frames Brand Nubian's message and establishes an appropriate atmosphere for the rest of the album to come.[31]

In another example, Killarmy takes advantage of both musical and sound effect samples to establish an atmosphere of warfare for its "5 Stars." The lyrics of "5 Stars" are filled with war imagery best illustrated by the chorus: "Five-star general giving killing orders / Militant assassins surround the headquarters." But this war narrative would not be interesting or distinctive without its accompanying soundtrack. As mentioned above, Killarmy samples chunks of "Suicide is Painless," the theme song from *M*A*S*H*, the popular television sitcom of the 1970s and early 1980s, for use in the new song. Each episode of *M*A*S*H* begins with a brief introduction on guitar (see example 5.1) and Killarmy preserves this order by beginning the song with the same guitar introduction. With only a few exceptions (mm. 21–22, 26, 34, 44, 56, 60, and 92–96), the two-measure guitar introductory theme plays throughout the song. The primary melody of the *M*A*S*H* theme also follows the guitar entrance in "5 Stars," but whereas the guitar is sampled, this second theme is reproduced on a synthesizer and appears intermittently throughout the song (see example 5.2).

4th Disciple, the producer of "5 Stars," uses the borrowed melodies to help define the boundaries of verse and chorus form, a typical strategy in sample-based rap. He includes the second half of the primary theme at the end of the song's introduction, but withholds the theme in its entirety until the beginning of Beretta 9's verse in measure 25. Measures 3–6 of the primary theme return during the first chorus. The theme returns once again in measures 38–56, this time bridging the last two lines of ShoGun Assassin's verse and the second statement of the chorus, enlarged here to six measures to accommodate the eight-measure theme. Measures 5–8 of the theme return in Dom Pachino's verse and are immediately followed by the entire theme (mm. 61–72). The theme does not return again until the final chorus and coda of the song, skipping over guest MC Masta Killah's verse. The final chorus begins with the last two measures of this theme, followed by a full statement of the theme and the beginning of another statement as the song fades out. In short, 4th Disciple varies the borrowed tunes throughout the song, and does so in a way that adheres to sampling conventions. Furthermore, he has chosen a singularly appropriate sample, musically calling to mind the war imagery of a popular television show still in syn-

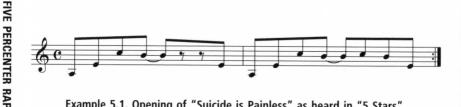

**Example 5.1. Opening of "Suicide is Painless" as heard in "5 Stars"**

**Example 5.2.** "Suicide Is Painless" main theme as heard in "5 Stars"

dication and highly present in public cultural memory.[32] But 4th Disciple also samples sound effects to provide an important part of the song's atmosphere, extending the song's war-soaked narrative by evoking familiar warfare sounds: machine-gun fire, missiles flying toward targets, and the whirring of military helicopters.

In a similar vein, Brand Nubian makes use of gunshot sounds to support both the title and theme of "Pass the Gat," the group's ode to self-defense produced in the wake of the Rodney King affair and the Los Angeles rebellion in April 1992. In keeping with sampling conventions, these sampled gunshots also play a specific formal role: with a single exception, the gunshots are limited to the introduction and choruses. They tend to come on beat 4 or on the "and" (the mid-point) of beat 4 at the end of the choral phrase "pass me the gat, I gotta fight back / I ain't rollin' over on my motherfuckin' back," acting as a pickup to the next measure. Lord Jamar's verse provides the exception. As he begins his verse "pass me the gat, and just like that / I squeeze like a man possessed from the Old West," his second line is punctuated by a gunshot in beat 4, a bit of word painting to add to the atmosphere. Despite the seemingly obvious relationship between music and text in this example, the text itself of "Pass the Gat" must be treated carefully. The lyrics suggest Brand Nubian advocates unchecked violence in the name of self-defense: in hip-hop slang, a gat is a gun. But as hip-hop journalist Jennifer Perry reminds us, GAT can also spell God Allah's Truth using the Supreme Alphabet. Lord Jamar himself has suggested, in an interview with Perry, that the latter reading may be appropriate: "people put tags on whatever they want. They say you're a nigga or a thug, they want you to be a gangsta. I'll be a gangsta. A gang is good if used correctly. We gangstas in the sense that we got a gang of Gods who get together for social equality to deal with one common course."[33]

Brand Nubian's "The Godz Must Be Crazy" also makes use of a special effect intended to add to the song's meaning. Lord Jamar and Sadat X here protest that their anti-Christianity and pro-black stance has earned them the label "crazy," and use metaphors of mental instability throughout the song. Samples play an important role in solidifying the song's overall theme. Brand Nubian draws spoken dialogue dealing with insanity and psychosis from movies and television and layers these samples throughout the choruses and coda. But the group also supports this theme musically with the use of a special effect that sounds something like a pitched siren, used throughout the introduction and choruses behind the sampled text. The "siren" has a pattern much like that of emergency vehicles: over two measures the siren ascends from a high E-flat to a B-flat and then descends again to E-flat. The transition between these two notes resembles a glissando, moving toward B-flat after two beats of E-flat, and returning to E-flat by beat 2 of the second measure. The siren sound not only evokes images of emergency vehicles and sickness, but also provides a musical contrast with the other layers of the song. All other musical elements are clearly delineated rhythmically, and the only other pitched layer, that of the bass, remains clearly pitched throughout its one-measure pattern. By contrast, the "siren" is unstable, thus lending musical meaning to the text's suggestion of mental instability.

### Interpreting Tropes: Sampling Lyrics, Speeches, Sermons, Film, and Television

Whereas instrumental and sound effect samples add to a song's ethos in a general way, sampled and quoted texts of various sorts bring specific meanings to their new settings, a sort of reverse troping. In the classic sense of troping, new material comments on or "glosses" old material; hip-hop troping instead uses snippets of borrowed material to comment on new texts and music. Like other vocal samples, verbal tropes reinforce common rap forms, usually appearing in the introduction, chorus, or coda, or are used as verbal interjections. Eric B. and Rakim's classic "In the Ghetto" provides an excellent example of lyrical troping. Here Eric B. reinforces Rakim's lyrics with two lines from 24 Carat Black's "Ghetto: Misfortune's Wealth": "in the ghetto" and "where you gonna see smiles in hell?"[34] Clearly Eric B. considered the impact of these lines when juxtaposed against Rakim's descriptions of ghetto life: "it seems like I'm locked in hell"; "I thought the ghetto was the worst that could happen to me"; "I got my back, my gun's on my side / It shouldn't have to be like that."

Ghostface Killah and Raekwon of the Wu-Tang Clan tell another ghetto tale in Ghostface's "Motherless Child." The song's title comes not from the spiritual of the same name, but from one of the samples RZA (the producer) uses for his new texture, the soul version of "Motherless Child" as performed by O. V. Wright (listeners familiar with the traditional tune may hear Ghostface's version as a modern reading of a very old song tradition). Raekwon and Ghostface together narrate a cinematic tale of ghetto violence and death, a tale that ends with "what the fuck? This shit is horrible." Before and after Ghostface's extended verse, RZA places a single line of the sampled song: "sometimes I feel like a motherless child" (yet again, a sample reinforces formal elements). We might be tempted to believe that Raekwon and Ghostface glorify violence with their song, but framing Ghostface's verse with the sample clearly places the narrative in a context: Raekwon and Ghostface, with RZA's sampling help, here decry the devastating results of never-ending cycles of violence.

Sampled lyrics in Poor Righteous Teachers' "We Dat Nice" extend Wise Intelligent's themes of boasting and toasting. Wise Intelligent illustrates how "nice" (or talented) he is both by his complex flow and by reinforcing his message in each chorus with carefully chosen samples.[35] The first sampled line, "take these words home and think it through," comes from Prodigy's verse in Mobb Deep's "Shook Ones Pt. II," and the second sampled line, "yo, I hate to brag, but damn I'm good," comes from Big Daddy Kane's "Just Rhymin' with Biz." Together these samples continue Wise's quest to illustrate his dominance over other MCs: in an ultimate act of ventriloquism, Wise Intelligent uses the voices of other highly respected MCs to proclaim his own greatness.

Big Daddy Kane samples from Kool Moe Dee for similar reasons. Kane fortifies the extended boasting of his song "Mortal Combat" by building the choruses from a single line from Kool Moe Dee's song "Let's Go"—"make you say daddy I don't want none"—as if giving voice to Kane's own (imaginary) vanquished foe. Kane's choice of sample is also significant because of the role Kool Moe Dee's song played in rap history. Throughout the late 1980s, veteran MC Kool Moe Dee and multi-platinum newcomer L. L. Cool J released extended battle raps, challenging each other for supremacy. Kool Moe Dee began the war of words with "How Ya Like Me Now," which L. L. Cool J answered with "Jack the Ripper." Kool Moe Dee's "Let's Go" answered "Jack the Ripper" and brought forth a new challenge from L. L. Cool J, "To the Break of Dawn." Kool Moe Dee ended the battle with "Death Blow."[36] "Let's Go," from which Big Daddy Kane samples, is a classic example of dissing. In "Let's Go," Kool Moe Dee accuses L. L. of being gay or, worse, a girl, and re-defined L. L.'s name with a series of now-infamous alliterative jabs, such as "Limp Lover," "Lack Luster," and "Lyrical Lapse." In sampling from "Let's Go," Big Daddy Kane not only recalls the extended battle, but also claims part of Kool Moe Dee's victory for himself.

In the case of Brand Nubian's two versions of "Wake Up," a vocal sample in the second version helps to establish a sort of dialogue—a narrative of change and personal growth—between the versions. The spoken introductions of the two versions are telling. The "Stimulated Dummies Mix" (the first version on the group's album *In God We Trust*) begins with a dialogue between Lord Jamar and Sadat X about Grand Puba. They would like to invite him into their "cipher," their circle of fellowship, but hesitate, mentioning his obsession for women ("skins") as evidence of weak moral fiber:

> Aiyo, God, we need somebody to come drop some science on this track
>   Word up, word up
> You know, tell it like it really is in the world today
>   Word up
> Aiyo, there go that brother Grand Puba, what's up with him?
>   Ah he don't know nothing, he don't know nothing
>   He be talking about skins all the time
>   You know what I'm sayin'?

By the time we reach the introduction of "Reprise in the Sunshine," the second version, Grand Puba has apparently experienced some personal growth:

> Peace to the Gods
>   Peace, Allah
> Aiyo, there go that brother Grand Puba. Heard that brother got knowledge of
>   self.
>     Yo, true indeed brother. Yo, let's have that brother come over and add on
>     to the cipher.

Yet Grand Puba is the featured MC in both versions: his lyrics and delivery are identical. So what has changed? Verse 1 of the remix contains a clue: heightened call-and-response between Grand Puba and his crew. As Grand Puba sets up his intention to "civilize the uncivilized" his crew encourages him with "speak on it, God." Grand Puba "drops science" (shares knowledge of self) in both versions, but in the temporal lapse between the original (at track 8) and the remix (at track 15) Sadat X and Lord Jamar have recognized him as an equal, as a fellow God, according to their shared belief in Five Percenter doctrine. Their acceptance thus prompts the remix version of "Wake Up"; in a fellowship of three they can now together "wake up" the masses. Furthermore, a prominent sample from Roy Ayers's "Everybody Loves the Sunshine" provides the hook for the remix: "Sunshine, everybody loves the sunshine, / folks get down in the sunshine." This sample sets up a significant intertextual reference to the Five Percent Nation's metaphor of man, woman, and child as sun, moon, and star respectively. The "sunshine" of the remix thus not only reflects Grand Puba's growth and salvation, but also the collective sunshine emanating from Brand Nubian's "godly," and decidedly male, fellowship.

In keeping with compositional conventions, sampled texts usually become refrains in their new settings. But textual samples can also frame the lyrics to come. Grand Puba's "Lickshot," an extended humorous boast detailing his verbal and sexual prowess, begins with a sampled introduction: "Alright y'all! I want y'all to put your hands together and to bring on a brother that's bound to lay more dips in your hips, more glide in your stride. And if you don't dig what's next you got the wrong damn address."[37] This sample does more than simply fill the introductory space: it introduces Grand Puba's very persona. Before he drops a single rhyme, Grand Puba has established the appropriate atmosphere for his boast with the help of a sample.

Producer Pete Rock does the same in "Anger in the Nation," adding depth to C. L. Smooth's diatribe against racial inequality and call for unity ("Together we can rise and now's the opportunity") by introducing the song with a sample of the introduction from Les McCann's "Talk to the People": "You know, nowadays it seems like there's a lot of bad things going on and I guess a lot of it, from the way I see it, seems to still stem from lack of feelings on our parts, it's . . . and how we relate or communicate with our fellow brothers and sisters." An additional lyrical sample in the chorus of "Anger in the Nation" also builds on the song's theme. Pete Rock here samples a single line from James Brown's "Funky President," "let's get together and raise," and loops the sample to create the chorus.

By contrast, instead of sampling an appropriate textual trope for his ode to children, "Children R the Future," Big Daddy Kane chooses instead to quote— not sample—the first few lines of Whitney Houston's hit song "Greatest Love of All."[38] After rapping gently to and about his young listeners for three verses, Big Daddy Kane finishes the song by singing, reggae style,

> I believe the children are the future
> Teach them well and let them lead the way
> Show them all of the beauty they possess inside
> Give them a sense of pride
> to make it easier, let the children's laughter
> remind us how we used to be.

Instead of finishing his song with new lyrics, Big Daddy Kane adds a final punch to his message by quoting the lyrics of a well-known popular song.

Lyrical samples also sometimes reveal intertextual tensions between the borrowed source and the new song, as illustrated by Poor Righteous Teachers' "Miss Ghetto." For the chorus of their new song they sample a single line from Mobb Deep's "Survival of the Fittest": "No matter how much loot I get I'm staying in the projects." Mobb Deep's song glorifies material wealth, violence, and drug culture, and this single line reveals their allegiance to this lifestyle. The line shows up in all three statements of "Miss Ghetto's" chorus, starkly contrasting with Wise Intelligent's vehemently rapped desire to get out of the ghetto, to not get caught up in the ghetto lifestyle, here personified in the form of a mythical "Miss Ghetto": "I ain't marrying Miss Ghetto again / first chance I get to bounce, word life I'm bouncin'."[39] Between statements of the chorus Wise Intelligent paints an unflattering, honest vision of ghetto life, including images of drugs, teenage pregnancy, and violence. By sampling Mobb Deep's "Survival of the Fittest," Poor Righteous Teachers here deftly reverse and criticize both the theme and the intent of the original song.[40] And in fact, for some producers, challenging the sampled source, as Poor Righteous Teachers do here in "Miss Ghetto," is in itself a key motivation for sampling. As Kool Akiem declares, "changing of context with the use of sampling" is "highly important and the essence of the art. . . . In fact, to not do so is pretty much cheating."[41]

Generally speaking, samples of speeches, sermons, films, and television follow the same conventions as samples of lyrics: they typically appear in introductions, choruses, and codas, and often extend the new song's meaning. Kool Akiem, for example, sampled a single line from an Eldridge Cleaver speech— "this is all that we know that we have"—for use in the chorus of the Micranots' "Culture."[42] Poor Righteous Teachers' "Word from the Wise" contains sampled excerpts from at least two separate speeches. The first textual sample, an excerpt from a Malcolm X speech, occurs just before the first verse, serving as the introduction: "One of the first things that I think young people, especially nowadays, should learn how to do, is think for yourself, and, uh, listen for yourself."[43] Each subsequent chorus introduces a slightly different theme with the help of samples from different speeches (or perhaps several excerpts from a single speech) by a new speaker (likely Louis Farrakhan). Over sampled saxophones and guitar from James Brown's "The Boss," the first chorus is militant: "We wanna bring people and [unintelligible] people [repeated]. And if it means that we have to take the head of those who oppose a righteous life for our people then we are ready to go to war. Now!" The second chorus opposes excessive materiality: "I know you, brother. Me and you are brothers. We flesh of each other's flesh, bone of each other's bone. I know why you fakin': because you got a greater desire to be known. And you have a desire to have money." The third chorus urges unity and brotherhood: "The problem is this: you have no unity, you don't see that your unity is the key to your success. Because you so divided, so disunited, so full of petty envy and jealousy, you don't see that your unity is the key to your success." And the final chorus encourages children to gain knowledge of self: "Ask my brother: what is he saying? He's telling black kids to get a good education. He's telling black kids to learn the knowledge of themselves so they can love themselves." Each sample taps into prominent and ever-present Poor Righteous Teachers themes: black unity, knowledge of self, and anti-materialism.[44]

Likewise, Lakim Shabazz's "Black Is Back" also uses a speech fragment— taken from Malcolm X's famous "Message to the Grass Roots" speech—for each chorus, although here DJ Mark the 45 King, the song's producer, uses the same fragment for both statements of the chorus.[45] The 45 King scratches the sample in and manipulates it so that certain words recur in different patterns, a DJ-ing technique known as cutting.[46] The first statement of the chorus repeats the first two words twice: "Concerning the . . . concerning the . . . concerning the difference between the black revolution and the Negro revolution." The final chorus, however, repeats not only the first two words, but then also the entire phrase: "Concerning the . . . concerning the . . . concerning the . . . concerning the . . . concerning the difference between the black revolution and the Negro revolution . . . concerning the difference between the black revolution and the Negro revolution." By re-configuring the original phrase, the 45 King suggests there must indeed be a difference between a "Negro revolution" and a "black revolution," a difference that extends beyond mere nomenclature.[47]

Brand Nubian's "Meaning of the 5%" is an obvious exception to this "rule": it contains no rapped lyrics, but instead simply samples a pre-existing speech or sermon on the topic of the Lost-Found Lessons.[48] "Meaning of the 5%" is a recording of a Louis Farrakhan speech set to a sample from Marvin Gaye's "T Stands for Trouble." The music under this speech is through-composed, although there are a few changes in texture: handclaps on the backbeats fade in and out and saxophones punctuate the downbeats of each measure. Most importantly, the crowd listening to the speech has also been sampled, and their reactions to the speaker's exhortations—again in call-and-response fashion—thicken as he warms to his chosen text: the Lost-Found Lessons. Brand Nubian thus uses borrowed musical tracks to highlight doctrine, choosing to set an already powerful "performance" of the Lost-Found Lessons in a way that will appeal to audiences familiar with African American worship traditions.

By contrast, both the lyrics and the melody of Brand Nubian's "Allah and Justice" are borrowed (not sampled) from pre-existing sources. Indeed, the lyrics of "Allah and Justice," with a different but clearly related melody, constitute the Five Percent Nation's anthem, a song collectively sung during Five Percenter gatherings.[49] A home video of the summer 1999 Five Percent Nation convention, the annual Show and Prove, posted to the Five Percent Nation's Website early in 2000, depicts a group performance of this anthem.[50] About six and a half minutes into the video, a young woman on a stage with a baby on her hip proclaims, "OK, on the count of three we're gonna do this. On the count of understanding: knowledge, wisdom, understanding," and then leads the choir on stage and the congregation in the audience in a collective "performance" of this anthem. Whereas the song is sung throughout in the collective performance, Brand Nubian raps the numerical section of the text, yet also weaves some of the original melody in counterpoint underneath the rap. By adapting this song, a borrowed tune and borrowed lyrics all Five Percenters should know, Brand Nubian makes public many of the ideological touchstones of Five Percenter faith, including the importance of the Science of Supreme Mathematics.

Producers also sample from film and television sources in their search for intertextual references. Both RZA and his protégé 4th Disciple draw frequently from films and television. As discussed above, for Killarmy's "5 Stars," 4th Disciple uses the theme song of the television series *M\*A\*S\*H\**; drawing audio clips from war films and war-themed television programs is one of his trademarks.[51] Among rap fans, RZA's frequent sampling of clips from kung fu movies is well known. His samples are primarily intended to make a connection between kung fu philosophy and the Wu-Tang collective, but in some cases the particular textual clips he borrows trope the themes of a song. "Wu-Revolution," for example, brings Five Percenter knowledge to the masses in an attempt to indoctrinate the uninitiated (see chapter 4 for a detailed discussion of this song). Poppa Wu makes this intention clear in measures 17–19: "This is the training that's gonna be given to you by the Wu, brothers and sisters." After presenting a "sermon" drawn from Five Percenter lessons, the song gives way to a kung fu clip that also speaks of finding new members: "I have given it much thought. It seems disaster must come, at best, only postponed. Shaolin Kung Fu, to survive, must now be taught to more young men. We must expand, get more pupils so that the knowledge will spread."

Brand Nubian's use of film samples also clearly sets up intertextual references for the group's song "The Godz Must Be Crazy." Making the most of the theme of insanity, Brand Nubian samples various textual chunks such as "paranoid"; "Too bad you can't cure a psychotic"; "Would you be willing to come forward and accept psychiatric help without any cost?"; a character laughing maniacally and saying "Beautiful! That's beautiful!"; and "I don't need you, doc! I don't need anybody," among others. Brand Nubian places these textual samples only in the choruses and throughout the samples weaves an additional original refrain, "the Godz must be crazy," as well as sound effects that heighten the insanity theme.[52]

### Sampling as Historical Dialectic

When sampling from vinyl, DJs tend to avoid taking from hip-hop's own history unless there is a specific reason to do so. As several songs in this study illustrate, however, sampling rap vocals in order to pay homage to rap's historical heavyweights is clearly acceptable.[53] Aceyalone pays a sort of homage to Ed O. G. and da Bulldogs with his "I Got to Have It Too," musically re-visiting their hit song "I Got to Have It." Despite their titles, both songs eschew empty materiality, instead promoting spiritual health, family devotion, and community involvement. Each of Ed O. G.'s verses end with the title line, and it is this line Aceyalone (or his producer Fat Jack) samples for the new song. Each line of Aceyalone's chorus lists one thing he must have—including knowledge of self, plenty of records, sufficient food for his family, money, and even "the wind underneath my wings"—and each item is followed by Ed O. G.'s voice intoning, "I got to have it." Thus Aceyalone not only pays homage to Ed O. G. in his introduction with a "shout-out," but also shows his respect by using Ed O. G.'s own voice.

Some voices are an indelible part of rap history, as is true of Flavor Flav, Chuck D's trickster sidekick in Public Enemy. Known for his bizarre behavior and obscure rhymes, and for the huge clocks that dangle from his neck, Flavor is a ready source of audio and visual samples. Brand Nubian takes advantage of Flavor's renown by sampling his voice in "Drop the Bomb." The sample is used only in the chorus, as DJ Alamo scratches in Flavor saying, "Drop it."

Whereas these two examples call upon significant voices in rap history, for other songs producers are careful to sample Five Percenter artists. Poor Righteous Teachers, for example, sample Mobb Deep for "Miss Ghetto" and both Mobb Deep and Big Daddy Kane for the chorus of "We Dat Nice." They draw again from Five Percenter artists for the chorus of "Gods, Earths and 85ers," this time also sampling lines of text that make reference to the Five Percent Nation. The first half of the chorus, rapped by guest artist Nine, clearly establishes the didactic nature of the song:

> Whatever happened to the Gods and the Earths.
> They thirst for a pot of gold God worth his birth
> Knowledge is worth more than diamonds.
> When the mind is shining, surprises for Gods, Earths and 85ers.

The second half of the chorus is built from two samples. The first is from Wu-Tang member Raekwon's solo song "Can It All Be So Simple (Remix)": "Dedicated to the Gods and the Earths." And the second is a single line from Grand Puba's final verse in Brand Nubian's "Wake Up": "Dip dip dive-a, civilize an 85er."

Ultimately, sampling voices from rap's past adds a depth of historical reference that new lyrics alone simply could not provide. Sampling rap history not only produces aesthetically pleasing results, but also reinforces ties between rap's past and present. And when Five Percenters sample from other Five Percenters, they construct a tight communal web built around a shared understanding of their musical and spiritual past.

Because of sampling's startling compositional possibilities, referential potential, and legal ramifications, it is easy to forget that sampling is only one of many compositional tools in the hands of capable producers. Yet as these few God Hop examples illustrate, samples can effectively perform a number of functions: samples help delineate song form, provide a fluid musical canvas for the

MC, and add to a song's overall meaning. Indeed, the many uses for samples inspired scholar Russell Potter (borrowing from Henry Louis Gates, Jr.) to differentiate between "unmotivated sampling"—those samples used primarily for sonic, aesthetic, or structural reasons—and "motivated sampling"—those samples which clearly trope, comment upon, or reverse the song's meaning.[54]

Whether or not Gates's terminology fits sampling practices in the way Potter describes, producers have clearly developed a set of conventions for sampling use. If we allow that all musical and aesthetic decisions relevant to the production of a song are both conscious and deliberate, we should also grant that creators intend at least some of the intertextual meanings that result from sampling. But authorial intent is not the only measure of a song's meaning. A song's meaning is not a static object, and each listener (or scholar) will bring to a song singular "interpretive moves," a dialogic interaction between a listener's past experiences and present encounter with (in this case) a musical work.[55] Sampling is one of the many bridges rap musicians use to build a rap tradition firmly entrenched in the musical past; the most effective sampling depends on the listener's historical and cultural knowledge.

These God Hop examples are merely a microcosm of hip-hop music, yet they clearly illustrate how rich a musical message can be when coupled with the weight of hip-hop's history. Indeed, the messages of these God Hop examples would not be as effective without the added musical and intellectual depth sampling adds to the mix. Appropriate samples and quotations thus offer yet another strategy, another musical method by which young souls can be reached. And for sample-based God Hop producers, that is precisely the point.

# 6 Album Packaging and Organization

In addition to textual and musical devices, Five Percenters also have an arsenal of other cues with which to direct their audience to doctrine. In this chapter, I investigate some of the ways albums can be arranged and decorated to guide the thoughts of a listener. I will first consider visual cues in the album's packaging, such as "shout-outs," commentary within liner notes, and album art, both in the pages of liner notes and on the faces of the compact discs themselves. I will then move to more abstract and less visible issues of album organization. Because they are neither visible nor readily audible, organizational cues are set apart both from the album's packaging and from its music. Yet in combination with music and lyrics, album packaging and organization both enrich and complicate the Five Percent Nation's message of redemption.

## Packaging: Shout-outs, Liner Notes, and Iconography

Album liner notes frequently contain references to the Five Percent Nation in the form of "shout-outs," acknowledgments of friends and colleagues by name. Nearly every rap album includes a section of thank-yous and album dedication, and many MCs use this space to thank their musical influences, mention the names of others in their extended crew, and recognize other figures in their lives who have helped push the production of the album in some way. Yet within these otherwise standard shout-outs, Five Percenters also leave hints of their faith. Busta Rhymes, Malik B of The Roots, Kool Akiem of the Micranots, 9th Prince of Killarmy, Prince Paul of the Gravediggaz, and Self Scientific all thank Allah in their albums.[1] Busta Rhymes also blesses others in the name of Allah in the liner notes to *When Disaster Strikes*.[2] Frukwan is careful to identify Clarence 13X as the latest manifestation of Allah in the liner notes to the Gravediggaz' *The Pick, the Sickle and the Shovel* and thanks "Allah and Justice for mentally preparing me as well as physically, everyday waking up and destroying negativity, an endless lifelong task of saving babies." Kool Akiem also thanks Clarence 13X in the Micranots' *Obelisk Movements*.[3]

Many Five Percenters use their liner notes to thank Gods and Earths in general, the Nation of Gods and Earths as a whole, and sometimes the Nation of Islam.[4] And some MCs and crews, such as Grand Puba, Killarmy, and the Wu-Tang Clan, are careful to thank their Earths and seeds. Other shout-outs mention specific Five Percent Nation and Nation of Islam leaders, as well as other black nationalist leaders Five Percenters admire. On the back of the liner notes to *One for All*, for example, Brand Nubian includes the following extended shout-out:

> Brand Nubian would like to extend peace and blessings to the following: Master Faraad [sic] Muhammad, the Honorable Elijah Muhammad, the Father Allah and Justice, Marcus Garvey, Anoble [sic] Drew Ali, Martin Luther King, Kwame Toure, Haile Selassie, Minister Louis Farrakhan, Huey P. Newton, Assata Chukur [sic], Fred Hampton, Malcolm X, Immam Isa and most of all we would like to give thanks to the original black mentality which manifested all things in existence.

In a few cases, the wording of thank-yous hints at specific Five Percenter teachings or code words. Supreme of Killarmy, for example, specifically wishes "peace to the Gods for enlightening me with supreme mathematics." And in the liner notes to *It Was Written,* Nas thanks his father (modern jazz trumpeter Olu Dara) for teaching him knowledge, wisdom, and understanding. Lord Jamar of Brand Nubian wishes "knowledge knowledge" instead of peace in the notes to *One for All* (as explained in chapter 3, "knowledge knowledge" means "peace"). Finally, Masta Killah wishes peace to Medina (Brooklyn) on *Wu-Tang Forever.*

In one instance, Five Percenter doctrine is hinted at not only in shout-outs but also with extended liner notes. The final two pages of the album liner to Poor Righteous Teachers' *The New World Order* include the following text, likely borrowed from an unknown source:

> The world has been under the dominion of sin for six thousand years. The spirit of confusion has reigned supreme throughout the whole world. The races and nations have changed over the centuries, but the spirit has stayed the same. Today the whole earth is under the yoke of sin, led by the pernicious western world powers. They have influenced the people of the earth contrary to the laws of God. The world is polluted with their wickedness. They have polluted the air, water, earth and the minds of men. Through powerful deception, the evil powers have made good seem evil and evil seem good. Only the forces of God can end the tight grip that Satan has upon the earth. It will take the force of God, a kingdom of disciplined men and women under God's rule who are dedicated to the return of the creation to the proper cycles of God. This kingdom will declare judgement through the word of God at the end of the age called the Great Tribulation. And, this Godly force will put an end to the dominion of sin.

The text is printed over a picture of piles of Revelationary, conspiratorial, historical, and theological literature with titles such as *The Illuminati 666; The Rise
and Fall of the Great Powers; Chemical and Biological Warfare; The Architect of
Genocide; Secret Societies Unmasked;* and *Holy Bible.* Positioned below the extended quotation is a verse from Revelations (13:18): "Here is the wisdom. Let
him that hath understanding count the number of the beast: for it is the number
of a man; and his number is six hundred threescore and six."

Although Five Percenter theology does not speak of a Great Tribulation, nor
of Satan as a physical and spiritual entity, the concept of Armageddon, a holy
war to end all wars and civilization as we know it, lies at the very core of Five
Percenter and Nation of Islam eschatology. Of particular interest here is the claim
"it will take the force of God, a kingdom of disciplined men and women under
God's rule who are dedicated to the return of the creation to the proper cycles
of God." Surely this is meant to describe the Nation of Gods and Earths, men
and women who seek the restoration of the black man's (read: God's) rightful
place in the universe. Too, the evil dominion to be extinguished has reigned for
six thousand years, the same amount of time allowed in Elijah Muhammad's
teachings for the devil's civilization to flourish. Thus, before the first rhymes and
beats find their way to willing ears, Poor Righteous Teachers' message is clear:
their mission is to reach the uncivilized before it is too late.

Even before God Hop consumers read shout-outs and commentary in liner
notes, they have seen album art, in which artists can also leave traces of their
faith. (This assumes, of course, that fans purchase the albums and do not first
encounter the music through the Internet, digital media, or bootleg recordings.)
Album art is not often considered a relevant artifact for musical analysis, yet as
scholar Paul Gilroy has argued, it can be a powerful tool, capable not only of
influencing dress and fashion, but also of more political acts such as encouraging
people to register to vote, or conveying information to "a specially targeted
audience which is not the same as the one in which the record company is
interested," which in turn "may also help solicit this audience into specific modes
of cultural and political identification."[5] Hip-hop and cultural scholar Todd Boyd
has also studied album art, and has asserted that that album art on Ice Cube's
1991 album *Death Certificate* contains cues to Ice Cube's political and ideological
stance. Of particular interest here is Boyd's claim that Ice Cube's clothing and
hairstyle, as well as a picture of Ice Cube reading an issue of the *Final Call,* all
point to Ice Cube's then newly formed affiliation with the Nation of Islam.[6]

The power of visual images is clearly not lost on God Hop artists. Front and
back covers of albums, inner leaves of album liners, and even the faces of compact discs can be adorned to symbolically represent the artists' spiritual priorities.
Some of these visual cues project an aura of general spirituality not directly

related to the Five Percent Nation or to al-Islam. The back cover of *Mecca and the Soul Brother,* for example, shows Pete Rock and C. L. Smooth seated at a lunch counter in a restaurant. Their heads are bowed, and their palms are cupped upward in a suppliant position, clearly suggesting the two men are praying and thus emphasizing their spirituality.

Album art can also suggest Pan-Africanism—connections with the African diaspora—through reference to Egypt. For his album *The Lost Tribe of Shabazz,* Lakim Shabazz convinced his record company to pay for a trip to Egypt, and the liner notes to his album show Lakim among pyramids and temple remains, wearing native dress (see figure 6.1). Computer-generated graphics of camels, hieroglyphics, and stylized musicians on the front cover further enhance Lakim's Egyptian theme. Lakim's presence in this setting does not suggest his particular allegiance to the Five Percent Nation, but it does align him with the black nationalist longing to connect with the ancient and present African civilization. Indeed, the video for "The Lost Tribe of Shabazz" was also filmed in Egypt, specifically in Luxor, Cairo, and Aswan. Of filming his video in Egypt, Lakim remembers, "It was my dream come true. I always wanted to go to the Motherland. I couldn't think of a more righteous place to make my video than Egypt. I got a mystic feeling come over my body standing that close to the pyramids. I

**Figure 6.1. Lakim Shabazz, from cover of The Lost Tribe of Shabazz**
Photo courtesy of Joe DiGennaro

wanted to show that we were the builders of the pyramids, that our people invented science and mathematics."[7]

An Egyptian obelisk graces the front cover and disc face of the Micranots' *Obelisk Movements* (see figure 6.2), and Egyptian icons such as hieroglyphics and burial sarcophagi intertwine with graffiti and futuristic images throughout the liner notes. In the center of the notes, the Micranots (specifically, Kool Akiem) clarify the relationship they see between Egyptian obelisks and hip-hop:

> Throughout ancient times the peoples of Egypt and Ethiopia built giant stone monuments, towering shafts crowned with a pyramid. During colonialism the European nations took these [obelisks] as prizes, moving them to European and American cities by the dozen. Not only were the physical structures stolen and moved, but the symbolic meaning was also appropriated and changed to fit this other mindset. Thus OBELISK MOVEMENTS represents this cultural struggle that is directly related to, and parallel to, general trends in Hip-Hop Culture today.

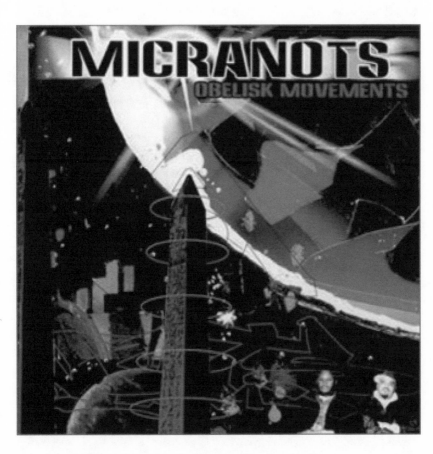

**Figure 6.2. Cover of the Micranots' Obelisk Movements**
Reproduced courtesy of Akiem Scott

In other words, just as the obelisk was a symbol of cultural and political colonialism, hip-hop is at risk of being artistically colonized. Through their album art and explanatory notes, the Micranots hope to fight artistic colonialism and political hegemony.

Whereas these recognizable icons illustrate general spirituality and Pan-Africanism, others create direct ties to Five Percenter theology or to Islamic traditions. For instance, on the front cover of Poor Righteous Teachers' *Black Business,* Wise Intelligent, Culture Freedom, and Father Shaheed sit below a logo that shows the universal flag of the Five Percent Nation within a star of David. The universal flag appears twice more within the album's liner notes, and also decorates the disc face. On the back page of the liner notes, Wise Intelligent lounges with his bandmates, holding a copy of a brochure entitled "Allah's School."

With its stylized loops and angles, Self Scientific's logo, reproduced on the outside cover and final page of the liner notes as well as on the face of the group's disc *The Self Science,* resembles Arabic calligraphy, and particularly calligraphic compositions around a central axis.[8] The ancient Arabic art of stylized calligraphy also seems to have inspired the art on the face of the Gravediggaz' *The Pick, the Sickle and the Shovel* (see figure 6.3). However, the calligraphic decoration, written around a central axis in two rows of text, not only closely resembles Arabic calligraphy written in the ancient Kufic script, but actually replicates the face of a tenth-century earthenware bowl (compare figures 6.3 and 6.4).[9] The text of both can be translated as follows: "He who believes in God's mercy is generous; and to whatever you accustom yourself, you will get accustomed to. Blessings to the owner."[10]

## Album Organization

Whether or not the visual and conceptual references of album art, shout-outs, and album liner commentary come through clearly to God Hop fans, these concrete cues are far more likely to make an impression than the more abstract ones embodied in album organization. Nevertheless, positioning tracks on an album and maintaining momentum between tracks by means of skits (spoken dialogues) or musical interludes can have a significant effect on a song's (and album's) reception and ultimately can influence the delivery of doctrine and references to doctrine. A number of concerns can determine track order. Tracks may be organized according to some desired meta-narrative or album concept, or may be grouped according to musical style.[11] For large crews, careful track organization can create shifting moods and styles by cycling through featured MCs. And in the case of God Hop, overall album organization can emphasize or de-emphasize

Figure 6.3. Disc face of the Gravediggaz' The Pick, the Sickle and the Shovel

Figure 6.4. Persian Bowl, Samanid dynasty (819-1005), 10th century Glazed earthenware, 6.0 cm H × 46.8 diameter
Reproduced with permission of Freer Gallery of Art, Smithsonian Institution, Washington, D.C.: Purchase, F1952.11

Album Packaging and Organization

messages of redemption through contextual relationships, numerologically appropriate positioning, and intertextual relationships with skits between songs.

Hip-hop producers often conceive of an album's organization in terms of song sets, alternating spoken tracks with groupings of songs. Consider, for example, the first album of Rakim's double-disc set *The 18th Letter* (see figure 6.5). The intro, skits, and outro are all excerpts from an interview between Rakim and an unidentified interlocutor. With the exception of the outro, the spoken tracks are each less than thirty seconds long. These brief respites between songs give insight into Rakim's personality and motivations: he speaks of wanting to give back to the community, of his struggles to return to rap after a lengthy hiatus and his warm welcome from eager fans, and of his desire to be remembered for the power of his words long after his death. The third skit not only explains Rakim's motivations, but also sets up a thematic link with the following musical track. Within this skit Rakim rejoices that his fans recognize him on the street as "the God." He makes the most of this theme as he investigates the nature of God in the following song, "The Mystery (Who Is God)."

Brand Nubian's *Foundation* also illustrates this sort of organization. After a brief (twenty-two second) musical introduction entitled "Here We Go" built over the Isley Brothers' "Here We Go Again," the remaining songs and "interludes" alternate in an even pattern (see figure 6.6). Each of the interludes is less than one minute long, and at least two of the three interludes are extended samples from motion pictures.[12] The only doctrine-filled song on this album, "I'm Black and I'm Proud," falls at track 12, the first song of the third grouping of songs. "I'm Black and I'm Proud" follows a skit entitled "Black on Black Crime," a scene from the film *Don't Be a Menace to South Central While Drinking Your Juice in the Hood.* In direct contrast to the song that follows it, this skit is a study in extreme (and exaggerated) black self-loathing: the narrator exclaims he hates black skin, black pants, black pepper, black piano keys, Whoopi Goldberg's lips, and the back of Forrest Whittaker's neck. Thus, "I'm Black and I'm Proud,"

```
"intro"
1 song
skit
3 songs
skit
4 songs
skit
4 songs
"outro"
```

**Figure 6.5. Formal layout of Rakim's The 18th Letter**

FIVE PERCENTER RAP

```
introduction
3 songs
Interlude
5 songs
Interlude
3 songs
Interlude
5 songs
```

Figure 6.6. Formal layout of Brand Nubian's Foundation

with its celebration of all things black, neatly overturns the self-hate of the interlude.

Brand Nubian's first album, *One for All,* seems to be organized according to relative density of doctrine. The first five songs of the album contain nothing more than brief references to Five Percenter theology, but the three subsequent songs—"Dance to My Ministry," "Drop the Bomb," and "Wake Up (Stimulated Dummies Mix)"—are heavy with doctrine. The five songs that follow this doctrine-heavy set seem to have little or nothing to do with Five Percenter teachings. Curiously, this set of five songs is also the most musically eclectic section of the album, drawing from rock, reggae/dancehall, R&B, and funk. The album then finishes with two doctrine-related songs—"Brand Nubian" and a remix of "Wake Up"—and "Dedication," a song that functions as an extended musical shout-out to Brand Nubian's musical heroes. The album thus begins and ends firmly anchored in Five Percenter doctrine, but moves away from doctrine momentarily in order to keep the attention of a diverse fan base.

Brand Nubian's second album, *In God We Trust,* continues the tight formal construction of the first: each of the first ten tracks of the album contains at least a few references to Five Percenter theology, while the final four tracks have few if any references. This album is also a good case study of the depths of contradiction present in God Hop albums. Four doctrine-filled songs come from this album, including "Ain't No Mystery," "Meaning of the 5%," the Five Percent Nation's anthem "Allah and Justice," and "The Godz Must Be Crazy." The album begins with "Allah u Akbar," which samples the Muslim call to prayer.[13] But the efficacy of their preaching in these tracks must be weighed against other songs from the album, such as their misogynistic "Steal Ya Ho'," homophobic "Punks Jump Up to Get Beat Down," and the violent "Pass the Gat" and "Black and Blue." Ultimately, fans must be left with the sense that Brand Nubian is not always primarily concerned with spreading the Five Percent gospel.

In some cases, producers isolate doctrine-related offerings from the rest of the album's secular content. Consider GZA's "B.I.B.L.E.," the only track not produced by RZA on GZA's *Liquid Swords.* Although a few other songs from the album contain brief references, "B.I.B.L.E." is GZA's heaviest message song on the album, and it holds the final album track, providing a sort of benediction. On the other hand, the single doctrine-based song of the Wu-Tang Clan's double-disc set *Wu-Tang Forever,* "Wu-Revolution," begins the set, thus introducing the message and motivation for the rest of the album. Likewise, Lakim's Shabazz's *The Lost Tribe of Shabazz* opens with the title track, one of only two doctrine-related songs on the album. The other theologically minded song from this album, "Brothers in Action," holds the penultimate track, perhaps in an effort to bring his listeners back to the point before the end of the album. Grand Puba includes two doctrine-filled songs on his album *Reel to Reel,* and places them together at tracks 10 and 11. Puba follows these doctrinal messages with three songs containing no references to doctrine (but plenty of braggadocio and references to cash and women), and a remix of "360°," a song with only a handful of Five Percenter references. The Micranots also clearly considered the rhetorical impact of careful track placement. Their disc *Obelisk Movements* contains only two songs with references to Five Percenter theology: "Culture" and "Sun Salutations."[14] The latter song ends the album, but "Culture's" placement has a deeper significance. In keeping with the Science of Supreme Mathematics, Kool Akiem placed "Culture" as the fourth track.

The Micranots are not the only crew to keep mathematics in mind when constructing an album. The title track of Scaramanga Shallah's album *Seven Eyes, Seven Horns,* for example, is placed at track 7. Brand Nubian's "The Godz Must Be Crazy" is track 7 on *In God We Trust,* another obvious link between title and number meaning (since 7 means "God"). And for track 7 of their album *Blowout Comb,* Digable Planets carefully chose "Dial 7 (Axioms of Creamy Spies)," a song that makes no secret of their belief in the divinity of black men with lines such as "we are God pieces" and "we are God's sequels."[15]

Track 7 of Rakim's CD, labeled simply "skit," is also placed according to the Science of Supreme Mathematics. Rakim introduces the song that follows this skit, "Guess Who's Back," with the following insight:

> Kinda glad I ain't come out in this, you know, the last few years. . . . Right now I think everybody want a change back to hip-hop . . . rhyme skills and things of that nature. So the timing man, the timing is perfect. Plus this is '97, which is born-God, you know what I mean? And I'm back, straight up.

Rakim's *18th Letter* was released in 1997, the born-God year, an appropriate time for the "God" to make his comeback, or be re-born in the music industry.[16] And this insight into the god's motivations falls squarely on track 7, corresponding to the God number.[17]

The "skits" and brief spoken dialogues or monologues between musical tracks serve a variety of functions. They can be mini-dramas, as for example on Wu-Tang albums when various Wu members assume crime boss personas and "perform" scenes of drug deals. Skits can also be extended samples, as are the interludes on Brand Nubian's *Foundation.* Skits can explain motivations, as illustrated by Rakim's "Born-God" skit. Skits can introduce concepts or themes to be presented in the following song, or sum up themes in the previous song. And finally, skits can introduce listeners to the persons behind the MC personas. In God Hop, some MCs use their skits to emphasize doctrine, or at least to position themselves as righteous. The following examples from three God Hop albums—Busta Rhymes's *When Disaster Strikes,* Killarmy's *Silent Weapons for Quiet Wars,* and Nas's *It Was Written*—will illustrate just a few examples of the complex roles skits play on albums.

The majority of Busta Rhymes's *When Disaster Strikes* could be described as "hardcore": dense, dissonant production tracks and street-wise (and extremely clever) lyrics with continuous warnings to competitors.[18] Yet one song defies this hardcore mentality. The only song on the album that even makes reference to the Five Percenter way of life, "One," is softer both in subject matter and in musical style. "One" features R&B songstress Erykah Badu, who weaves her melodies over Busta's rapping and gently raps a few lines herself. The music under the vocal lines is soothing and continuous, built on a looped sample of Stevie Wonder's "Love Is in Need of Love Today" and featuring a cooing background chorus. But the skit following this track reminds us that the soft stylings and family orientation of "One" are not Busta's typical mode. Acting as a radio announcer who segues between songs, a woman (probably Rah Digga of Busta's Flipmode Squad) abruptly breaks the familial mood:

> Aiight. We gonna bounce back into this hot shit and keep this motherfucker movin'. Yeah, in case you don't realize by now, shit gets extremely "Dangerous" when you fuck with any of the Flipmode niggas. Fuck around if you want, bitches, but you better off actin' like you know.

The skit thus contextualizes "One's" message while introducing the next song, "Dangerous." By moving from "One" back into "hot shit," Busta clearly identifies "One" as an anomaly. The message of Five Percenter family values is thus buried in the midst of hardcore songs, and those fans who value Busta's "hardcore" persona can forgive him for his momentary softness.

The entirety of track 7 on Killarmy's *Silent Weapons for Quiet Wars,* entitled "Love, Hell or Right," is also a skit, although not labeled as such. The track consists of various Killarmy and Sunz of Man members in dialogue over a simple piano and trumpet accompaniment, and it introduces the next song, "Wake Up," featuring Sunz of Man. The subject of their minute-long skit seems to be the efforts required to "make it" in the music business and their decision to exclude (unknown and unnamed) others from their circle. The skit contains several references to Five Percenter rhetoric. They repeatedly address each other as Gods, and the phrase "It's like we had to go though hell to come out right" both gives the title to the skit and makes reference to the Supreme Alphabet: "Love, Hell or Right" corresponds to the letter L in the Supreme Alphabet. Several speakers address a secondary theme: all things happen for a reason. The final lines of the dialogue sum up the conversation: "It seems like when niggas got cut our shit came stronger together. It's for the better." These lines also set the mood and provide motivation for "Wake Up." Unified and strong, the members of Killarmy and Sunz of Man use the song directly following this explanatory skit to reach the masses with a message of redemption before it is too late, and their war imagery underscores going through hell to come out right.

Nas opens his album *It Was Written* with a skit featuring himself and another voice (probably AZ of The Firm). The skit envisions the two men as slaves awakening to the horrors of their situation and captures the moment they seek freedom. Their flight will not be easy: an unknown voice yells after them, "get the hounds, we gonna have ourselves a hangin' tonight!" Before the next track (the first song) begins, Nas and his companion begin another dialogue, this one in the present. Yet this half of the track makes it clear that although slavery has long ended, African Americans still struggle in American society. Nas and his compatriot use a card metaphor to make their point, claiming that whereas African Americans may be dealt a fifty-two-card deck, majority (white) society plays with a fifty-four-card deck that includes jokers:

> *AZ:* "How we playin'? . . . They dealt us in, son. They playin' with the fifty-four deck ya see with the jokers in it and everything, you know what I'm saying?"
> *Nas:* "Son, I'm playin' with the fifty-two."

The point is that African Americans have few tools to overcome the trickery, or "stacked deck," of white society. Additionally, Nas and his friend make repeated reference to their belief in predestination, that our fate is already written and nothing is "accidental or coincidental," a prominent theme they share with the Killarmy skit described above. Nas ends this skit with a reference to the Qur'an: "In the Qur'an it says Nas, the man," finding an Arabic precedent for his name.[19] The entire skit ends with the line "It was written," thus providing the title for the album. All events, past and future, are recorded in the Qur'an; Nas's task is to tell the story of the streets as it is written every day.

Later in this same album Nas provides a different context for the song that follows, "Nas Is Coming," produced by legendary California producer Dr. Dre. The introductory skit is a conversation between Dr. Dre and Nas. They share "chronic" (marijuana) and discuss how to make money in the industry and protect their creative ventures. Dr. Dre has no known ties to the Nation of Gods and

Earths, yet Nas hails Dr. Dre as "god" throughout the skit. In its entirety, the skit illustrates some of the tensions Five Percenter MCs face in the music industry. On the one hand, they value their faith, a belief system that decries the use of drugs and other stimulants. Yet on the other hand, mainstream rap flaunts drinking, partying, and drugs, especially marijuana in a variety of forms. The skit itself thematically introduces "Nas Is Coming," a song devoid of additional references to the Five Percent Nation (except for a brief mention of Louis Farrakhan), lauding Nas's prowess on the microphone and his material wealth.

Nas's quickness to both identify himself as a god and yet publicly endorse drugs and a "bling bling" lifestyle has caused confusion among listeners eager to learn more about the Nation of Gods and Earths. Take, for example, the case of American Taliban soldier Jonathan Walker Lindh, whose struggle with rap's contradictions is now public knowledge. According to a *Newsweek* article profiling Lindh not long after his arrest in Afghanistan, Lindh had expressed his confusion on a hip-hop Website: "In a 1997 message to a hip-hop site, [Lindh] demanded to know why a rapper named Nas 'is indeed a "God"? If this is so,' [Lindh] indignantly asks, 'then why does he smoke blunts, drink Moet, fornicate, and make dukey music? That's a rather pathetic "god," if you ask me.' "[20] Nas should not be singled out as a scapegoat for the Five Percent Nation's conflicting representation in God Hop, and Lindh is not the only rap fan to be troubled by these inconsistencies. Five Percenter fans are surely the most troubled by waffling representation of their Nation. As one Five Percenter fan (and journalist) recognized, "Not to judge or discredit anyone, but there have been and still are many MC's that claim to have Islam, or be god, but appear to continuously contradict the very principles that we stand on."[21]

In some cases, album art, liner notes, and album organization enhance the delivery of doctrine, but considering individual God Hop songs within the context of their respective albums also illustrates that friction between righteousness and commercial success is a common facet of God Hop. Album art and liner notes can very well project a message contradicted by songs, and vice versa. Ultimately it is up to God Hop consumers to make sense of the complex combination of lyrics, music, album organization, and the packaging in which they are wrapped.

# Reaching the Blind, Deaf, and Dumb

In a 1991 interview, legendary MC Big Daddy Kane described his vision of using rap music as a powerful tool to teach black youth:

> so many brothers and sisters are out here listening to [rap music]. And for those who won't listen to a Farrakhan speech, or won't play a Malcolm X tape, or don't go to any type of Islamic school whatsoever, and only have knowledge coming from the book teachings about a white god[,] they can learn through rappers like myself, KRS-One, Public Enemy, and Rakim.[1]

But the God Hop message is only effective if listeners hear, understand, and respond to the music. Unfortunately, rap fans may easily miss the God Hop message when it is buried beneath heavily coded doctrinal language. Indeed, lyric transcriptions posted by ardent fans on various Websites suggest that fans may be missing the point. On one Website, for example, the line "or their origins in the world" from the Wu-Tang Clan's "Wu-Revolution" reads "and all the orchards in the world," an interpretation that completely obscures the Lost-Found Lessons embedded in the Wu-Tang's lyrics.[2] When compiling lyrics for this study, I found it necessary to check transcriptions against the recordings or produce my own, since Website versions of passages loaded with doctrine too often offered fanciful texts, wide of the doctrinal mark. And even with Five Percenter lessons in front of me, many lyrics were simply unintelligible. Perhaps only the most dedicated, curious, and patient fans take the time to find meaning in the lyrics. And as Jonathan Walker Lindh's struggle illustrates, uncovering the meaning can sometimes lead to even more confusion.

On the other hand, reviews of God Hop albums reveal that at least some fans have heard and responded positively to the Five Percenter message of redemption and self-knowledge. Take, for example, an anonymous review of Brand Nubian's *One for All,* posted to Amazon.com in May 2000:

> This album LITERALLY changed my life. It exposed me to the teachings of The Nation of Gods and Earths (also known as the 5% Nation of Islam or the Five

Percenters). Like the song "All for One" when Lord Jamar says "All your life you must teach truth, of the true and LIVING God, not a mystery spook!" This really affected me because at that time, I was enslaved by the remnant of the slavemaster's religion that he gave slaves to control them. I was BLIND, DEAF, and DUMB like 85% of the population and I was DEAD to the REALITY of God and how he relates to me and my people until I analyzed this album which led me on a quest to learn the teachings of the 5%. This album is ABSOLUTELY one of the BEST hiphop/rap albums ever made second ONLY (in my opinion) to PUBLIC ENEMY's 2nd album *It Takes a Nation of Millions to Hold Us Back*.[3]

Brand Nubian's messages of living black godhood, self-knowledge, and white "tricknology" evidently found a mark with this Los Angeles listener. Especially significant is the reviewer's confession that Brand Nubian's message led him or her to seek out knowledge beyond what is offered on the album.

Another rap fan, Gregory Parks, was moved by Public Enemy's lyrics to attend a lecture at his local Nation of Islam mosque.[4] Parks subsequently not only joined the Nation of Islam, but also publicly committed himself to the "rise and liberation of the black man." Before graduating from high school, Parks compiled and published a handful of Elijah Muhammad's teachings and basic Islamic concepts—such as appropriate foods, times for prayer, the five pillars (here called "principles") of Islam, and a brief history of slavery—in a small pamphlet he entitled *Freedom, Justice, and Equality: The Teachings of the Nation of Islam.* Public Enemy's music also affected the life of Daniel Muhammad, who converted to Elijah Muhammad's teachings in the early 1990s. In a 2002 interview with the *Source,* Daniel Muhammad remembers, "it was the music that led me to the Nation. If you remember, it was Public Enemy who used to sample Minister Farrakhan."[5] And DJ Kool Akiem recalls hearing of the Five Percent Nation first from MCs such as Just-Ice, Big Daddy Kane, and King Sun.[6] Clearly "conscious" rap lyrics (and samples) sometimes fall on ready ears. Even on such an individual scale, it seems Wise Intelligent is right when he claims, "we ain't just rappers / we changers of black situation" ("We Dat Nice").

Yet we are still left with the question: why should the Five Percent Nation entrust its redemptive message to such a controversial genre of popular music? Historical and cultural expectations offer some insight. Linguist Geneva Smitherman argues, for example, that teaching is expected of MCs: "The rapper is a postmodern African griot, the verbally gifted storyteller and cultural historian in traditional African society. As African America's 'griot,' the rapper must be lyrically/linguistically fluent; he or she is expected to testify, to speak the truth, to come wit it [sic] in no uncertain terms."[7] In other words, because of their verbal virtuosity, rappers are understood to have a distinct cultural role; they have a special duty to bring knowledge to the masses.

Cornel West, on the other hand, attributes this expectation not just to MCs as inheritors of griot traditions, but to all African American musicians: "since black musicians play such an important role in Afro-American life, they have a special mission and responsibility: to present beautiful music which both sustains and motivates people and provides visions of what black people should aspire to."[8] Paul Gilroy, too, sees a special cultural role for black music: "[Black] music has thus often been prized more for its sublimity and the racial probity of its witness to their lives than for its precarious status as a disposable and replaceable fragment of pop culture."[9]

The point here is that Smitherman, West, and Gilroy, all respected scholars of African American and diasporic black culture, credit black music with a special power to reach deep into the lives of its audience. Black music taps into collective social consciousness, the "soul" of African America. And this point is not lost on rap musicians. As Chuck D explains,

> [Soul] is what the essence of black music is all about. And it's a term that was once used and hasn't been used in a long time for black music, cause the white media has convinced us into thinking that this is a derogatory term. And that is the true meaning of soul. Rap music is soul. What is soul? It's inside man. It's something that moves you whether it be lyrics or music, or whatever.[10]

Five Percenter and Nation of Islam rappers are clearly aware that the quickest way to the souls of their intended audience—black American youth—is through African America's cultural soul: black music.

David Toop would perhaps argue that rap is a more effective tool than other popular music genres—even other popular music genres infused with elements of African American musical traditions—because of its unique relationship between lyrics and accompaniment:

> It has always been debatable just how much listeners take in the lyrics of a song. Sung vocals have a tendency to blend into the instrumental music, so that often the only words that are remembered are those in the title. . . . Rap vocals, on the other hand, have a separation from the music—it is possible to communicate in more detail and with a greater directness.[11]

In other words, Toop believes we hear rap lyrics better because they are foregrounded, set apart from the "music." While he is correct that rap vocals hardly blend into the musical tracks, rap lyrics do not function separately from the music, as I hope this study has shown. The interaction between music and text in these God Hop examples is a complex, orchestrated negotiation of musical layers, polyrhythms, timbres, and message, and all of these layers contribute to the dissemination of the Five Percent Nation's message.

As one of the most popular forms of American youth music, rap music is perhaps the most effective tool to reach the souls of young black folk and lead them to redemption and "knowledge of self." Within its layers, rap music carries both oral and musical traditions. As chapter 3 illustrates, God Hop lyrics not only bring Five Percenter doctrine to the public, but also extend a number of black intellectual traditions: God Hop lyrics draw on centuries of black nationalist and Pan-Africanist rhetoric and celebrate self-sufficiency, the family, and cultural unity. And in their music-making, God Hop (and other rap) musicians cling to and perpetuate long traditions of African American music, including call-and-response interaction, heterogeneous instrumental layering, and polyrhythmic percussion patterning. Sampling the rich history of African American music adds further depth to this dialogue with African America's cultural past.

Yet it is important to remember that even though Five Percenter MCs have a distinct mission, they nevertheless are very much a part of hip-hop culture. Just like other MCs, Five Percenter MCs develop their rhyme skills and flow styles through hard work, years of practice, and battling (competitive, freestyle rhyming). It should come as no surprise, then, that themes long associated with rap lyrics in general should also find their way into God Hop lyrics. These themes include oral traditions of "toasting" (ritualized boasts) and "dissing" (ritualized insults); fascination with material wealth and Mafioso lifestyles; and nostalgia for "pure" hip-hop culture. Obviously these themes have little to do with the Five Percenter mission. Likewise, DJs and producers associated with the Five Percent Nation, such as RZA, are concerned with matters beyond God Hop beats. Although I have harnessed specific analytical methods and interpretive frameworks in order to emphasize the messages behind the music in this study, proselytism is but one of many reasons these musicians take up the microphone and turntables.

Furthermore, although the MCs I have discussed in this study all use Five Percenter rhetoric to a certain extent, not all of these rappers are Five Percenters. As I demonstrated in chapter 3, much of Five Percenter rhetoric has become common parlance within the hip-hop community. A number of these musicians claimed by the Five Percent Nation may or may not consider themselves Five Percenters. Chace Infinite and DJ Khalil of the group Self Scientific, for example, are identified on the Five Percent Nation's Website as Five Percenters, but Chace Infinite is more closely allied with the Nation of Islam (his aunt is Minister Farrakhan's chief of protocol) and DJ Khalil, whose full name is Khalil Abdul Rahman, follows the *hadith* (teachings) of Sunni Muslims.[12] Why, then, would the Five Percent Nation consider these musicians to be part of their community? Chace Infinite offered me this explanation: "although every song that we do is influenced by Islam in some way we make an effort not to represent one fraction but rather the totality, from Al-Islam to the Nation of Gods and Earths."[13] Given that Five Percenters themselves do not agree on whose voice is authentic and whose voice is hypocritical, I decided early in this study that I was not equipped to make such decisions either. Therefore, instead of belaboring my discussion with judgment calls, I have instead focused on Five Percenter rhetoric and rap music's efficacy as a carrier of the Nation's message. Ultimately, understanding the nature of the Five Percent Nation's message and the extent to which that message permeates rap music is far more valuable than identifying which musicians are truly "authentic" Five Percenter voices.

Conscious texts fell from popularity by the mid-1990s for a variety of reasons, replaced by "bling-bling," booty-shaking southern raps, and MCs from all corners of the country concerned with "keeping it real," telling "true" stories from the streets. Anti-Islamic sentiment in the 1990s did not help the cause of conscious rap, and the current "War on Terror" has encouraged the American public to be leery of all things even vaguely Islamic. But, as I hope this study has shown, God Hop is concerned first and foremost not with preaching war and hate, but with teaching and uplifting black men and women. Or in the words of Chace Infinite: "Islam deals with peace, and ultimately, through our music, that's what we're trying to achieve—peace."[14]

# Appendix: Five Percenter Rap Musicians

These list is taken, slightly edited, from "God Hop: Striving Righteous Brothers and Sisters in Hip-Hop," available on the Five Percent Nation's Website at http://www.ibiblio.org/nge/ under the link "Plus Info" and then "God-Hop," accessed 15 July 2004 (last updated 8 May 2000). The parenthetical notes appear on the Web page; "still studying" means the person is "still doing research/hasn't make a commitment but uses the 'language.'" The bracketed annotations are my own. Musicians and groups discussed in this study are indicated in **boldface** type.

A+
**Aceyalone** [solo artist and member of **Freestyle Fellowship**]
**Akiem Allah [Akiem Allah Elisra]** from **Micranots**
Andre the Giant (ShowBiz and A.G.)
Artifacts
**AZ** (past) [associated with **The Firm**, which at various times has also included **Nas, Foxy Brown, Cormega**, and Nature]
**Big Daddy Kane** [formerly of the Juice Crew]
**Black Thought** (from **The Roots**)
Boot Camp Clique
**Brand Nubian** [includes **Grand Puba, Lord Jamar, Lord Sincere**, and Sadat X]
BuckShot (**Black Moon**)
**Capone and Noreaga**
**C Knowledge (Doodlebug)** from **Digable Planets** [the group also includes possible Five Percenters **Ladybug Mecca** and **Butterfly**]
**C. L. Smooth** [MC associated with DJ and producer **Pete Rock**]
Channel Live
Chino XL
C.I.A.S. (Central Indiana Attack Squad)
Company Flow
C-rayz Walz
Cru

Dark Poets
Divine Life Allah
DJ Clark Kent
Dred Poets Society
E. Bros.
Erule
**Erykah Badu** (past)
Fanatic
**Frukwan** [formerly of **Stetsasonic**; member of **Gravediggaz**, which also includes **Prince Paul, RZA**, and Poetic (deceased)]
Future Sound
God Sunz
**Gravediggaz**
Guru from Gangstarr (still studying)
Invisees
J-Live
John Forte [formerly associated with the **Fugees**]
**Killarmy** [includes **Beretta 9, Dom Pachino, 9th Prince, 4th Disciple,** Killa Sin, and Islord; loosely affiliated with the **Wu-Tang Clan**]
King Just
**King Sun** [also known as Born Sun Al-lah]
Kwame'
**Lakim Shabazz** [formerly of the Flavor Unit, which included Chill Rob G, Apache, Lord Alibaski, Latee, and **Queen Latifah**]

Leaders of the New School [Busta **Rhymes**, Dinco D, and Charlie Brown]

Lil Soldiers (No Limit Records)

Lord Finesse

M.A.R.S. (from the Roots)

Massive Influence

MC Shan [member of the Juice Crew]

Medina Green

Mic Geronimo

MF Doom

**Mobb Deep** [including Prodigy and Havoc]

Mother Superia

Movement X

Mystidious Misfits

**Nas** [associated with **The Firm,** which at various times has also included **AZ, Foxy Brown, Cormega,** and Nature]

**Nine**

Now Born Click

Nu*Born Records

Omniscience

**Pete Rock**

Phenomena

Poets of Darkness

**Poor Righteous Teachers** [includes **Wise Intelligent, Culture Freedom,** and **Father Shaheed**]

Powerule

Prime Meridian

**Queen Latifah** (past member) [formerly of the Flavor Unit, which included Chill Rob G, Apache, Lord Alibaski, Latee, and **Lakim Shabazz**]

**Rakim**

Rampage [member of the **Flipmode Squad,** which also includes **Busta Rhymes**, Rha Digga, Serious, and Spliff Star]

Red Head Kingpin

Rough House Survivors

**Scaramanga Shallah** [also known as Sir Menelik]

Self Jupiter [of **Freestyle Fellowship,** which also includes **Aceyalone,** P.E.A.C.E., and Mikah 9]

**Self Scientific** [**Chace Infinite** and **DJ Khalil**]

7ods

Shorty Long

Smif-n-Wessun [Tek and Steele, both formerly of Boot Camp Clique]

Solar Panel

Supernatural (still studying)

Superstar Quam Allah

Sun Risers

**Sunz of Man** [includes 60 Sec Assassin, Killah Priest, Prodigal Sunn, and Hell Razah; loosely affiliated with the **Wu-Tang Clan**]

3rd Eye Cipher

Top Quality

Two Kings in a Cipher

Universal

Wise Born [of **Stetsasonic,** which also includes **Daddy-O, Prince Paul, Frukwan,** Delite, and DBC]

Wizdom Life

World's Reknown

**Wu-Tang Clan** [includes **RZA, GZA, Ghostface Killah, Raekwon, Masta Killah, U-God, Method Man, Inspectah Deck,** and Ol' Dirty Bastard; also loosely affiliated with **Sunz of Man** and **Killarmy**]

YGz (Young Gunz)

**Bling Bling:** ostentatious display of wealth; the shine from diamonds and platinum.

**Biting:** imitating or copying the work of other hip-hop musicians without giving due credit. A pejorative term.

**Chopping:** altering a sampled phrase by dividing it into smaller segments and reconfiguring them in a different order.

**Conscious:** addressing the reality of a situation as the rapper perceives it. Conscious rap encompasses both black nationalist rap and gangsta rap. Its musical style varies widely, but this genre is marked by complex examples of what Krims calls speech-effusive flow.

**Crew:** a loose collection of MCs, DJs, producers, often b-boys (breakdancers), and other hangers-on. The size of a crew varies and is usually in flux at any given time. The Wu-Tang Clan, for example, contains several essential members, including GZA, RZA, Ghostface Killah, Method Man, Ol' Dirty Bastard, Raekwon, U-God, Inspectah Deck, and Masta Killah, but at any given time a number of other MCs and DJs move along the periphery of the crew and can show up in guest spots on a Wu-Tang album.

**Digging in the Crates, Digging:** the process of searching through old, rare, out-of-print vinyl records to discover obscure, fresh sounds for use in a new composition.

**Disc Jockey, DJ:** the "musician" of rap music. The DJ spins the records and has some control over the production of musical sounds (although in modern hip-hop the distinctions between DJs and producers are growing). DJs typically work with two turntables but can also use a soundboard. DJs differ from producers in that they often perform live, but most producers have DJ experience. Virtuoso DJs often refer to themselves as "turntablists."

**Dissing (Dissin'):** insulting an opponent; derives from oral traditions such as signifying and the dozens.

**Dropping Science:** sharing knowledge; teaching.

**Flow:** the quality and style of vocal delivery and rhyme. Flow is the signature stylistic marker of a particular MC.

**Freestyle:** to improvise rhymed lyrics.

**Gangsta:** a type of conscious or reality rap with west-coast origins. Gangsta rap differs from black nationalist rap in that the former tends to address the "reality" of ghetto life (including frequent references to guns, gangs, and illegal drugs), while the latter looks more to social issues (such as racism, illiteracy, and drug and alcohol abuse) for lyrical inspiration. Nationalist rap and gangsta rap share similar hard-edged musical styles and use complex patterns of flow.

**Hip-Hop:** the "culture" comprising the four elements of MC-ing, DJ-ing, writing (graffiti), and b-boying (breakdancing). According to MC and hip-hop philosopher KRS-One, "Rap is something you do, hip-hop is something you live."

**Hook:** a repeated, unifying element of a song; can be rapped, sung, or instrumental.

**Looping:** sampling one or more measures and repeating the sampled material throughout a song, with little or no alteration.

**Mack:** a genre of rap music typically concerned with women, fast cars, and ostentatious displays of wealth.

**MC:** originally an abbreviation for "master of ceremonies," but has been redefined by hip-hop practitioners as standing for "mic controller" or "move the crowd." The MC is therefore the "rapper" (although hardcore MCs consider the term "rapper" pejorative and commercial).

**Outro:** the concluding material after the final chorus or final verse of a song. The word was coined as a counterpart to "intro," for introduction. The outro is typically a place for MCs to give "shout-outs" to friends and compatriots.

**Phat:** of high value or quality.

**Punch-Phrasing:** using the cross-fader to insert a short musical segment from one song into another song being played on the opposite turntable. A musical segment which is "punched" into another song can be as short as one beat, or much longer.

**Rap:** the musical product of hip-hop culture. Rap typically features an MC who "spits" the lyrics and a DJ or producer who lays down the musical tracks under the MC's lyrics and may interact with the MC on the recorded product. Rap music exists in many genres; only a small percentage of rap is actually recorded for commercial release.

**Sampling:** the act of extracting a chunk of pre-recorded material for re-use in a new composition. Once the borrowed material is stored in a sampler, it can then be "looped," "chopped," or otherwise manipulated.

**Science of Supreme Mathematics:** an esoteric, mystical numerological system that plays a key role in Five Percenter doctrine. The numbers one to ten each have specific meanings and can also make reference to the Supreme Alphabet.

**Scratch, Scratching:** moving a record back and forth under the needle to produce rhythmic or melodic sounds. The technique was invented in the mid-1970s by Grand Wizard Theodore.

**Shout-Out:** a form of acknowledgment and respect. MCs give shout-outs to friends and colleagues by mentioning their names in song lyrics and album liner notes.

**Supreme Alphabet:** a system of assigning mystical meanings, or explanatory phrases or parables, to the letters of the alphabet. Five Percenters frequently use the Supreme Alphabet to find the "true" meanings of words by treating them as acronyms: the word "Allah," for example, reveals *A*rm *L*eg *L*eg *A*rm *H*ead, supporting the Five Percenter idea that God is not invisible but takes human form in each black man.

**Underground:** traded, sold, and performed in minor, local, and non-traditional venues. Underground hip-hop music tends to have primarily local appeal.

# Notes

## Introduction

1. One of the most important early hip-hop DJs, Kool Herc (né Clive Campbell), was in fact Jamaican-born.

2. Rap music developed within a nascent inner-city culture known as hip-hop. From its earliest days, rap—made up of a combination of MC-ing and DJ-ing—was associated with two additional artistic forms, "writing" (graffiti) and "b-boying" (breakdancing). (Like DJ-ing, "writing" and "b-boying" preceded the development of rap music.) Rap then forms merely one pillar of a larger cultural construct which today includes fashion, film, journalism, advertising, trendy foods and beverages, and even politics.

3. My description here of rap genres is necessarily abbreviated. Instead of providing a comprehensive discussion of all rap genres, I want to simply situate conscious rap within rap's overall development.

4. Quoted in Joseph D. Eure and James G. Spady, eds., *Nation Conscious Rap* (New York: PC International Press, 1991), 60.

5. Colin Soloway, Evan Thomas, Karen Breslau, and Ron Moreau, "A Long, Strange Trip to the Taliban," *Newsweek,* 17 December 2001, http://www.msnbc.com/news/669825.asp#BODY, accessed 15 December 2001 (page no longer available). For related articles, see Dan Eggen and Brooke A. Masters, "U.S. Taliban Fighter Spared Death Penalty in Indictment," *Washington Post* 121, no. 68 (16 January 2002), available at http://www-tech.mit.edu/V121/N68/walker_68.68w.html, accessed 8 July 2004; David Orland, "The Paradox of Taliban John," *Boundless Webzine,* available at http://www.boundless.org/2001/features/a0000542.html, accessed 8 July 2004; and Kevin Potvin, "Fear Leaves American Hero Hanging," *The Republic: Vancouver's Opinionated Newspaper* 2, no. 32 (21 February 2002), http://1rev.net/archive/32repub/repub_32_fear.html, accessed 17 June 2002 (page no longer available).

6. Mark Goldblatt, "Hip Hop's Grim Undertones," *USA Today,* 29 October 2002, available at http://www.usatoday.com/news/opinion/2002-10-29-oped-goldblatt_x.htm, accessed 8 July 2004. For additional commentary linking the snipers and Five Percenter rap, see William Norman Grigg, "Weapons of Mass Insurrection," *New American* 18, no. 24 (2 December 2002), available at http://www.thenewamerican.com/tna/2002/12-02-2002/vol8no24_insurrection_print.htm, accessed 8 July 2004; John Leo, "Search for the Snipers Was Too PC," *New York Daily News,* 3 November 2002, available at http://www.nydailynews.com/news/col/jleo/story/32492p-30785c.html, accessed 8 July 2004; Marc Morano, "Black Muslims Create 'Explosive Mix' in Terror War, Says Author," *Nation,* 14 November 2002, available at http://www.cnsnews.com/Nation/archive/200211/NAT20021114a.html, accessed 8 July 2004; and Cedric Muhammad, "Rap COINTELPRO XI: *Meet the Press* and Tim Russert Connect the Sniper Shootings with Hip-Hop and the 5 Percent Nation Of Islam," *BlackElectorate.com,* 1 November 2002, available at http://www.blackelectorate.com/articles.asp?ID 32, accessed 8 July 2004.

7. Hip-hop solo artists and crews typically take a stage name, but those of Five

Percenters are especially notable. Some Five Percenters take names that resonate with Nation of Islam ideology: Sadat X of Brand Nubian, for example, uses "X" to signify his unknown African name. As initiates complete their Nation of Islam indoctrination, they replace their last names (also sometimes called "government names" or "slave names") with an X, and sometimes replace their given first names with a name that carries African resonance. Other Five Percenters adopt names that show the influence of the Supreme Alphabet, in which every letter carries a symbolic meaning. Complete words are treated as acronyms to reveal their "true" meaning. In this system, KRS-One's name means "Knowledge Reigns Supreme Over Nearly Everybody," and Big Daddy Kane's name becomes Big Daddy "King Asiatic Nobody Equals." Yet others choose as names attributes they wish to emulate or embody, for example, Wise Intelligent and Culture Freedom of Poor Righteous Teachers (Culture Freedom's name also comes from the Science of Supreme Mathematics). The Supreme Alphabet will be further discussed in chapters 2 and 3.

8. See "Farrakhan Acknowledges Sniper as Member of NOI," *NewsMax.com,* 28 October 2002, available at http://www.newsmax.com/archives/articles/2002/10/26/222128 .shtml, accessed 8 July 2004.

9. Quoted in Dasun Allah, "Civilized People: Five Percenters 'Build' on Negative Press," *Village Voice,* 13–19 November 2002, available at http://www.villagevoice.com/ issues/0246/allah.php, accessed 8 July 2004. See also Chuck Creekmur's interview with Busta Rhymes in "Rage against the Machine," *Source,* no. 161 (February 2003): 80–82.

10. Quoted in Dasun Allah, "Civilized People."

11. For histories of the early development of rap music, see Mark Dery, "Rock is Dead: Rap!" *Keyboard* 14, no. 11 (November 1988): 32–55; S. H. Fernando, Jr., "Back in the Day, 1975–1979," in Alan Light, ed., *The Vibe History of Hip Hop* (New York: Three Rivers Press, 1999), 13–21; S. H. Fernando, Jr., *The New Beats: Exploring the Music, Culture, and Attitudes of Hip-Hop* (New York: Anchor Books, 1994), chapter 1; Jim Fricke and Charlie Ahearn, *Yes Yes Y'all: The Experience Music Project Oral History of Hip-Hop's First Decade,* with an introduction by Nelson George (Cambridge, Mass.: Da Capo Press, 2002); William Eric Perkins, "The Rap Attack: An Introduction," in *Droppin' Science: Critical Essays on Rap Music and Hip Hop Culture,* ed. William Eric Perkins (Philadelphia: Temple University Press, 1996), 1–45; Tricia Rose, *Black Noise: Rap Music and Black Culture in Contemporary America* (Hanover, N.H.: Wesleyan University Press, 1994); and David Toop, *The Rap Attack 2: African Rap to Global Hip Hop* (London: Serpent's Tail, 1991).

12. According to the Nation of Islam's Lost-Found Muslim Lesson no. 1, question 9, Caucasians (here called "devils") must devote thirty-five to fifty years to the Nation of Islam before being considered eligible to wear the Nation's emblems. See Fard Muhammad, "The Supreme Wisdom Lessons," available at http://www.thenationofislam.org/ supremewisdom.html, accessed 8 July 2004.

## 1. Building a Nation

1. See Peter Lamborn Wilson, "Shoot-Out at the Circle Seven Koran: Noble Drew Ali and the Moorish Science Temple," *Gnosis* 12 (summer 1989): 44. According to the bio attached to the Gnosis article, Wilson is an exilarch of the Moorish Orthodox Church of America. Because of his insider status, Wilson is currently one of the best sources for information on Noble Drew Ali and the history of the Moorish Church. Wilson also writes under the name Hakim Bey (I am grateful to Joe Schloss for bringing this to my attention).

2. Ibid.

3. Mattias Gardell, *Countdown to Armageddon: Louis Farrakhan and the Nation of Islam* (London: Hurst and Company, 1996), 37.

4. Moorish Orthodox Church of America, "History & Catechism of the Moorish Orthodox Church of America," *Deoxyribonucleic Hyperdimension*, available at http://www.deoxy.org/moorish.htm, accessed 8 July 2004.

5. Wilson, "Shoot-Out at the Circle Seven Koran," 44.

6. Whereas Wilson upholds the gypsy story, the Moorish Orthodox Church of America claims Noble Drew Ali traveled as a circus magician. Compare Wilson, "Shoot-Out at the Circle Seven Koran," 44; and Moorish Orthodox Church of America, "History & Catechism."

7. Wilson, "Shoot-Out at the Circle Seven Koran," 45.

8. For scholarly studies of lynching and racial violence in the Jim Crow south, see Leon F. Litwack, *Trouble in Mind: Black Southerners in the Age of Jim Crow* (New York: Alfred A. Knopf, 1998), especially chapter 6; and Orlando Patterson, *Rituals of Blood: Consequences of Slavery in Two American Centuries* (New York: Basic Civitas, 1998), chapter 2.

9. Any aspirations beyond mere subsistence also met with resistance, as Matthew Wilson shows in his study of the careers of poet and novelist Paul Laurence Dunbar, painter Henry O. Tanner, and novelist Charles W. Chestnutt. Wilson sums up the few choices available to African American artists around the turn of the twentieth century: invisibility, spectacle, and a complex inversion of spectacle that allowed African American artists to both play upon and subvert white expectations. Although he is primarily concerned with these three key figures in African American arts and letters, Wilson's argument is far-reaching: no matter what life path southern African Americans chose in the era of Jim Crow, they all confronted the unyielding machinery of white expectations and prejudices. See Matthew Wilson, "The Advent of 'The Nigger': The Careers of Paul Laurence Dunbar, Henry O. Tanner, and Charles W. Chestnutt," *American Studies* 43, no. 1 (spring 2002): 13.

10. Litwack, *Trouble in Mind*, 380.

11. Wilson, "Shoot-Out at the Circle Seven Koran," 45.

12. Ibid., 47.

13. Ibid. Like Moorish initiates, members of fraternal orders also endured strict rules of conduct and dress. Litwack suggests that rather than considering such strict codes and rituals disagreeable, members welcomed them: "The rituals, titles, and uniforms that characterized the fraternal orders gave members a welcome respite from their daily routine and made them feel like somebody in a society that insisted they were nobody" (Litwack, *Trouble in Mind*, 375).

14. Wilson, "Shoot-Out at the Circle Seven Koran," 47.

15. According to Wilson, oral histories recall an earlier version of *The Holy Koran* called the *Circle 7 Koran* ("Shoot-Out at the Circle Seven Koran," 45).

16. As defined by Wilson Jeremiah Moses and adopted by other scholars of black nationalism, "classical" black nationalism reached its peak between 1850 and 1925, culminating in Marcus Garvey's charismatic teachings. See Wilson Jeremiah Moses, *The Golden Age of Black Nationalism, 1850–1925* (Hamden, Conn.: Archon Books, 1978); and Wilson Jeremiah Moses, ed., *Classical Black Nationalism: From the American Revolution to Marcus Garvey* (New York: New York University Press, 1995). For detailed discussions of the literary bases and "borrowings" of *The Holy Koran*, see Wilson, "Shoot-Out at the Circle Seven Koran," and Gardell, *Countdown to Armageddon*.

17. "The Moabites from the land of Moab who received permission from the Pharaohs of Egypt to settle and inhabit North-West Africa; they were the founders and are

**148**  the true possessors of the present Moroccan Empire. With their Canaanite, Hittite, and Amorite bretheren [*sic*] who sojourned from the land of Canaan seeking new homes. Their dominion and inhabitation extended from North-East and South-West Africa, across great Atlantis even unto the present North, South, and Central America and also Mexico and the Atlantis Islands; before the great earthquake, which caused the great Atlantic Ocean" (Noble Drew Ali, *The Holy Koran of the Moorish Science Temple of America* [n.p., (1927?)], 47:7–8, available at http://www.geocities.com/Athens/Delphi/2705/koran-index.html, accessed 8 July 2004). See also Hakim Bey [Peter Lamborn Wilson], "Preface," *Journal of the Moorish Paradigm* 1, no. 1 (January 2001), available at http://www.mu-atlantis.com/jmp1/, accessed 8 July 2004.

18. Prince-A-Cuba, Wilson, and Claude Andrew Clegg all maintain Noble Drew Ali's influence on the Nation of Islam. See Prince-A-Cuba, "Black Gods of the Inner City," *Gnosis,* fall 1992, 56–63, also available at http://www.ibiblio.org/nge/innercity.html, accessed 8 July 2004; Wilson, "Shoot-Out at the Circle Seven Koran"; and Claude Andrew Clegg III, *An Original Man: The Life and Times of Elijah Muhammad* (New York: St. Martin's Press, 1997), 19–20.

19. Prince-A-Cuba, "Black Gods of the Inner City."

20. Gardell, *Countdown to Armageddon,* 51–52.

21. Noble Drew Ali, *The Holy Koran,* 48:3.

22. Adib Rashad, *Islam, Black Nationalism and Slavery: A Detailed History* (Beltsville, Md.: Writers' Inc. International, 1995), 172. It is worth noting that Garvey's demands for repatriation have been recently revived by Minister Louis Farrakhan, who has proposed two alternative ideas: the United States government could give land within the country's boundaries to African Americans as partial reparation for slavery, or African countries could donate land to African Americans to atone for their role in the slave trade. See Gardell, *Countdown to Armageddon;* and Lawrence Mamiya, "From Black Muslim to Bilalian: The Evolution of a Movement," *Journal for the Scientific Study of Religion* 21, no. 2 (1982): 142–43. On the phrase "Asiatic Blackman," see note 27 below.

23. See Wilson, "Shoot-Out at the Circle Seven Koran," 48; and Moorish Orthodox Church of America, "History & Catechism."

24. Adam Edgerly and Carl Ellis, "Emergence of Islam in the African-American Community," *ReachOut* 7, nos. 3–4, also available at http://answering-islam.org.uk/ReachOut/emergence.html, accessed 8 July 2004. The Moorish Orthodox Church of America identifies Sheik Timothy Givins El as Noble Drew Ali's chauffeur; see Moorish Orthodox Church of America, "History & Catechism." Wilson supports the chauffeur story, but gives the name John Givens El. Wilson also mentions additional factions led by R. German Ali, Daddy Grace, and Elijah Mohammed [*sic*] (Wilson, "Shoot-Out at the Circle Seven Koran," 48).

25. See Gardell, *Countdown to Armageddon,* 50–55; C. Eric Lincoln, *The Black Muslims in America* (Boston: Beacon Press, 1973), 12–13; and Steven Tsoukalas, *The Nation of Islam: Understanding the "Black Muslims"* (Phillipsburg, N.J.: P&R Publishing, 2001), 20–22. All three sources explain Fard's multiple possible "histories" at length.

26. Erdmann Doane Beynon, "The Voodoo Cult among Negro Migrants in Detroit," *American Journal of Sociology* 43 (May 1938), 896.

27. Elijah Muhammad taught that "all nations of the earth are recognized by the name by which they are called. By stating one's name, one is able to associate an entire order of a particular civilization simply by name alone" (Elijah Muhammad, *Message to the Blackman in America* [Chicago: Muhammad Mosque of Islam No. 2, 1965], 54–55). Given the importance of nation naming, Elijah Muhammad rejected contemporary names such as "Negro," and referred to his people variously as the "so-called Negro," the

"Original" man, the "Asiatic Nation," or the "Asiatic Blackman" (see *Message to the* *Blackman in America,* passim). In discussing Elijah Muhammad's teachings, I will use his terminology and capitalization.

28. Gardell, *Countdown to Armageddon,* 53–54, 155–56.

29. Edgerly and Ellis, "Emergence of Islam in the African-American Community"; Ted Swedenburg, "Islam in the Mix: Lessons of the Five Percent," paper presented at the Anthropology Colloquium, University of Arkansas, 19 February 1997, available at http://comp.uark.edu/tsweden/5per.html, accessed 8 July 2004 (cited with permission from the author); Lincoln, *The Black Muslims in America,* 12; and Prince-A-Cuba, "Black Gods of the Inner City," quoting E. U. Essien-Udom, *Black Nationalism: A Search for Identity* (Chicago: University of Chicago Press, 1962), 43, respectively.

30. Clegg, *An Original Man,* 14–15.

31. Edgerly and Ellis, "Emergence of Islam in the African-American Community," quoting Clifton Marsh, *From Black Muslims to Muslims: The Transition from Separatism to Islam* (Metuchen, N.J.: Scarecrow Press, 1984), 53.

32. Edgerly and Ellis, "Emergence of Islam in the African-American Community."

33. Prince-A-Cuba, "Black Gods of the Inner City." Although Prince-A-Cuba's studies seem to be supported by other similar approaches, the Five Percent Nation has posted his article "Black Gods in the Inner City" on their Website with the following disclaimer: "This 'brother' Prince-A-Cuba claims to B a part of the Nation of Gods And Earths. However he has disgruntled attitudes towards the physical foundation of our Nation in the Wilderness of North America, which is Allah School in Mecca (Harlem). This material is presented here as a form of general information, but is not exclusively condoned by the Nation of Gods and Earths universally, and is the sole responsibility of Prince-A-Cuba. Peace."

34. Gardell, *Countdown to Armageddon,* 54.

35. Ibid., 58. Several theories have appeared to account for Fard's disappearance. Rumors suggest that Fard met with foul play and was killed, but other sources give accounts of journeys: Elijah Muhammad claimed that Fard fled to Mecca after being ordered out of America, and various newspaper sources claimed Fard traveled to either Australia, New Zealand, or Europe. According to Prince-A-Cuba, a recent report proposes that Fard was still alive as of 1992, living in California as an orthodox Muslim (Prince-A-Cuba, "Black Gods of the Inner City"). Adib Rashad reports, however, that Imam Warith Deen Mohammad (see note 44 below) announced Fard's death to his congregation in 1993 and claimed Fard had been serving as an imam in California under Warith Deen's leadership prior to his death (Rashad, *Islam, Black Nationalism and Slavery,* 227).

36. According to Beynon, the congregation had already been divided by Abdul Mohammed, one of Fard's temple officers, who objected to Fard's insistence that their collective allegiance should be only to the "Moslem" flag and not to the United States. Abdul Mohammed seceded with a few followers and proclaimed allegiance to the Constitution and the American flag. Other troubles arose when Robert Karriem, one of Fard's followers, took Fard's lessons concerning sacrificing "Caucasian devils" too literally and "sacrificed" his tenant, John J. Smith (Beynon, "Voodoo Cult," 903).

37. Edgerly and Ellis, "Emergence of Islam in the African-American Community."

38. For detailed scholarly discussions of Elijah Muhammad's teachings, see Edgerly and Ellis, "Emergence of Islam in the African-American Community"; Gardell, *Countdown to Armageddon,* 59 and especially chapter 7; and Prince-A-Cuba, "Black Gods of the Inner City."

39. Gardell, *Countdown to Armageddon,* 171–72, emphasis in the original.

40. *Message to the Blackman; How to Eat to Live; How to Eat to Live, Book Two; The Fall of America;* and *Our Saviour Has Arrived* are all available at http://www

.seventhfam.com/temple/elijah_books.htm, accessed July 8, 2004. This site is hosted by the Nation of Islam, Settlement No. 1, which does not recognize the authority of Louis Farrakhan and considers his organization heretical.

41. See especially *The Autobiography of Malcolm X,* as told to Alex Haley (New York: Ballantine Books, 1964). See also Clegg, *An Original Man,* chapter 8; and Gardell, *Countdown to Armageddon,* 65–85. The following discussion is based on these sources.

42. For a biographical account of Clarence 13X's early years, see Beloved Allah, "The Bomb: The Greatest Story Never Told," *Word* 1, no. 1 (July 1987); 1, no. 3 (August–September 1987); and 1, no. 4 (October–November 1987), also available at http://www.ibiblio.org/nge/thebomb.html, accessed 8 July 2004. Primary and secondary sources disagree on the year of Clarence 13X's departure from Temple #7. Prince-A-Cuba, a self-described "insider," maintains that the Five Percent Nation was founded "around 1964" (Prince-A-Cuba, "Black Gods of the Inner City"). Mattias Gardell, Swedenburg, and Beloved Allah all give 1963; see Gardell, *Countdown to Armageddon,* 224; Swedenburg, "Islam in the Mix"; and Beloved Allah, "The Bomb." The anonymous author of a "symbol quiz" attached to the Web journal *Blackseven.com* (a Five Percenter journal based in the United Kingdom, now defunct) claims Clarence 13X left the Temple in 1969; see http://www.geocities.com/cheybazz/symbol_quiz.html, and http://www.geocities.com/cheybazz/symbol_quiz_answers.html, accessed 7 October 2001 (pages no longer available).

43. Following President Kennedy's death, Elijah Muhammad instructed his ministers to either remain silent on the issue or, if pressed by the media, to reply, "No comment." A few days after the assassination, Malcolm X spoke at the Manhattan Center in New York. When asked his opinion of the assassination, Malcolm replied that it was a case of "the chickens coming home to roost." He went on to say that "the hate in white men had not stopped with the killing of defenseless black people, but that hate, allowed to spread unchecked, finally had struck down this country's Chief of State" (*The Autobiography of Malcolm X,* 307–308).

44. After Elijah Muhammad's death in 1975, Wallace took over the leadership of the Nation of Islam and promptly moved his congregation in the direction of orthodox Islam, eventually re-naming his organization the World Community of al-Islam in the West and later the American Muslim Mission. Wallace Muhammad, now known as Imam Warith Deen Muhammad, is today a respected leader in orthodox Islamic world affairs.

45. As leader of the Hanafi Muslims, McGhee was known as Hamaas Abdul Khaalis. He is best known as the mentor of former professional basketball star Kareem Abdul Jabbar, a convert to the Hanafi Muslims, but also came to public attention in the early 1970s due to his ongoing rivalry with the Nation of Islam. After Khaalis circulated an open letter in which he criticized Elijah Muhammad and the Nation of Islam, unidentified assailants—assumed to be renegade followers of Elijah Muhammad—attacked Khaalis's residence in Washington D. C. in January 1973, killing seven Hanafis, including five children. See Gardell, *Countdown to Armageddon,* 189; and Clegg, *An Original Man,* 262–64.

46. Swedenburg, "Islam in the Mix: Lessons of the Five Percent."

47. Beloved Allah, "The Bomb."

48. Gardell, *Countdown to Armageddon,* 224.

49. Prince-A-Cuba, "Black Gods of the Inner City." An editorial in the *Washington (D.C) Sunday Star* printed after Clarence 13X's death claims Malcolm X expelled him from Temple #7 but gives no reason for the punishment ("Police Seek Aid to Solve Killing of Clarence 13X," *Sunday Star,* 15 June 1968, sec. A, p. 25, reprinted in Prince-A-Cuba, *Our Mecca Is Harlem: Clarence 13X (Allah) and the Five Percent* [Hampton, Va.: United Brothers and United Sisters Communication Systems, 1995], 36–37).

50. Barry Gottehrer, *The Mayor's Man: One Man's Struggle to Save Our Cities* (Garden City, N.Y.: Doubleday, 1975), 93. Gottehrer's book is notoriously difficult to find. Prince-A-Cuba, who reprints part of it in his pamphlet *Our Mecca is Harlem,* hints that the book has been deliberately hidden from public sight: "Barry Gottehrer's book, *The Mayor's Man,* has served as a major source of information. It is included here because the book from which the chapter is drawn is no longer in print, and copies of it have been stolen from most public libraries, only to be hidden by the priests (10%)" (Prince-A-Cuba, *Our Mecca is Harlem,* 5). Whatever the reason behind the book's scarcity, I finally—in July 2001—located a used copy for sale through Amazon.com after searching for nearly four years. Unfortunately, the third-party seller contacted me several days later to apologize: she could not ship the book because it was suddenly missing from her stock. Four months later, however, I located another copy on Amazon.com, and the book did arrive a few days later.

51. Beloved Allah, "The Bomb."

52. Beloved Allah offers a psychological reason for the nickname "Father": "They called Allah, 'The Father' because many of them were the products of broken homes and this was the only father they knew" (ibid.).

53. "Harlem Hit by Five Percenters," *New York Amsterdam News,* 16 October 1965, p. 1. Gottehrer reported that by the time he first met Allah in May 1967, police estimated that Allah's followers numbered between two and five hundred, while Allah placed the number closer to eight hundred (Gottehrer, *The Mayor's Man,* 93).

54. "Harlem Hit by Five Percenters," 2.

55. "A New Harlem Hate Group? Police Chilly," *New York [Post?]* (15 October 1965), n.p. This article comes from a microfiche clipping file entitled "Five Percent Nation" located at the Schomburg Center for Research in Black Culture in New York.

56. Gardell, *Countdown to Armageddon,* 224.

57. See FBI file 157-6-34, "Five Percenters." According to Gardell, by 1968 the FBI had established five specific long-range goals for COINTELPRO: "(1) 'prevent the coalition of militant black nationalist groups' that 'might be the first step toward a real "Mau Mau" in America, the beginning of a true black revolution'; (2) 'prevent the rise of a "messiah" who could unify and electrify the militant black nationalist movement'; (3) 'prevent violence' by identifying 'potential troublemakers and neutraliz[ing] them'; (4) 'prevent militant black nationalist groups and leaders from gaining respectability, by discrediting them'; and (5) 'prevent the long range growth of black nationalist organizations, especially among youth' " (Gardell, *Countdown to Armageddon,* 224, quoting FBI file 100-448006-17, dated 4 March 1968).

58. Gardell, *Countdown to Armageddon,* 224, quoting FBI file 157-33 76-6.

59. FBI file 157-6-34, "Five Percenters."

60. Ibid.

61. Ibid. See also FBI file 100-444636, "Clarence 13X Smith." According to Gottehrer, Clarence 13X was "grateful" to the hospital for "validating his status": " 'They know I'm Allah,' he told me. 'They gave me proof.' He pulled out the waistband of his prison underwear to show the name Allah inked on it. 'This was my name in the hospital,' he said. 'If they didn't believe I was Allah, why did they let me out? Would they let out a crazy person?' " (Gottehrer, *Mayor's Man,* 99–100).

62. See, for example, "Harlem Hit by Five Percenters," 1–2; and Alex Todorovic, "They Call Themselves Five Percenters," *POINT: South Carolina's Independent News-monthly* 7, no. 77 (April 1996), available at www.mindspring.com/~scpoint/point/9604/p06.html, accessed 8 July 2004.

63. A. Cortez (God Allah Shah) and C. Goodwin (God Adew Allah), "In the Defense

of the Five Percenters," *Black News* 3, no. 13 (October 1976): 21. One of my consultants, Akiem Allah Elisra (DJ Kool Akiem), offered a different view: "I won't pretend that the NGE never acted exactly like a gang, as it still does in many instances now. I don't see anything wrong with a 'gang,' only the negative images applied to them, regardless of activity" (personal communication, 24 May 2003).

64. Gardell, *Countdown to Armageddon,* 85.

65. Gottehrer, *The Mayor's Man,* 91–108. Barry Gottehrer is still active in New York City politics and has also worked as a political consultant for the television sitcom *Spin City.*

66. Ibid., 92.

67. Father Allah's obituary in the *Washington Post Times Herald* also describes him as a peace-loving moderate, noting that "the Five Percenters were militant when they were organized about five years ago but have become increasingly moderate and willing to cooperate with City Hall in various ghetto projects." The article further reports that Father Allah played a major role in calming the African American community in Harlem after the assassination of Dr. Martin Luther King, Jr. ("Harlem Moderate Is Murdered," *Washington Post Times Herald,* 14 June 1969, reprinted in Prince-A-Cuba, *Our Mecca is Harlem,* 32–33). According to Gottehrer, Gloria Steinem wrote a similar piece for *New York* magazine lauding Allah's role in promoting peace after King's death. Gottehrer's description of the magazine's cover art is telling: "on the cover was a picture of the Empire State Building in flames, flanked by Allah and Mayor Lindsay, who were presumably putting out the fire together" (Gottehrer, *The Mayor's Man,* 215).

68. Five Percenters habitually re-name geographic locations. Other examples include Medina (Brooklyn), the Desert (Queens), and Pelan (the Bronx); New Jerusalem for New Jersey; Love Allah for both Los Angeles and Louisiana; West Asia for San Francisco; New Heaven for New Haven; Allah's Garden for Atlanta; and C-God for Chicago (see the Five Percent Nation's homepage at http://www.ibiblio.org/nge/ under the link "Allah's Atlas," accessed 8 July 2004). Such re-naming is an example of what linguists call "semantic inversion," defined by Geneva Smitherman—a celebrated linguist and champion of African American Vernacular English—as "a process whereby African American Language speakers take words and concepts from the English American Language [that is, standard English] lexicon and either reverse their meanings or impose entirely different meanings" on them. Smitherman calls "semantic inversion" an "act of linguistic empowerment." See Geneva Smitherman, " 'The Chain Remains the Same': Communicative Practices in the Hip Hop Nation," *Journal of Black Studies* 28, no. 1 (September 1997): 17.

69. Gardell, *Countdown to Armageddon,* 61. Although called universities, these schools served the educational needs of children of all ages. The Universities of Islam opened under Elijah Muhammad were closed down after his death, when his son Wallace Muhammad chose to move the Nation of Islam closer to mainstream Islam. Universities of Islam were re-opened in 1989 under the leadership of Louis Farrakhan. While the majority of these "universities" are elementary schools, the Chicago University of Islam also provides secondary education (Gardell, *Countdown to Armageddon,* 323).

70. Gottehrer, *The Mayor's Man,* 101.

71. Although it could be argued that verbal ability is and has been valued throughout the African American community, Nuruddin and Swedenburg place special emphasis on the verbal abilities gained by Five Percenters during their indoctrination; see Yusef Nuruddin, "The Five Percenters: A Teenage Nation of Gods and Earths," in *Muslim Communities in North America,* ed. Yvonne Yazbeck Haddad and Jane Idleman Smith (Albany: State University of New York Press, 1994), 111; and Swedenburg, "Islam in the Mix." Compelling oratory may also be part of Father Allah's legacy. According to Beloved Allah, Clarence

13X was known as a fiery speaker: "he had a speaking style that was unique to him, a slow methodical cadence stressing syllables that normally aren't. It was hypnotic" (Beloved Allah, "The Bomb"). Gottehrer, too, noted Allah's idiosyncratic speech style: "Allah's speech pattern was uniquely his own, with its own pitch and rhythm. He would start a sentence, 'I am neither pro-black or anti-' and then he would pause. He'd add, 'whi-i-ite,' stretching the emphasis on that last syllable" (Gottehrer, *The Mayor's Man*, 93).

72. Gottehrer, *The Mayor's Man*, 239–41.

73. See FBI file 100-444636.

74. Charlie Ahearn, "The Five Percent Solution," *Spin* 6 (February 1991): 57.

75. Beloved Allah, "The Bomb."

76. Gottehrer, *The Mayor's Man*, 245–46.

77. Beloved Allah, "The Bomb."

78. Quoted in Ahearn, "The Five Percent Solution," 57.

79. Quoted in Fricke and Ahearn, *Yes Yes Y'all*, 26.

80. Quoted in Eure and Spady, *Nation Conscious Rap*, 359.

81. Louis Farrakhan broke from Wallace Muhammad's World Community of al-Islam in the West in 1978 in order to return to Elijah Muhammad's teachings. Calling his splinter group the Nation of Islam in honor of Elijah Muhammad, Farrakhan quickly gained supporters and today leads the largest congregation of black Muslims in America.

82. Quoted in Eure and Spady, *Nation Conscious Rap*, 271.

83. Minister Farrakhan was invited to speak again at another hip-hop summit, held in Los Angeles in February 2002, where he was joined by notables such as Congresswoman Maxine Waters. Here he spoke again of the responsibility rap musicians have to teach the young. For one hip-hop journalist's perspective on the event, see Davey D., "The West Coast Hip Hop Summit: Who? What? Where? Why? & How?" *Hip Hop News: FNV Newsletter*, 19 February 2002, available at http://www.daveyd.com/westcoasthiphop summarticle.html, accessed 8 July 2004.

84. Quoted in Richard Muhammad, "Farrakhan to Rappers: 'You Have Been Chosen to Lead,'" *Final Call*, 26 June 2001, available at http://www.finalcall.com/national/rapsummit06-26-2001b.htm, accessed 8 July 2004.

85. Quoted in Fahiym Ratcliffe, "Common Ground," *Source*, no. 144 (September 2001): 72.

## 2. The Five Percenter "Way of Life"

1. The full set of lessons is available in Felicia M. Miyakawa, "God Hop: The Music and Message of Five Percenter Rap" (Ph.D. diss., Indiana University, 2003).

2. The catechism-styled lessons of the Nation of Islam and the Five Percent Nation bear a striking resemblance to lessons fashioned by Noble Drew Ali for his followers. A list of 101 lessons he drew up, entitled "Koran Questions for Moorish Children," includes questions pertaining to Noble Drew Ali's background, the founding of the Moorish Science Temple of America, the paternity of Jesus and his status as a prophet, the nature of the self, and definitions of words such as "Black," "Colored," "Negro," and "Ethiopia." Like the lessons later fashioned by Elijah Muhammad, Noble Drew Ali's lessons include both question and answer (Noble Drew Ali, "Koran Questions for Moorish Americans," folder 4 of 7, special collection on the Moorish Science Temple of America, Schomburg Center for Research in Black Culture, New York).

3. Clegg, *An Original Man*, 27. "Actual Facts," the "Student Enrollment Lessons," the "Lost-Found Lessons," and "English Lesson no. C1" are all available in Master Fard Muhammad, "The Supreme Wisdom Lessons."

4. See "The Eight Planes of Study to Be Born as Revealed to Us by Allah," available at http://www.angelfire.com/ga/9thJewel/8planesofstudy.html, accessed 8 July 2004.

5. Akiem Allah Elisra (DJ Kool Akiem) corrected my original placement of 0 (cipher) before 1 (knowledge) with the following explanation: "Cipher comes after Born [9], it represents completeness. The decimal system, base ten, uses the '0' as a place holder, meaning as a written indicator—there is no value, but the number to the left is multiplied by 'ten.' . . . So in the decimal system it represents the completion of the cycle through all the numbers 1–9" (personal communication, 24 June 2003).

6. Beloved Allah, "The Bomb."

7. Nuruddin, "The Five Percenters," 127; the bracketed explanation is by Nuruddin.

8. Divine Ruler Equality Allah, "Solar Factorization," available at http://www.ibiblio.org/nge/ under the "Plus Info" link, accessed 8 July 2004. Divine Ruler Equality Allah holds a master's of science in physics from Purdue University (personal communication, 14 October 2003).

9. The flag was designed by Universal Shaamgaud Allah, one of Father Allah's "First Born." See "Universal Flag of Islam," available at http://www.ibiblio.org/nge/ under the "Plus Info" link, accessed 12 July 2004.

10. Nuruddin, "The Five Percenters," 115–16. See also Master Fard Muhammad, "The Supreme Wisdom Lessons."

11. Nuruddin, "The Five Percenters," 117.

12. In the early stages of the development of Islam, Islamic mystics codified a system of cosmology and numerology based on the writings of Greek philosophers, particularly Ptolemy. See John David North, *The Norton History of Astronomy and Cosmology* (New York: Norton, 1994), 179; chapters 8 and 9 include a detailed description of the use of astronomy and cosmology in early Islam.

13. Nuruddin also suggests that the Supreme Alphabet finds a parallel in the Kabbalistic science of the Path of Letters and notes that the Science of Supreme Mathematics shares common concepts with Sufism, Kabbala, and Pythagorean numerology. See Nuruddin, "The Five Percenters," 122–23.

14. Gardell, *Countdown to Armageddon,* 176–81. Gardell also offers examples of numerology at work in Nation of Islam theology.

15. This is also true of *Hurufa-i-jay-Hurufa-Ab-jay;* for example, the third letter of the Arabic alphabet,     (transliterated as "ta"), is associated with the number 400. See Gabriel Mandel Khan, *Arabic Script: Styles, Variants, and Calligraphic Adaptations,* trans. Rosanna M. Giammanco Frongia (New York: Abbeville Press Publishers, 2001).

16. See Gardell, *Countdown to Armageddon,* 225.

17. Sincere Allah Merciful God, "Why We Are Not Muslims," available at http://www.ibiblio.org/nge/ under the "Plus Info" link, accessed 8 July 2004.

18. Gardell, *Countdown to Armageddon,* 144.

19. Quoted in Eure and Spady, *Nation Conscious Rap,* 65–66.

20. Nuruddin, "The Five Percenters," 129.

21. Akiem Allah Elisra (Kool Akiem), personal communication, 29 May 2003.

22. Gardell, *Countdown to Armageddon,* 225.

23. Quoted in Ahearn, "The Five Percent Solution," 57.

24. Nuruddin, "The Five Percenters," 117.

25. Lincoln, *The Black Muslims in America,* 75.

26. Akiem Allah Elisra (Kool Akiem), personal communication, 24 June 2003.

27. Gottehrer, *The Mayor's Man,* 97.

28. The Nation of Islam is also concerned with proper eating. Elijah Muhammad published two books on healthy eating, and Minister Farrakhan has declared a "war on

obesity" and advocates exercise and a vegetarian diet. See Louis Farrakhan, "Declare War on Obesity (Fat)!" *Final Call,* 22 July 1991, and "Exercise to Stay Alive," *Final Call,* 19 August 1991. See also Abdul Allah Muhammad, "Eat to Live—Or Else!" *Final Call,* 13 August 2002, http://www.finalcall.com/columns/eleven.html, accessed 16 August 2002 (page no longer available).

29. Quoted in Eure and Spady, *Nation Conscious Rap,* 72.

30. For the history and theology of the Ansaaru Allah Community, see Gardell, *Countdown to Armageddon,* 225–31.

31. Quoted in Charlie Ahearn, "Lakim Gets Busy Dropping Science," *New York City Sun* 6, no. 17 (26 April 1989): 19.

32. Quoted in Eure and Spady, *Nation Conscious Rap,* 65.

33. Quoted in Ahearn, "The Five Percent Solution," 76.

34. Sha-King Ceh' um Allah, "Social Equality?" *National Statement,* http://www.nationalstatement.com/e/sha-kingAllah_pg1.htm, accessed 14 October 2001 (page no longer available).

35. Nuruddin, "The Five Percenters," 128. See also Beloved Allah, "The Bomb."

36. Gottehrer suggests another reason for the heavy emphasis on reproduction: "Allah [Clarence 13X] believed that one way for Five Percenters to inherit the earth was to produce more children than any other group and outpopulate the competition" (*The Mayor's Man,* 96).

37. Anne Campbell, *The Girls in the Gang,* 2nd ed. (Cambridge, Mass.: Basil Blackwell, 1991), 191 and passim.

38. Gottehrer, *The Mayor's Man,* 104.

39. Born Allah, "The Undisputable Truth," *National Statement,* http://www.nationalstatement.com/e/AllahB-tUT_pg1.htm, accessed 14 October 2001 (page no longer available).

40. Lord Natural Self Allah, "The Five Percent Dilemma," available at http://www.ibiblio.org/nge/ under the "Prison Outreach" link; accessed 8 July 2004.

41. See Paul von Zielbauer, "Inmates Are Free to Practice Black Supremacist Religion, Judge Rules," *New York Times,* 18 August 2003, available at http://www.nytimes.com/2003/08/18/nyregion/18PRIS.html, accessed 8 July 2004. I wish to thank Travis Jackson for bringing this article to my attention.

42. Akiem Allah Elisra (Kool Akiem) explained that photocopies play an integral role in passing down lessons: "I was given my Lessons by going to Kinkos and copying them. First I was given the Math and Alphabet orally to write down and memorize. Later I was given photocopies of Math and Alphabet that went along with all the rest of the Lessons. Now I have several different photocopied versions, including versions photocopied directly from NOI sources. Photocopying is routine, usually lesson by lesson starting with the Math and ending with Solar Facts" (personal communication, 30 July 2003).

43. "What We Teach," *Word* 1, no 2 (July 1987), 12, quoted in Nuruddin, "The Five Percenters," 113.

44. In the interest of keeping the text uncluttered with editorial brackets, I have silently corrected spelling and punctuation in documents taken from the Internet.

45. "What We Teach" and "What We Will Achieve" are linked off the Five Percent Nation's homepage at http://www.ibiblio.org/nge/, accessed 8 July 2004. (The link for "What We Will Achieve" is labeled "What We Achieve.") "What We Teach" and "What We Will Achieve" (here titled "What We Achieve" and omitting "Peace") are also included in *All Eye Seeing,* a Five Percenter Web journal, volume 4, pp. 11–12 (available at http://www.ibiblio.org/nge/thealleyeseeing/volume4/page11.html and http://www.ibiblio.org/nge/thealleyeseeing/volume4/page12.html, accessed 8 July 2004).

46. See for example, the Gravediggaz' song "Twelve Jewelz" from their album *The Pick, the Sickle and the Shovel.*

47. The Five Percenter Web journal *All Eye Seeing* includes narrative explanations of all of the "Twelve Jewels" except Happiness. Knowledge "is to know, look, listen observe and respect. To retrieve information based on fact and record that which is true." Wisdom "is wise words based on facts, to speak what you know. Wisdom is wise ways, actions and thoughts used to educate others on what is true." Understanding "is to comprehend what one hears and sees. Understanding is to have insight as well as eye sight." Freedom is "to release from obligation and control. To have the ability to progress without hindrance." Justice "is to reward the good and correct the wrong." Equality "is to have equal opportunity to express ones thoughts and or ideas; whether wrong or right. One must take that which is of quality (good) to aid in the development and growth of ones self (Nation)." Food "is that which nourishes the body, physically as well as mentally." Clothing "is the garments one wears on the outside to show what one sees on the inside. The moral and decent coverings [one] wears to protect them from shame." Shelter "is a place of refuge in the wilderness to protect one from the elements of the jungle." Love "is to desire for your brother or sister what you want for yourself." And Peace "is the absence of confusion. Peace is the goal of the righteous and the way of life of the civilized man." See "Twelve Jewels," http://www.ibiblio.org/nge/thealleyeseeing/volume4/page10.html, accessed 8 July 2004.

48. World Wide Web sources suggest that the Nation has also begun to spread internationally. For example, *Blackseven.com,* an online magazine devoted to Five Percenters and their teachings, was based in the United Kingdom.

49. Gardell, *Countdown to Armageddon,* 295.

50. The Five Percent Website at http://www.ibiblio.org/nge/, under "Other Links," offers information on and links to both commercial and underground acts.

51. The Five Percent Nation is also heavily represented in the "underground" hip-hop scene (that is, hip-hop that is not generally available through mainstream commercial outlets), but since underground rap is very difficult to track, it is beyond the scope of the present study.

52. Quoted in Eure and Spady, *Nation Conscious Rap,* 69.

## 3. Lyrics

1. Jonathan "Gotti" Bonanno, "Last Man Standing," *Source,* no. 126 (March 2000): 217.

2. Muhammad, *Message to the Blackman in America,* 44. See also Lost-Found Lesson no. 2, questions 18–20, in Muhammad, "The Supreme Wisdom Lessons."

3. Culture Freedom made a similar point in an interview with S. H. Fernando, Jr.: "To teach anybody anything, you gotta be able to speak the language. . . . You gotta know the language before you can talk the talk. You gotta walk like the people and talk like the people before you can be accepted by those people sometimes. Because people be like 'How the hell you gonna try to tell me something, for one, you ain't never been in the ghetto, for two you ain't never had shit stolen, you ain't never had any welfare cheese, how can you come in here and tell me[?]' " Quoted in Fernando, *The New Beats,* 262.

4. A "blunt" is a specific type of cigar popular in hip-hop circles, produced by carefully slitting open a cigar, emptying it of tobacco, replacing the tobacco with marijuana, and resealing the cigar.

5. The speaker is not identified in the liner notes of this album and I have not been

able to find a printed copy of this speech. My conclusion that the speaker is Farrakhan is **157**
based on my own comparisons with other Farrakhan speeches as well as on my conversations with other Nation of Islam scholars who have reached the same conclusion.

6. For other contractions of this lesson, see Ghostface Killah's "Motherless Child," Black Moon's "Buck 'em Down," and Grand Puba's "Lickshot."

7. The second phrase of this line could be interpreted as number play. The twelfth jewel is happiness (see chapter 2). With this phrase Wise Intelligent could be suggesting that happiness is the product of the digits of 13, which mean knowledge and understanding. In other words, true happiness is attained only through a combination of knowledge and understanding.

8. Using the Supreme Alphabet—to be explained later in this chapter—"now-cipher" means simply "no."

9. Brand Nubian's first album, *One for All,* contains two versions of "Wake Up": the first is subtitled "Stimulated Dummies Mix," while the second, featuring nearly identical lyrics but different musical tracks, is subtitled "Reprise in the Sunshine." Unless otherwise noted, the shortened title "Wake Up" refers to characteristics that both versions share.

10. The year 2004 marks the fortieth anniversary of the Five Percent Nation's founding, if 1964 is taken as the founding date. According to the Nation of Islam, however, 2004 is the year 15,091. The Nation of Islam dates the beginning of the present Islamic civilization from the year it was predicted that Yacub would create the grafted Devil. In that year, the twenty-three scientists outlined the next 15,000 years: Yacub was to be born in the year 8,400, would take 600 years to perfect his grafted devil, and the devil's civilization would then flourish for 6,000 years. In western dating, 1914 marked the end of the devil's civilization. Thus, according to the Nation of Islam's eschatology, the devil's civilization continues on borrowed time and is due to expire at any moment. See Lost-Found Lesson no. 2, questions 21–36, in Muhammad, "The Supreme Wisdom Lessons"; and Muhammad, *Message to the Blackman in America.*

11. To "fall off" implies selling out, or losing popularity and public recognition.

12. RZA appears in a brief cameo role near the end of the 1999 film *Ghost Dog: The Way of the Samurai* (he also produced the soundtrack). RZA's character greets Forrest Whitaker's character with this wish for peace: "knowledge knowledge." It has also been suggested to me that "knowledge knowledge" suggests a meaning of "peace" through a different association. If one accompanies the phrase "knowledge knowledge" with a particular hand gesture—that of raising first the index finger and then the middle finger on the same hand with the pronouncement of each word—the resulting hand shape is the familiar peace sign.

13. "Trife" derives from "triflin' " or "to trifle." Here "we got trife" means our lives became focused on the trivial and unimportant.

14. The genesis of "Mystery (Who Is God)" further underlines Louis Farrakhan's significance in the Five Percenter community. In a interview with Wakeel Allah of the Allah Team on 11 April 1998, Rakim credited Minister Farrakhan with inspiring "The Mystery": "Farrakhan, he always drops science and if you listen, he be telling you that the Black Man is God! . . . He's the one that kind of pushed me to do 'Who is God' . . . I heard something that Farrakhan was speaking on, and he made it simple and plain, because he went to Mecca and put it on the table, and they couldn't even question him. . . . So you know he did his thing, he let them know that the Black Man is God! So I said it's time right now" (Wakeel Allah, "It's Been a Long Time: Interview with Rakim Allah," http://www.allahteam.com/rakim_interview.htm, accessed 11 October 2001 [page no longer available]).

15. According to the Five Percent Nation's homepage (http://www.ibiblio.org/nge, under the links "Plus Info" and then "God-Hop"), Erykah Badu is a former member of the Nation. Nevertheless, even Badu's most recent lyrics are still dense with references to Five Percenter doctrine.

16. See Gardell, *Countdown to Armageddon,* 180.

17. "Ryzarector" is one of many aliases for RZA, producer of Killarmy's "Wake Up."

18. See also "7XL," "Anger in the Nation," and "Dial 7 (Axioms of Creamy Spies)" for additional references to "devils" and "devil civilization."

19. "Phat" means "good" or "of high quality."

20. For a detailed discussion of black nationalist rhetoric in Five Percenter lyrics, see Felicia M. Miyakawa, " 'The Duty of the Civilized Is to Civilize the Uncivilized': Tropes of Black Nationalism in the Messages of Five Percent Rappers," in *Understanding African American Rhetoric: Classical Origins to Contemporary Innovations,* ed. Ronald Jackson and Elaine Richardson (New York: Routledge, 2003), 171–85.

21. Imanuel Geiss, *The Pan-African Movement: A History of Pan-Africanism in America, Europe and Africa,* trans. Ann Keep (New York: Holmes and Meier, 1974), 96.

22. Muhammad, *Message to the Blackman in America,* 31.

23. The title of Brand Nubian's song is a reference to James Brown's hit song "Say It Loud (I'm Black and I'm Proud)." As Kyra Gaunt has pointed out, James Brown continues to be one of the most revered and heavily sampled musical predecessors of hip-hop. See Kyra D. Gaunt, "The Veneration of James Brown and George Clinton in Hip-Hop Music: Is It Live! Or Is It Re-memory?" in *Popular Music: Style and Identity,* ed. William Straw (Montreal: The Centre for Research on Canadian Industries and Institutions, 1995), 117–22.

24. Muhammad, *Message to the Blackman in America,* 39.

25. A "gat" is a gun or weapon.

26. Again, "knowledge" is used as an imperative verb.

27. Five Percenters and members of the Nation of Islam draw much of their doctrine from the Qur'an, but also quote frequently from both the Old and New Testaments of the Bible. In his *Message to the Blackman in America,* Elijah Muhammad frequently uses the Bible to argue his main points.

28. In mentioning Casio and Rolex watches Wise Intelligent also makes reference to time, a frequent trope of conscious rap. Public Enemy and other conscious groups frequently exhort their listeners to know "what time it is": time for African Americans to rise up and fight for equality. Flavor Flav of Public Enemy is known for wearing huge clocks around his neck to emphasize his awareness of "Nation Time." Poor Righteous Teachers make an explicit reference to this trope in "Rock Dis Funky Joint" as Wise explains his distance from "brothers" who "didn't know the time" (m. 109).

29. Quoted in Ahearn, "Lakim Gets Busy Dropping Science," 13.

30. Allah, "It's Been a Long Time."

31. Akiem Allah Elisra (Kool Akiem), personal communication, 28 May 2003.

32. Some producers do acknowledge the possibility that well-constructed songs can speak both to the mainstream and also to those listening for a deeper message. Pharell Williams of the Neptunes (also known as N.E.R.D., one of hip-hop's current production wonder teams) recently admitted that their songs "Lap Dance"—a song about strippers—and "I Just Wanna Love U" (performed by Jay-Z)—a song about hustling—both contain hidden messages, and are not their only songs to do so. According to Williams, "kids don't want to be preached to"; he has found instead that subliminal messages are a far more effective tool to reach the youth. See Billy Johnson, Jr., "Revenge of the Nerds," *Source,* no. 139 (April 2001): 129.

## 4. Flow, Layering, Rupture, and Groove

1. Rose, *Black Noise,* 88.

2. Ibid., 39.

3. Ibid.

4. I am indebted here to Adam Krims, who uses beat-class analysis to map flow styles. Krims's own flow maps, however, take a slightly different form. See Adam Krims, *Rap Music and the Poetics of Identity* (New York: Cambridge University Press, 2000), 59–60. Jean-Marie Jacono has also recently written on flow (although he does not use the term) and visually maps the lyrics and 4/4 meter (although he is concerned only with how syllables fall on main beats and not on subdivisions of beats). His ultimate purpose, however, is not to relate flow and musical tracks, but to illustrate his theory that in French rap, accent is not concerned with typical French accentuation but instead corresponds to poetic structure. He also notes that virtuoso MCs are quick to create new accents in the French language to produce a signature flow style. See Jean-Marie Jacono, "Pour une analyse des chansons de rap," *Musurgia* 5, no. 2 (1998): 65–75.

5. Krims, *Rap Music and the Poetics of Identity,* 48.

6. Ibid., 49–52.

7. Ibid., 50. As Krims notes, most hip-hop music is organized in duple or quadruple meters. Friedrich Neumann agrees, and proposes that most rap could be charted in some version of 4/4 meter. See Friedrich Neumann, "Hip Hop: Origins, Characteristics and Creative Processes," *World of Music* 42, no. 1 (2000): 57.

8. Krims, *Rap Music and the Poetics of Identity,* 49.

9. *Source,* no. 138 (March 2001): 244, 248, and 258 respectively.

10. Robert Walser, "Rhythm, Rhyme, and Rhetoric in the Music of Public Enemy," *Ethnomusicology* 39, no. 2 (1995): 204.

11. Ibid. Walser's examples attend specifically to the interplay between Chuck D's flow and the Bomb Squad–produced tracks under "Fight the Power," but his observation is true in general of hip-hop music. Hank Shocklee, one of the Bomb Squad's producers, has also spoken of the importance of matching music and lyrics: "we think about trying to complement the vocal situation by making the backing tracks as aggressive as possible. Whatever you bring up as a sample, whatever beat you work with, has to be an exclamation point to the situation" (quoted in Tom Moon, "Public Enemy's Bomb Squad," *Musician,* October 1991, 70).

12. My analyses for this chapter rest in part on the assumption that MCs and producers collaborate in methodical ways in order to produce expressive meaning. This is certainly true in some cases, especially when an MC and a producer have a consistent partnership. For example, in his discussion of his own collaboration (as producer) with a Canadian Cree MC named Bannock, Adam Krims describes a collaborative moment when Bannock asked Krims if he could "do something special in the musical realm" to highlight a particular line of text; Krims complied by "[thinning] out the layering a bit at that moment, to foreground the vocals" (Krims, *Rap Music and the Poetics of Identity,* 196). Yet as Joseph Schloss has recently pointed out, not all collaborations work in this manner. An MC may visit a producer and write lyrics or freestyle over a track the producer has recently "composed"; or an MC may visit a producer with lyrics already written, looking for a "beat" to match the lyrics. In many cases the music is composed first, and MCs write lyrics to match the ethos they perceive in the song (Joseph G. Schloss, "Making Beats: The Art of Sample-Based Hip-Hop" [Ph.D. diss., University of Washington, 2000]," 193–95). RZA, for example, prefers to compose a "beat" and then choose an MC or several MCs to write lyrics for the beat (see Kim Osario, "Operation W: Back at the Front,"

*Source,* no. 136 [January 2001]: 167). Surely a different collaborative method exists for each musical partnership. Insider accounts of the production process would do much to clarify how hip-hop musicians make their musical choices.

13. Producer Hank Shocklee describes himself as an architect and his fellow Bomb Squad producers as builders: "I'm thinking about arrangements—putting in the chorus at times you don't really expect a chorus, coming up with that little extra interruption" (quoted in Moon, "Public Enemy's Bomb Squad," 70).

14. In a 1987 interview, producer Rick Rubin (noted especially for his work with Run DMC and the Beastie Boys) hinted that the hip-hop practice of associating signature sounds and textures with a particular moment of a song's structure owes something to his production style: "I use beats to achieve the dynamics of melodies without melodies. . . . drum parts are the parts of the song: one beat happens during the verse, different pauses bring you into the chorus, then the chorus gets filled out—something is added or taken away. I create a song structure. This is the thing I might have brought to rap music." Quoted in Havelock Nelson, "Rick Rubin: Def Jam's Man with the Plan," *Musician,* no. 103 (May 1987): 39.

15. My statements about form here rely primarily on data gleaned from the songs analyzed for this study, but these generalities hold for rap at large as well.

16. DJ Kool Akiem (Akiem Allah Elisra) of the Micranots disagrees with this argument, noting that "MCs always used a hook, in fact what they do evolved from a 'hook,' that call and response at the party, that's the first thing they did, the hook, then came the verses and so on as they took more of the spotlight" (personal communication, 24 June 2003).

17. See Nelson George, *Hip Hop America* (New York: Penguin, 1999), 95.

18. A few songs, such as Lakim Shabazz's "The Lost Tribe of Shabazz" and Brand Nubian's "Drop the Bomb," have unusually long introductions (twenty-four and twenty measures respectively).

19. Consistent verse lengths seem not to be of great importance. Few songs analyzed for this study have verses of identical measure lengths. See, for example, Grand Puba's "Proper Education," Poor Righteous Teachers' "Word from the Wise," Brand Nubian's "The Godz Must Be Crazy" and "Sincerely," Scaramanga's "7XL," Lakim Shabazz's "Black is Back," and Aceyalone's "I Got to Have It Too."

20. Friedrich Neumann has made similar observations about verse-chorus form in rap, although he also notes that "the musical material of the strophes, refrains and all other sections is the same," which, as I will argue in the following pages, is not always true (Neumann, "Hip Hop," 52).

21. Although they typically do, choruses or hooks need not follow immediately after verses. Rakim's "The 18th Letter," for example, reserves the hook for the end of the song. After one long verse broken into five chunks delineated by an eight-measure bass guitar pattern, Rakim offers a four-measure chorus that he promptly repeats and follows with an instrumental coda.

22. My concept of the groove continuum is based primarily on Adam Krims's layering graph technique, first introduced in his analysis of Ice Cube's "The Nigga Ya Love to Hate." Each line of his layering graph shows the layering of what he terms "configurations" (stable combinations of tracks), "upbeats" (one-measure combinations of tracks that precede key moments of the song), and "adjuncts" (one or more tracks superimposed over configurations or refrains) over the formal sections of verses and refrains. In other words, Krims's layering graph addresses how the discrete chunks of musical material used in "The Nigga Ya Love to Hate" are layered both simultaneously and successively. Krims

conceives of each moment of musical activity in terms of cells and charts the interaction of all timbres and instruments throughout the song as one cell gives way to another. His approach is thus primarily (and artificially) vertical: he looks for stacks of timbres and pitches at any given moment rather than for continuity of sounds and groove between moments and across broader temporal expansions. See Krims, *Rap Music and the Poetics of Identity,* chapter 3 ("The Musical Poetics of a 'Revolutionary' Identity").

23. The bass line and the synthesizer melody (melodic layer 4), as well as additional sound effects, are sampled from Tavares's "Bad Times."

24. Because this second pattern is modulatory, it lacks the repetition necessary for a concise transcription. I have chosen to not transcribe this section in order to keep the groove continuum on a single page.

25. Rose, *Black Noise,* 39.

26. See Olly Wilson, "Black Music as an Art Form," *Black Music Research Journal* (1983): 1–22; and Olly Wilson, "The Heterogeneous Sound Ideal in African-American Music," in *New Perspectives on Music: Essays in Honor of Eileen Southern,* ed. Josephine Wright (Warren, Mich.: Harmonie Park Press, 1992), 327–38.

27. Similar changes occur to emphasize formal divisions between verses and choruses in Brand Nubian's "Wake Up (Stimulated Dummies Mix)" and Poor Righteous Teachers' "We Dat Nice" and "Word Iz Life."

28. Four-measure kick drum patterns seem to be of particular structural importance to Father Shaheed, Poor Righteous Teachers' DJ and usual producer. By contrast, RZA and his protégé 4th Disciple prefer larger organizational structures, frequently opting for eight-measure phrases delineated by melodic layers (in "A Better Tomorrow," for example). Phrasing greatly affects the form of a song, but before we can fully understand how hip-hop music works, we need to know much more about producers' individual compositional proclivities.

29. Neumann calls the break "an important structural element in rap music" and defines a rap "break" as "a short general rest during which the rapper is completely alone for a half- or whole beat. In this way, important statements can be accentuated, and so the exact timing of a break depends on the text" (Neumann, "Hip Hop," 54).

30. The bass and keyboard are both sampled from 24 Carat Black's "Ghetto: Misfortune's Wealth."

31. RZA and 4th Disciple are the only producers listed for GZA's album *Liquid Swords.*

32. The only exception is the sampled tenor sax riff from Eddie Harris's "Superfluous," but this sax riff only occurs in the choruses and thus does not play a primary structural role other than distinguishing chorus from verses. See chapter 5 for a further discussion of this sample.

33. For additional songs in which melodic layers are clearly associated with form, see Brand Nubian's "Brand Nubian," "Pass the Gat," and "I'm Black and I'm Proud"; Lakim Shabazz's "Brothers in Action"; Poor Righteous Teachers' "Holy Intellect," "Strictly Ghetto," "Word from the Wise," and "Rock Dis Funky Joint"; Grand Puba's "Proper Education"; Big Daddy Kane's "Children R the Future"; Aceyalone's "I Got to Have It Too"; and Self Scientific's "The Long Run."

34. The verses vary in length: AZ begins with a twelve-measure verse, followed by Cormega's fourteen-measure verse, Nas's twelve-measure verse, and Foxy Brown's extended thirty-two-bar verse.

35. James Snead, "Repetition as a Figure of Black Culture," in *Black Literature and Literary Theory,* ed. Henry Louis Gates, Jr. (New York: Routledge, 1984), 67.

36. Ibid.

37. Rose, *Black Noise,* 38.

38. Charles Keil and Stephen Feld, *Music Grooves: Essays and Dialogues* (Chicago: University of Chicago Press, 1994), 23.

39. Ibid., 109.

40. Ibid., 23. Samuel Floyd explains a similar phenomenon but uses the term "time line" (borrowing from Nketia) instead of "groove": "The time line is an integral part of the music itself and is therefore more complex than a single accompanying pulse. . . . It is against the time line that the other instruments play the multilinear rhythms that yield the exciting interlocking, cross-rhythmic, and polyrhythmic configurations of African music" (Samuel A. Floyd, Jr., *The Power of Black Music: Interpreting Its History from Africa to the United States* [New York: Oxford University, 1995], 28–29).

41. Keil and Feld, *Music Grooves,* 22. An entire body of literature has developed in response to Keil's idea of "participatory discrepancies," those tensions of rhythm and timbre musicians play with and against when musicking together. Although his theory is compelling, I will not dwell on it here since my chief concern is with the interplay between music and audience and not between musicians themselves in the act of creation. Furthermore, it could be argued that groove applies differently to hip-hop music since hip-hop music is typically not created by live musicians interacting on acoustic instruments.

42. See Christopher Small, *Music of the Common Tongue: Survival and Celebration in Afro-American Music* (New York: Riverrun Press, 1987; reprint, Hanover, N.H.: Wesleyan University Press), especially chapter 2 ("On the Ritual Performance").

43. Keil and Feld, *Music Grooves,* 111.

44. True 54, "Interview with Micranots," *Thrasher,* December 1999, 120, http://www.micranots.com/m2000/words/thrasher.html (page no longer available).

45. Keil and Feld, *Music Grooves,* 91.

46. Ibid.

## 5. Sampling, Borrowing, and Meaning

1. See, for example Jeffrey R. Houle, "Digital Audio Sampling, Copyright Law and the American Music Industry: Privacy or Just a Bad 'Rap'?" *Loyola Law Review* 37, no. 4 (winter 1992): 879–902; Jason H. Marcus, "Don't Stop That Funky Beat: The Essentiality of Digital Sampling to Rap Music," *COMM/ENT: Hastings Journal of Communications and Entertainment Law* 13, no. 4 (summer 1991): 767–90; and Thomas G. Schumacher, " 'This Is a Sampling Sport': Digital Sampling, Rap Music and the Law in Cultural Production," *Media, Culture & Society* 17 (1995): 253–73. Friedrich Neumann's brief discussion of sampling in his article "Hip Hop: Origins, Characteristics and Creative Processes" is also primarily concerned with copyright problems. Although the title of Michael Ashburne's *Sampling in the Record Industry* (Oakland, Calif.: Law Offices of Michael Ashburne, Esq., 1994) implies that he is concerned with sampling in all popular music, this slim volume is devoted primarily to the process of clearing samples for rap recordings. Ashburne, an Oakland-based music industry legal expert, includes sample forms for clearance procedures, as well as a copy of the landmark 1991 federal court decision against Biz Markie for sampling Gilbert O'Sullivan's "Alone Again Naturally" without permission.

2. See especially Richard Shusterman, "The Fine Art of Rap," in *Pragmatist Aesthetics: Living Beauty, Rethinking Art,* 2nd ed. (Oxford: Rowman & Littlefield, 2000); and Russell A. Potter, *Spectacular Vernaculars: Hip-Hop and the Politics of Postmodernism* (Albany: State University of New York Press, 1995), chapter 1. Additionally, within an article otherwise concerned with copyright issues, Marcus includes a section titled "Sampling as a Postmodern Art Form," and advocates sampling practices *because* they give

evidence of post-modernism (Marcus, "Don't Stop That Funky Beat," 772). Susan McClary **163** closes a chapter on post-modernism in her book *Conventional Wisdom* with a discussion of the intertextual, multivalent borrowings in Public Enemy's song "Nighttrain." Although compelling and cogent, McClary's reading of "Nighttrain" insists on meaning and does not address the possibility that the borrowed sounds could be valued for their purely sonic value. See McClary, *Conventional Wisdom: The Content of Musical Form* (Berkeley: University of California Press, 2000), 159–66.

3. Nikitah Okembe-Ra Imani and Hernan Vera see sampling as both resistance and re-contextualization. They argue, for example, that "the technique of digital sampling [is] itself a form of cultural resistance. By sampling African cultural heroes, the DJ mapped the symbolic discourse of those sampled onto the new record, recontextualizing and modernizing the original sample" (Imani and Vera, "War at 33 1/3: Exploring Hip-hop (Rap) Music," in *All Music: Essays on the Hermeneutics of Music,* edited by Fabio B. Dasilva and David L. Brunsma [Brookfield, Vt.: Ashgate, 1996], 170). See also J. D. Considine, "*Larcenous Art?*" *Rolling Stone,* 14 June 1990, reprinted in *Rap on Rap: Straight-up Talk on Hip-Hop Culture,* ed. Adam Sexton (New York: Dell Publishing, 1990), 58–61; and Smitherman, " 'The Chain Remains the Same,' " 15–17.

4. See Gaunt, "The Veneration of James Brown and George Clinton in Hip-Hop Music," 117; George, *Hip Hop America,* 96; Rose, *Black Noise,* 79; Smitherman, " 'The Chain Remains the Same,' " 15–16; and Robert Walser, "Rhythm, Rhyme, and Rhetoric in the Music of Public Enemy," *Ethnomusicology* 39, no. 2 (1995): 196. In addition to advocating sampling as a valuable post-modern practice, Marcus also proposes that it should be allowed because "through this medium, many artists pay homage to the strong roots of black American music" (Marcus, "Don't Stop That Funky Beat," 773). Considine sees sampling as both re-contextualization and homage, arguing, for example, "what makes sampling so attractive isn't that it's easier to pinch a James Brown scream than to learn how to make that sound yourself. Rather, it's the fact that there's something immediately recognizable about that scream, that it carries a specific association: Soul Brother No. 1 " (Considine, "Larcenous Art?" 59).

5. "The practice of sampling expresses the impulse to collage [that] characterizes the best of black musical traditions, particularly jazz and gospel. Sampling is also post-modernist activity that merges disparate music and cultural forms to communicate an artistic message. Sampling is a transgressive activity because rappers employ it to interrupt the narrative flow and musical stability of other musical texts, producing a new and often radically different creation" (Michael Eric Dyson, *Reflecting Black: African-American Cultural Criticism* [Minneapolis: University of Minnesota Press, 1993], 14).

6. http://www.micranots.com/m2000/words/samp.html, accessed 6 January 2002 (page no longer available).

7. Quoted in Moon, "Public Enemy's Bomb Squad," 69.

8. "Talkin' All That Jazz" was itself Stetsasonic's angry response to criticism of sampling practices. According to Nelson George, in 1988 producer-songwriter and political activist Mtume "blasted" hip-hop's sampling practices on a New York City radio show, calling songs produced from samples "nothing but Memorex music." Daddy-O, founder of Stetsasonic, heard the show, and the members of Stetsasonic collectively responded with "Talkin' All That Jazz," a verbal defense of sampling ("You said it wasn't art / So now we're gonna rip you apart") delivered over a musical track constructed from several samples, including a sample from Mtume's own "Juicy." See George, *Hip Hop America,* 88–91.

9. Cheryl L. Keyes, "At the Crossroads: Rap Music and Its African Nexus," *Ethnomusicology* 40, no. 2 (1996): 240.

10. Schloss, "Making Beats," 77. Schloss uses the term "sample-based producers" throughout his study to clearly differentiate those producers who value sampling as a compositional practice from those who do not. In Schloss's view, the difference between sample-based hip-hop and non-sample-based hip-hop is one of genre, rather than of methodology or compositional style. See Schloss, "Making Beats," 7–8.

11. Toop, *The Rap Attack 2*, 192.

12. David Metzer, *Quotation and Cultural Meaning in Twentieth-Century Music* (Cambridge: Cambridge University Press, 2003), chapter 5 ("Sampling and Thievery"). In this chapter, Metzer presents a useful binary to understand how sampling has been used in popular music: first, musicians sample isolated instrumental sounds which are later recombined with other sounds into the tapestry of a new song; and second, musicians have sampled longer chunks of sounds—often polyphonic—that are inserted intact into the new song. He identifies the second form of sampling as closer to the other practices of borrowing he discusses elsewhere in the book.

13. The sources of miscellaneous samples, such as those from speeches, are frequently unidentified. Those identified in this chapter are the product of my own research. The Sample FAQ was originally located at http://www.members.accessus.net/xombi/intro.html, and has now moved to http://www.the-breaks.com.

14. Schloss, "Making Beats," 201.

15. C.f. fn. 12 above. My distinction between borrowing and sampling differs somewhat from Metzer's. Metzer's two categories of digital borrowing do not take into account the possibility of re-performing borrowed material in a new song, rather than digitally sampling from a previous source.

16. See Potter, *Spectacular Vernaculars*, 43; and Toop, *The Rap Attack 2*, 191–92.

17. Toop, *The Rap Attack 2*, 194.

18. Schloss, "Making Beats," 125–54.

19. Ibid., 121 and passim.

20. Ibid., 143.

21. Quoted in ibid., 142.

22. See also "Gods, Earths and 85ers"; "I Got to Have It Too"; "Motherless Child"; "Mortal Combat"; "Wake Up (Reprise in the Sunshine)"; and "We Dat Nice." Rakim's "The 18th Letter," a song without a typical refrain, nevertheless uses a vocal sample—a single, highly emotional "ahh" from the end of Lyn Collin's "Do Your Thing"—to help delineate eight-bar phrases.

23. Schloss, "Making Beats," 125.

24. "Word from the Wise" (1990) by Poor Righteous Teachers and "Get Down" (2002) by Nas (produced by Nas and Salaam Remi) also share a sample: the bass, guitar, and drum groove from James Brown's "The Boss." The producers of both of the new songs sample the bass, guitar, and drums polyphonically, using these instruments as the groove for the new songs. Both new songs also make occasional use of a sampled horn burst and a held horn crescendo; these monophonic samples punctuate some formal sections but otherwise occur primarily in the choruses. Nas and Salaam Remi also borrow James Brown exclaiming "Get down!"

25. See also the groove of Digable Planets' "Dial 7 (Axioms of Creamy Spies)," which is built over sampled bass and keyboard lines from Tavares's "Bad Times."

26. For additional examples of this type of sampling application, see Brand Nubian's "Dance to My Ministry" and "Drop the Bomb"; Eric B. and Rakim's "In the Ghetto"; Nas's "Life's a Bitch"; Mobb Deep's "Still Shinin' "; and Poor Righteous Teachers' "Word from the Wise."

27. Schloss, "Making Beats," 80. Schloss points out that finding beats for sampling

secondary functions of digging: to show commitment to hip-hop DJ-ing traditions; to "pay dues" in an appropriate manner; to learn about different styles of music; and to socialize with other DJs and producers (109–10).

28. Ibid., 60.

29. True 54, "Interview with Micranots."

30. Both quoted in Schloss, "Making Beats," 60.

31. As Ted Swedenburg notes, sampling Muslim worship practices is quite unusual, even for Islamic rap: "Orthodox Muslims consider setting the call to prayer (idhân) to music and drums harâm, forbidden, and many Muslims would be shocked by Brand Nubian's 'Allahu Akbar'. Technically, one 'chants' or 'recites' (tilâwa) the call to prayer, one does not 'sing' (ghanniya) it; 'recitation' and 'music' are seen as distinct categories which should be kept separate" (Swedenburg, "Islam in the Mix"). Furthermore, the very use of musical instruments is much debated in the Muslim community. For this reason the members of Native Deen, an orthodox Muslim rap group, use only percussion instruments in their music. According to their Website, "some scholars such as Sheikh Yusuf Qaradawi say that if the lyrics of the music [are] Islamic, then any type of musical instrument is permissible. However there are others that say that wind and string instruments must be avoided and only percussion (drums) instruments can be used. There [are] other scholars that say that only the duff (tambourine) can be used. Even others say no instruments at all are allowed. Since this is such a hot debate, we tried to use the least amount of instruments possible and still give the sound most American Muslim youth are used to" (http://www.nativedeen.com/faqs.htm, accessed 8 July 2004).

32. The *M*A*S*H** sample is a good example of what Frank Zappa would call an "Archetypal American Musical Icon," a compositional allusion widely recognizable to those familiar with American culture. See Christopher Smith, "Broadway the Hard Way: Techniques of Allusion in the Music of Frank Zappa," *College Music Symposium* 35 (1995): 37.

33. Jennifer Perry, "Bringing Truth to Light," *Source,* no. 42 (March 1993): 30.

34. The keyboard and bass groove of "In the Ghetto" also come from the 24 Carat Black source. See chapter 4, example 4.6.

35. Father Shaheed also illustrates his crew's talents musically, as discussed in chapter 4.

36. "Kool Moe Dee—Biography," available at http://www.oldschoolhiphop.com/artists/emcees/koolmoedee.htm, accessed 8 July 2004.

37. The source of this sample is unidentified.

38. "Greatest Love of All" was a hit song for musicians such as George Benson and Shirley Bassey long before Houston's cover on her debut album *Whitney.* Yet Houston's version, which appeared in 1985, is likely the most immediate reference for both Big Daddy Kane and his audience: his album appeared in 1989.

39. To "bounce" here means to leave.

40. One is reminded here of Harold Bloom's work with patterns of poetic influence and his resulting theory, known as the Anxiety of Influence. Bloom's analysis centers around six revisionary ratios—clinamen, tessera, kenosis, daemonization, askesis, and apophrades—each of which is paired with a rhetorical trope (irony, synecdoche, metonymy, hyperbole, metaphor, and metalepsis respectively). Although Bloom's theories are meant to apply to poetry, they can be applied to other patterns of artistic influence, as Kevin Korsyn has shown for music. Bloom's third revisionary ratio, kenosis, is particularly relevant for my reading of "Miss Ghetto." Korsyn defines kenosis as "a reaction against the precursor, a counter-movement." Bloom's Freudian readings of poetic influence may or may

not be a fruitful basis for further sampling scholarship, but at the very least, Bloom's kenosis reminds us that artistic influence does not always produce imitation: influence often inspires reactionary art, as we see in Wise Intelligent's critique of Mobb Deep. See Harold Bloom, *The Anxiety of Influence: A Theory of Poetry,* 2nd ed. (New York: Oxford University Press, 1997), 77–92; and Kevin Korsyn, "Towards a New Poetics of Musical Influence," *Music Analysis* 10, nos. 1–2 (1991): 47.

41. Akiem Allah Elisra (Kool Akiem), personal communication, 24 June 2003.

42. Ibid.

43. These are the opening lines from a speech Malcolm X gave at the Hotel Theresa in Harlem to a delegation of Mississippi youth on 1 January 1965. See *Malcolm X Speaks: Selected Speeches and Statements,* ed. George Breitman (New York: Pathfinder, 1989), 137.

44. Potter suggests that mingling sermons and music is not a new practice and points to early recordings of African American preachers framed by choruses of sacred songs as precedents (Potter, *Spectacular Vernaculars,* 42–43). Furthermore, in his work on Dr. Martin Luther King, Jr., Keith D. Miller argues not only that King inherited this oral preaching style ("like other folk preachers, King typically ended his oral sermons . . . by merging his voice with the lyrics of a spiritual, hymn, or gospel song") but also used this tradition of reaching for familiar songs to create both a personal voice and a collective, communal voice. See Keith D. Miller, "Martin Luther King, Jr. and the Black Folk Pulpit," *Journal of American History* 78, no. 1 (June 1991): 121–23. When sampling speeches and sermons, rap musicians reverse the process, borrowing spoken texts to give weight to their musical message.

45. Malcolm X delivered the "Message to the Grass Roots" to the Northern Negro Grass Roots Leadership Conference in Detroit on 10 November 1963. For an Africological analysis of this speech, see Jeffrey Lynn Woodyard, "Africological Theory and Criticism: Reconceptualizing Communication Constructs," in *Understanding African American Rhetoric: Classical Origins to Contemporary Innovations,* ed. Ronald Jackson and Elaine Richardson (New York: Routledge, 2003), 133–54.

46. As detailed in chapter 4, scratching frequently works as sonic quotation marks for samples.

47. "Black Is Back" appears in two versions on Lakim Shabazz's album *The Lost Tribe of Shabazz.* While DJ Mark the 45 King changes much of the instrumentation between versions, he deems the speech sample significant enough to appear in both versions. For additional examples of sampled speeches, see the Micranots' "Culture," Lakim Shabazz's "The Lost Tribe of Shabazz," and Poor Righteous Teachers' "Strictly Ghetto."

48. Although the occasion of the sermon is unknown, the speaker is likely Minister Louis Farrakhan.

49. See chapter 2 for a discussion of numbers in "Allah and Justice."

50. This video, which I accessed in spring of 2000 from http://www.ibiblio.org/nge/, is no longer available on the Website. Photos of the 1999 Show and Prove are still available (under "Other Links"). As the page of photos loads, Brand Nubian's "Wake Up (Reprise in the Sunshine)" serves as the soundtrack.

51. See "Bio—Killarmy," available at http://www.rollingstone.com/artists/bio .asp?oid-069&cf-069, accessed 8 July 2004.

52. The sources of these samples are unknown.

53. Schloss, "Making Beats," 135–36.

54. Potter, *Spectacular Vernaculars,* 41–42. Geneva Smitherman also distinguishes two types of sampling, but for her, the differences are between sampling "which triggers

duplicates that work" (Smitherman, "The Chain Remains the Same," 16).

55. I borrow the term "interpretive moves" from Stephen Feld: "Interpretive moves involve the discovery of patterns as our experience is organized by juxtapositions, inter-actions, or choices in time when we engage symbolic objects or performances" (Keil and Feld, *Music Grooves,* 86).

## 6. Album Packaging and Organization

1. *When Disaster Strikes; Do You Want More?; Obelisk Movements; Silent Weapons for Quiet Wars; The Pick, the Sickle and the Shovel;* and *The Self Science* respectively.

2. Shout-outs to God are almost obligatory in hip-hop albums and have become the object of parody. See, for example, "God Finally Gives Shout-Out Back to All His Niggaz," *Onion,* 5 September 2001, http://www.theonion.com. I would like to thank Dr. Daniel Melamed for bringing this article to my attention.

3. Clarence 13X here is actually listed as "Clearance 13X." Kool Akiem (Akiem Allah Elisra) blames the error on "a knucklehead at Subverse [Records] who was trying to spell check our LP and kept fiddling with proper names" (personal communication, 24 June 2003).

4. See, for example, Ghostface Killah's thanks in *Ironman;* Butterfly's and Doodle-bug's shout-outs in *Blowout Comb;* RZA's and Frukwan's thanks on the Gravediggaz' *The Pick, the Sickle and the Shovel;* Kool Akiem's thanks on the Micranots' *Obelisk Movements;* and Grand Puba's shout-outs on *Reel to Reel,* where he also thanks the Fruit of Islam.

5. See Paul Gilroy, "Wearing Your Art on Your Sleeve," in *Small Acts: Thoughts on the Politics of Black Cultures* (New York: Serpent's Tail, 1993), 245.

6. See Todd Boyd, *Am I Black Enough for You? Popular Culture from the 'Hood and Beyond* (Bloomington: Indiana University Press, 1997), 76–78.

7. Quoted in Ahearn, "The Five Percent Solution," 57.

8. For comparison, see Khan, *Arabic Script,* especially pages 142–43.

9. The Kufic script style emerged in the early history of Islam and for centuries remained the favored Qur'anic script style. For a thorough discussion of Arabic calligraphic scripts, see Khan, *Arabic Script.*

10. I wish to thank Massumeh Farhad, Associate Curator of Islamic Art at the Freer Gallery of Art, for providing this translation (personal communication, 22 October 2002). The liner in the bed below the CD of *The Pick, the Sickle and the Shovel* offers a slightly different translation: "He who professes the faith will excel: and to whatever you accustom yourself, you will grow accustomed to. Blessings to the owner."

11. Hip-hop production paradigms have shifted since the early 1990s. Up to that time, a majority of hip-hop albums featured a single producer or production team; for example, anything by Eric B. and Rakim, or Public Enemy and the Bomb Squad. In the second half of the 1990s the majority of hip-hop albums featured a variety of guest producers; for example, both Aceyalone's *Accepted Eclectic* (2000) and Brand Nubian's *Foundation* (1998) feature seven guest producers, and Busta Rhymes's *Anarchy* (2000) features a whopping eleven guest producers. Gone are the days when a particular MC could be identified by the style of the musical tracks over which he rhymed. Hip-hop fans now want to hear their favorite MCs grace a variety of musical styles.

12. Interlude 2 ("Black on Black Crime") comes from *Don't Be a Menace to South Central While Drinking Your Juice in the Hood* and interlude 3 ("The Ghetto") comes from *Rhyme & Reason.*

13. See chapter 5 for a discussion of this sample.

14. It should be noted that although Kool Akiem (Akiem Allah Elisra) considers himself "to be of the Five Percent" (although not necessarily a member of the Nation of Gods and Earths), I Self Devine, the MC of the group, has no known affiliations with any Black Muslim group.

15. "Dial 7" also falls squarely in the album's center: it is the seventh track of thirteen.

16. It is also worth noting that the internal sum of 97 is 7 ($9 + 7 = 16$; $1 + 6 = 7$), yet again reinforcing Rakim's choice to return to the recording studio in '97.

17. Rakim's *The 18th Letter* is a double-disc set; my album analysis applies only to the first disc, which contains new songs. Disc two is a collection of Rakim's classics, both with and without his former partner Eric B.

18. Krims includes the following in his definition of "hardcore" rap style: "a (pitchwise) unfocused but dominating bass (both in terms of balance and in terms of predominance in the mix); radically dissonant pitch combinations; and samples that foreground their own deformation and/or degrees of reproduction" (Krims, *Rap Music and the Poetics of Identity,* 72).

19. *Nās* in Arabic means people, or humans.

20. Soloway et al., "A Long, Strange Trip to the Taliban."

21. Allah, "It's Been a Long Time."

## Conclusion

1. Quoted in Eure and Spady, *Nation Conscious Rap,* 23.

2. See Lost-Found Lesson no. 2, question 14, in Muhammad, "The Supreme Wisdom Lessons."

3. Available at http://www.amazon.com, posted 4 May 2000; accessed 1 April 2002. I have retained the reviewer's emphases in capital letters, but have taken the liberty of silently correcting the spelling.

4. Gregory Parks, *Freedom, Justice, and Equality: The Teachings of the Nation of Islam* (Hampton, Va.: United Brothers and United Sisters Communications Systems, 1992).

5. Quoted in Brett Johnson and Malik Russell, "Time to Build," *Source,* no. 158 (November 2002): 122.

6. Personal communication, 29 May 2003.

7. Smitherman, " 'The Chain Remains the Same,' " 4.

8. Cornel West, "The Paradox of the Afro-American Rebellion," in *The Sixties without Apology,* ed. Sonya Sayres (Minneapolis: University of Minnesota Press, 1984), 56. West goes on to say that most Afro-American music falls short of this goal, but does allow that hip-hop can be part of this vision, singling out Grandmaster Flash and the Furious Five's classic hip-hop song "The Message" as a good step in the "repoliticization of the black working poor and underclass" (27).

9. Gilroy, *Small Acts,* 238–39.

10. Quoted in Eure and Spady, *Nation Conscious Rap,* 351–52.

11. Toop, *The Rap Attack 2,* 120.

12. Personal communication, 2 June 2003.

13. Ibid.

14. Quoted in Oliver Wang, "Self Scientific," *Source,* no. 140 (May 2001): 80.

Ahearn, Charlie. "The Five Percent Solution." *Spin* 6 (February 1991): 57.
————. "Lakim Gets Busy Dropping Science." *New York City Sun* 6, no. 17 (26 April 1989): 13, 19.
Allah, Dasun. "Civilized People: Five Percenters 'Build' on Negative Press." *Village Voice,* 13–19 November 2002. http://www.villagevoice.com/issues0246/allah.php.
Allah, Wakeel. "It's Been a Long Time: Interview with Rakim Allah." http://www.allah team.com/rakim_interview.htm (page no longer available).
Allen, Ernest Jr. "Making the Strong Survive: The Contours and Contradictions of Message Rap." In *Droppin' Science: Critical Essays on Rap Music and Hip Hop Culture,* ed. William Eric Perkins, 159–91. Philadelphia: Temple University Press, 1996.
Arnold, Eric K. "Metaphysical Graffiti." *Eastbay Express On Line,* 23 July–3 August 2000.
Asante, Molefi Kete. *The Afrocentric Idea.* Philadelphia: Temple University Press, 1987.
————. *Kemet, Afrocentricity, and Knowledge.* Trenton, N.J.: Africa World Press, 1990.
Ashburne, Michael. *Sampling in the Record Industry.* Oakland, Calif.: Law Offices of Michael Ashburne, Esq., 1994.
Baker, Houston A., Jr. *Black Studies, Rap and the Academy.* Chicago: University of Chicago Press, 1993.
Bambaataa, Afrika. "Bambaataa Explains the True Meaning of Hip Hop." *Davey D.'s Hip Hop Daily News,* 14 August 2002. http://www.daveyd.com/FullArticles/articleN1191 .asp.
Banfield, William C. "Some Aesthetic Suggestions for a Working Theory of the 'Undeniable Groove': How Do We Speak about Black Rhythm, Setting Text, and Composition?" In *This Is How We Flow: Rhythm in Black Cultures,* ed. Angela S. Nelson, 32–45. Columbia: University of South Carolina Press, 1999.
Beloved Allah. "The Bomb: The Greatest Story Never Told." *Word* 1, no. 1 (July 1987); 1, no. 3 (August–September 1987); and 1, no. 4 (October–November 1987). http://www.ibiblio.org/nge/thebomb.html.
Bernard, James. "Down on the Corner." *Village Voice* 35, no. 19 (8 May 1990): 86.
Beynon, Erdmann Doane. "The Voodoo Cult among Negro Migrants in Detroit." *American Journal of Sociology* 43 (May 1938): 894–907.
Bloom, Harold. *The Anxiety of Influence: A Theory of Poetry.* 2nd ed. New York: Oxford University Press, 1997.
Bohlman, Philip V. "Musicology as a Political Act." *Journal of Musicology* 11, no. 4 (fall 1993): 411–36.
Bonanno, Jonathan "Gotti." "Last Man Standing." *Source,* no. 126 (March 2000): 210–17.
Boone, Ida. "What the Five Percenters Believe." *What's Happening* (February–March 1967): 4–5.
Boyd, Todd. *Am I Black Enough for You? Popular Culture from the 'Hood and Beyond.* Bloomington: Indiana University Press, 1997.

**170**    ———. *The New H.N.I.C.: The Death of Civil Rights and the Reign of Hip Hop.* New York: New York University Press, 2003.

Bracey, J. M., Jr., A. Meier, and E. Rudwick, eds. *Black Nationalism in America.* Indianapolis: Bobbs-Merrill, 1970.

Brennan, Tim. "Off the Gangsta Tip: A Rap Appreciation, or, Forgetting about Los Angeles." *Critical Inquiry* 20, no. 4 (summer 1994): 663–93.

Campbell, Anne. *The Girls in the Gang.* 2nd ed. Cambridge, Mass.: Basil Blackwell, 1991.

Cheney, Charise. "Representin' God: Rap, Religion and the Politics of a Culture." *North Star* 3, no. 1 (fall 1999). http://northstar.vassar.edu/volume3/cheney.html.

Clegg, Claude Andrew, III. *An Original Man: The Life and Times of Elijah Muhammad.* New York: St. Martin's Press, 1997.

Considine, J. D. "Larcenous Art?" *Rolling Stone,* 14 June 1990. Reprinted in *Rap on Rap: Straight-up Talk on Hip-Hop Culture,* ed. Adam Sexton (New York: Dell Publishing, 1990), 58–61.

Cortez, A. (God Allah Shah), and C. Goodwin (God Adew Allah). "In the Defense of the Five Percenters." *Black News* 3, no. 13 (October 1976): 21, 31.

Craddock-Willis, Andre. "Rap Music and the Black Musical Tradition: A Critical Assessment." *Radical America* 23, no. 4 (October–December 1989): 29–37.

Creekmur, Chuck. "Rage against the Machine." *Source,* no. 161 (February 2003): 80–82.

Decker, Jeffrey Louis. "The State of Rap: Time and Place in Hip-hop Nationalism." In *Microphone Fiends: Youth Music and Youth Culture,* ed. Andrew Ross and Tricia Rose, 99–121. New York: Routledge, 1994.

Dery, Mark. "Rock Is Dead: Rap!" *Keyboard* 14, no. 11 (November 1988): 32–55.

DeSilva, Earlston E. "The Theology of Black Power and Black Song: James Brown." *Black Sacred Music: A Journal of Theomusicology* 3, no. 2 (1989): 57–67.

Durand, Alain-Philippe, ed. *Black, Blanc, Beur: Rap Music and Hip-Hop Culture in the Francophone World.* Lanham, Md.: Scarecrow Press, 2002.

Dyson, Michael Eric. "Performance, Protest, and Prophecy in the Culture of Hip-Hop." *Black Sacred Music: A Journal of Theomusicology* 5, no. 1 (spring 1991): 12–24.

———. *Reflecting Black: African-American Cultural Criticism.* Minneapolis: University of Minnesota Press, 1993.

Eggen, Dan, and Brooke A. Masters. "U.S. Taliban Fighter Spared Death Penalty in Indictment." *Washington Post* 121, no. 68 (16 January 2002). http://www-tech.mit.edu/V121/N68/walker_68.68w.html.

"The Eight Planes of Study to Be Born as Revealed to Us by Allah." http://www.angelfire.com/ga/9thJewel/8planesofstudy.html.

Eure, Joseph D., and Richard M. Jerome, eds. *Back Where We Belong: Selected Speeches by Minister Louis Farrakhan.* Philadelphia: PC International Press, 1989.

Eure, Joseph D., and James G. Spady, eds. *Nation Conscious Rap.* New York: PC International Press, 1991.

"Farrakhan Acknowledges Sniper as Member of NOI." *Newsmax.com.* http://www.newsmax.com/archives/articles/2002/10/26/222128.shtml.

Farrakhan, Louis. "Declare War on Obesity (Fat)!" *Final Call,* 22 July 1991.

———. "Exercise to Stay Alive." *Final Call,* 19 August 1991.

Federal Bureau of Investigation. File 100-444636, "Clarence 13X Smith."

———. File 157-6-34, "Five Percenters."

Feld, Stephen. "Sound Structure as Social Structure." *Ethnomusicology* 28, no. 3 (1984): 383–409.

Fernando, S. H., Jr. "Black Enterprise." *Vibe,* March 2001, 128–34.

————. *The New Beats: Exploring the Music, Culture, and Attitudes of Hip-Hop.* New York: Anchor Books, 1994.

Floyd, Samuel A., Jr. *The Power of Black Music: Interpreting Its History from Africa to the United States.* New York: Oxford University Press, 1995.

Forman, Murray. "Represent: Race, Space and Place in Rap Music." *Popular Music* 19, no. 1 (January 2000): 65–90.

Fricke, Jim, and Charlie Ahearn. *Yes Yes Y'all: The Experience Music Project Oral History of Hip-Hop's First Decade.* With an introduction by Nelson George. Cambridge, Mass.: Da Capo Press, 2002.

Gardell, Mattias. *Countdown to Armageddon: Louis Farrakhan and the Nation of Islam.* London: Hurst and Company, 1996.

Gaunt, Kyra D. "The Veneration of James Brown and George Clinton in Hip-Hop Music: Is It Live! Or Is It Re-memory?" In *Popular Music: Style and Identity,* ed. William Straw, 117–22. Montreal: The Centre for Research on Canadian Cultural Industries and Institutions, 1995.

Geiss, Imanuel. *The Pan-African Movement: A History of Pan-Africanism in America, Europe and Africa.* Translated by Ann Keep. New York: Holmes and Meier, 1974.

George, Nelson. *Buppies, B-Boys, Baps & Bohos: Notes on Post-Soul Black Culture.* New York: HarperCollins, 1992.

————. *The Death of Rhythm and Blues.* New York: Penguin Books, 1988.

————. *Hip Hop America.* New York: Penguin Books, 1999.

Gilroy, Paul. *Small Acts: Thoughts on the Politics of Black Cultures.* New York: Serpent's Tail, 1993.

"God Finally Gives Shout-Out Back to All His Niggaz." *Onion,* 5 September 2001. http:// www.theonion.com.

Goldblatt, Mark. "Hip Hop's Grim Undertones." *USA Today,* 29 October 2002. http:// www.usatoday.com/news/opinion/2002-10-29-oped-goldblatt_x.htm.

Gottehrer, Barry. *The Mayor's Man: One Man's Struggle to Save Our Cities.* Garden City, N.Y.: Doubleday, 1975.

Griffin, Monica Denise. "The Rap on Rap Music: The Social Construction of African-American Identity." Ph.D. dissertation, University of Virginia, 1998.

Grigg, William Norman. "Weapons of Mass Insurrection." *New American* 18, no. 24 (2 December 2002). http://www.thenewamerican.com/tna/2002/12-02-2002/vo18no24 _insurrection_print.htm.

"Harlem Hit by Five Percenters." *New York Amsterdam News* 54, no. 39 (16 October 1965): 1–2.

"Harlem Moderate Is Murdered." *Washington Post Times Herald,* 14 June 1969. Reprinted in Prince-A-Cuba, *Our Mecca Is Harlem,* 32–33.

Henderson, Errol A. "Black Nationalism and Rap Music." *Doula: The Journal of Rap Music and Hip Hop Culture* 1, no. 2 (winter 2001): 30–39.

Hoffmann, Frank W. "Popular Music and Its Relationship to Black Social Consciousness." *Popular Music and Society* 8, nos. 3–4 (winter 1982): 55–61.

Houle, Jeffrey R. "Digital Audio Sampling, Copyright Law and the American Music Industry: Privacy or Just a Bad 'Rap'?" *Loyola Law Review* 37, no. 4 (winter 1992): 879–902.

Imani, Nikitah Okembe-Ra, and Hernan Vera. "War at 33 1/3: Exploring Hip-Hop (Rap) Music." In *All Music: Essays on the Hermeneutics of Music,* ed. Fabio B. Dasilva and David L. Brunsma, 167–90. Brookfield, Vt.: Ashgate, 1996.

Jacono, Jean-Marie. "Pour une analyse des chansons de rap." *Musurgia* 5, no. 2 (1998): 65–75.

Johnson, Billy, Jr. "Revenge of the Nerds." *Source,* no. 139 (April 2001): 126– 29.

Johnson, Brett, and Malik Russell. "Time to Build." *Source,* no. 158 (November 2002): 118–22.

Keil, Charles, and Steven Feld. *Music Grooves: Essays and Dialogues.* Chicago: University of Chicago Press, 1994.

Kelley, Robin D. G. *Freedom Dreams: The Black Radical Imagination.* Boston: Beacon Press, 2002.

———. *Yo' Mama's Disfunktional!* Boston: Beacon Press, 1997.

Keyes, Cheryl L. "At the Crossroads: Rap Music and Its African Nexus." *Ethnomusicology* 40, no. 2 (spring–summer 1996): 223–48.

———. *Rap Music and Street Consciousness.* Urbana: University of Illinois Press, 2002.

———. "Rappin' to the Beat: Rap Music as Street Culture among African Americans." Ph.D. dissertation, Indiana University, 1991.

Khan, Gabriel Mandel. *Arabic Script: Styles, Variants, and Calligraphic Adaptations.* Translated by Rosanna M. Giammanco Frongia. New York: Abbeville Press Publishers, 2001.

Korsyn, Kevin. "Towards a New Poetics of Musical Influence." *Music Analysis* 10, nos. 1–2 (March–July 1991): 3–71.

Krims, Adam. *Rap Music and the Poetics of Identity.* New York: Cambridge University Press, 2000.

Leo, John. "Search for the Snipers Was Too PC." *New York Daily News,* 3 November 2002. http://www.nydailynews.com/news/col/jleo/story/32492p-30785c.html.

Levine, Lawrence W. *Black Culture and Black Consciousness: Afro-American Folk Thought from Slavery to Freedom.* New York: Oxford University Press, 1977.

Light, Alan, ed. *The Vibe History of Hip Hop.* New York: Three Rivers Press, 1999.

Lincoln, C. Eric. *The Black Muslims in America.* Boston: Beacon Press, 1973.

Litwack, Leon F. *Trouble in Mind: Black Southerners in the Age of Jim Crow.* New York: Alfred A. Knopf, 1998.

Mamiya, Lawrence. "From Black Muslim to Bilalian: The Evolution of a Movement." *Journal for the Scientific Study of Religion* 21, no. 2 (June 1982): 138–52.

Mapp, Ben. "Soul to Soul Brothers." *Village Voice* 37, no. 29 (21 July 1992): 69.

Marcus, Jason H. "Don't Stop That Funky Beat: The Essentiality of Digital Sampling to Rap Music." *COMM/ENT: Hastings Journal of Communications and Entertainment Law* 13, no. 4 (summer 1991): 767–90.

Maultsby, Portia K. "Africanisms in African-American Music." In *Africanisms in American Culture,* ed. Joseph E. Holloway, 185–210. Bloomington: Indiana University Press, 1990.

McClary, Susan. *Conventional Wisdom: The Content of Musical Form.* Berkeley: University of California Press, 2000.

———. *Rap, Minimalism, and Structures of Time in Late Twentieth-Century Culture.* Geske Lecture, presented in Lincoln, Nebraska, on 15 September 1998. Lincoln: University of Nebraska, 1998.

Metzer, David. *Quotation and Cultural Meaning in Twentieth-Century Music.* Cambridge: Cambridge University Press, 2003.

Miller, Keith D. "Martin Luther King, Jr. and the Black Folk Pulpit." *Journal of American History* 78, no. 1 (June 1991): 120–23.

Mitchell, Tony, ed. *Global Noise: Rap and Hip-Hop outside the USA.* Middletown, Conn.: Wesleyan University Press, 2001.

Miyakawa, Felicia M. " 'The Duty of the Civilized Is to Civilize the Uncivilized': Tropes of Black Nationalism in the Messages of Five Percent Rappers." In *Understanding African*

and Elaine Richardson, 171–85. New York: Routledge, 2003.
———. "God Hop: The Music and Message of Five Percenter Rap." Ph.D. dissertation, Indiana University, 2003.
———. Review of *Rap Music and the Poetics of Identity,* by Adam Krims. *Indiana Theory Review* 21 (spring–fall 2000): 223–30.
Moon, Tom. "Public Enemy's Bomb Squad." *Musician,* October 1991, 69–72, 76.
Morano, Marc. "Black Muslims Create 'Explosive Mix' in Terror War, Says Author." *Nation,* 14 November 2002. http://www.cnsnews.com/Nation/archive/200211/NAT20021114 a.html.
Moses, Wilson Jeremiah. *The Golden Age of Black Nationalism, 1850–1925.* Hamden, Conn.: Archon Books, 1978.
———, ed. *Classical Black Nationalism: From the American Revolution to Marcus Garvey.* New York: New York University Press, 1995.
Muhammad, Abdul Allah. "Eat to Live—Or Else!" *Final Call,* 13 August 2002. http:// www.finalcall.com/columns/eleven.html (page no longer available).
Muhammad, Cedric. "Rap COINTELPRO XI: *Meet the Press* and Tim Russert Connect the Sniper Shootings with Hip-Hop and the 5 Percent Nation of Islam." *Black-Electorate.com,* 1 November 2002. http://www.blackelectorate.com/articles.asp?ID 32.
Muhammad, Elijah [Elijah Poole]. *Message to the Blackman in America.* Chicago: Muhammad Mosque of Islam No. 2, 1965.
———. *The Supreme Wisdom: Solution to the So-called NEGROES' Problem.* Newport News, Va.: National Newport News and Commentator, 1957.
Muhammad, Fard. "The Supreme Wisdom Lessons." http://www.thenationofislam.org/ supremewisdom.html.
Muhammad, Richard. "Farrakhan to Rappers: 'You Have Been Chosen to Lead.' " *Final Call,* 26 June 2001. http://www.finalcall.com/national/rapsummit06-26-2001b.htm.
Nation of Islam. Settlement No. 1. http://www.seventhfam.com/.
Nelson, Angela S. "Theology in the Hip-Hop of Public Enemy and Kool Moe Dee." *Black Sacred Music: A Journal of Theomusicology* 5, no. 1 (spring 1991): 51–59.
———. "A Theomusicological Approach to Rap: A Model for the Study of African American Popular and Folk Musics." Ph.D. dissertation, Bowling Green State University, 1992.
———. "Rhythm and Rhyme in Rap." In *This Is How We Flow: Rhythm in Black Cultures,* ed. Angela S. Nelson, 46–53. Columbia: University of South Carolina Press, 1999.
Nelson, Havelock. "Rick Rubin: Def Jam's Man with the Plan." *Musician,* no. 103 (May 1987): 34–39, 58.
Neumann, Friedrich. "Hip Hop: Origins, Characteristics and Creative Processes." *World of Music* 42, no. 1 (2000): 51–64.
"A New Harlem Hate Group? Police Chilly." *New York [Post?],* 15 October 1965, n.p. "Five Percent Nation" file, Schomburg Center for Research in Black Culture, New York.
Noble Drew Ali. *The Holy Koran of the Moorish Science Temple of America.* N.p., [1927?]. http://www.geocities.com/Athens/Delphi/2705/koran-index.html.
———. "Koran Questions for Moorish Americans." Folder 4 of 7, special collection on the Moorish Science Temple of America. Schomburg Center for Research in Black Culture, New York.
Norfleet, Dawn Michaelle. " 'Hip-Hop Culture' in New York City: The Role of Verbal Musical Performance in Defining a Community." Ph.D. dissertation, Columbia University, 1997.

**174**  North, John David. *The Norton History of Astronomy and Cosmology.* New York: Norton, 1994.

Nuruddin, Yusef. "The Five Percenters: A Teenage Nation of Gods and Earths." In *Muslim Communities in North America,* ed. Yvonne Yazbeck Haddad and Jane Idleman Smith, 109–32. Albany: State University of New York Press, 1994.

Original Hip Hop Lyrics Archive. http://www.ohhla.com/.

Orland, David. "The Paradox of Taliban John." *Boundless Webzine.* http://www.boundless.org/2001/features/a0000542.html.

Osario, Kim. "Operation W: Back at the Front." *Source,* no. 136 (January 2001): 162–69.

Parks, Gregory. *Freedom, Justice, and Equality: The Teachings of the Nation of Islam.* Hampton, Va.: United Brothers and United Sisters Communications Systems, 1992.

Patterson, Orlando. *Rituals of Blood: Consequences of Slavery in Two American Centuries.* New York: Basic Civitas, 1998.

Perkins, William Eric. "Nation of Islam Ideology in the Rap of Public Enemy." *Black Sacred Music: A Journal of Theomusicology* 5, no. 1 (spring 1991): 41–50.

———, ed. *Droppin' Science: Critical Essays on Rap Music and Hip Hop Culture.* Philadelphia: Temple University Press, 1996.

Perry, Jennifer. "Bringing Truth to Light." *Source,* no. 42 (March 1993): 30–32.

"Police Seek Aid to Solve Killing of Clarence 13X." *Washington (D.C) Sunday Star,* 15 June 1968, sec. A, 25.

Porcello, Thomas. "The Ethics of Digital Audio-Sampling: Engineers' Discourse." *Popular Music* 10, no. 1 (January 1991): 69–84.

Potter, Russell A. "Not the Same: Race, Repetition, and Difference in Hip-Hop and Dance Music." In *Mapping the Beat,* ed. Thomas Swiss, John Sloop, and Andrew Herman, 31–46. Malden, Mass.: Blackwell Publishers, 1998.

———. *Spectacular Vernaculars: Hip-Hop and the Politics of Postmodernism.* Albany: State University of New York Press, 1995.

Potvin, Kevin. "Fear Leaves American Hero Hanging." *The Republic: Vancouver's Opinionated Newspaper* 2, no. 32 (21 February 2002). http://1rev.net/archive/32-repub/repub_32_fear.html (page no longer available).

Prince-A-Cuba. "Black Gods of the Inner City." *Gnosis,* no. 25 (fall 1992), 56–63. http://www.ibiblio.org/nge/innercity.html.

———. *Our Mecca Is Harlem: Clarence 13X (Allah) and the Five Percent.* Hampton, Va.: United Brothers and United Sisters Communication Systems, 1995.

Ramsey, Guthrie P., Jr. *Race Music: Black Cultures from Bebop to Hip-Hop.* Berkeley: University of California Press, 2003.

Rashad, Adib. *Islam, Black Nationalism and Slavery: A Detailed History.* Beltsville, Md.: Writers' Inc., 1995.

Ratcliffe, Fahiym. "Common Ground." *Source,* no. 144 (September 2001): 72.

Rose, Tricia. *Black Noise: Rap Music and Black Culture in Contemporary America.* Hanover, N.H.: Wesleyan University Press, 1994.

———. " 'Fear of a Black Planet': Rap Music and Black Cultural Politics in the 1990s." *Journal of Negro Education* 60, no. 3 (summer 1991): 276–90.

———. "Orality and Technology: Rap Music and Afro-American Cultural Resistance." *Popular Music and Society* 13 (winter 1987): 35–44.

Rose-Robinson, Sia. "A Qualitative Analysis of Hardcore and Gangsta Rap Lyrics: 1985–1995." Ph.D. dissertation, Howard University, 1999.

Sample FAQ. http://www.the-breaks.com.

Schloss, Joseph G. "Making Beats: The Art of Sample-Based Hip-Hop." Ph.D. dissertation, University of Washington, 2000.

Schumacher, Thomas G. " 'This Is a Sampling Sport': Digital Sampling, Rap Music and the Law in Cultural Production." *Media, Culture & Society* 17 (1995): 253–73.

Sexton, Adam. "Don't Believe the Hype: Why Isn't Hip-Hop Criticism Better?" In *Rap on Rap: Straight-Up Talk on Hip-Hop Culture,* ed. Adam Sexton, 1–13. New York: Delta, 1995.

Sha-King Ceh' um Allah. "Social Equality?" *National Statement.* http://www.national statement.com/e/sha-kingAllah_pg1.htm (page no longer available).

Shusterman, Richard. "The Fine .Art of Rap." In *Pragmatist Aesthetics: Living Beauty, Rethinking Art.* 2nd ed. Oxford: Rowman & Littlefield, 2000.

Sincere Allah Merciful God. "Why We Are Not Muslims." http://www.ibiblio.org/nge/.

Small, Christopher. *Music of the Common Tongue: Survival and Celebration in Afro-American Music.* New York: Riverrun Press, 1987. Reprint, Hanover, N.H.: Wesleyan University Press, 1998.

Smith, Christopher. "Broadway the Hard Way: Techniques of Allusion in the Music of Frank Zappa." *College Music Symposium* 35 (1995): 35–60.

Smith, Douglass. "The Five Percenters." *What's Happening,* February–March 1967, 4.

Smitherman, Geneva. " 'The Chain Remains the Same': Communicative Practices in the Hip Hop Nation." *Journal of Black Studies* 28, no. 1 (September 1997): 3–25.

———. *Talkin' and Testifyin': The Language of Black America.* Boston: Houghton Mifflin, 1977.

Snead, James A. "Repetition as a Figure of Black Culture." In *Black Literature and Literary Theory,* ed. Henry Louis Gates, Jr., 59–79. New York: Routledge, 1984.

Soloway, Colin, Evan Thomas, Karen Breslau, and Ron Moreau. "A Long, Strange Trip to the Taliban." *Newsweek,* 17 December 2001. http://www.msnbc.com/news/669825.asp#BODY (page no longer available).

Stephens, Ronald Jemal. "Keepin' It Real: Towards an Afrocentric Aesthetic Analysis of Rap Music and Hip-Hop Subculture (Michigan, Pennsylvania, New York)." Ph.D. dissertation, Temple University, 1996.

———. "The Three Waves of Contemporary Rap Music." *Black Sacred Music: A Journal of Theomusicology* 5, no. 1 (spring 1991): 25–40.

Stewart, Earl, and Jane Duran. "Black Essentialism: The Art of Jazz Rap." *Philosophy of Music Education Review* 7, no. 1 (spring 1999): 49–54.

Swedenburg, Ted. "Islam in the Mix: Lessons of the Five Percent." Paper presented at the Anthropology Colloquium, University of Arkansas, 19 February 1997. http://comp.uark.edu/tsweden/5per.html.

Sylvan, Robin. "Traces of the Spirit: The Religious Dimension of Popular Music." Ph.D. dissertation, University of California, Santa Barbara, 1998.

Todorovic, Alex. "They Call Themselves Five Percenters." *POINT: South Carolina's Independent Newsmonthly* 7, no. 77 (April 1996). http://www.mindspring.com/~scpoint/point/9604/p06.html.

Toop, David. *The Rap Attack 2: African Rap to Global Hip Hop.* London: Serpent's Tail, 1991.

Tsoukalas, Steven. *The Nation of Islam: Understanding the "Black Muslims."* Phillipsburg, N.J.: P&R Publishing, 2001.

True 54. "Interview with Micranots." *Thrasher,* December 1999, 120. http://www.micranots.com/m2000/words/thrasher.html (page no longer available).

von Zielbauer, Paul. "Inmates Are Free to Practice Black Supremacist Religion, Judge Rules." *New York Times,* 18 August 2003. http://www.nytimes.com/2003/08/18/nyregion/18PRIS.html.

**176**   Walker, Tshombe R. "The Hip Hop World View: An Afrocentric Analysis." Ph.D. dissertation, Temple University, 1998.

Walser, Robert. "Rhythm, Rhyme, and Rhetoric in the Music of Public Enemy." *Ethnomusicology* 39, no. 2 (spring–summer 1995): 193–218.

Wang, Oliver. "Self Scientific." *Source,* no. 140 (May 2001): 79–80.

West, Cornel. "The Paradox of the Afro-American Rebellion." In *The Sixties without Apology,* ed. Sonya Sayres, 44–58. Minneapolis: University of Minnesota Press, 1984.

———. *Prophetic Fragments.* Grand Rapids, Mich.: Eerdmans, 1988.

Wheeler, Elizabeth A. " 'Most of My Heroes Don't Appear on No Stamps': The Dialogics of Rap Music." *Black Music Research Journal* 11, no. 2 (fall 1991): 193–216.

Whitehead, Colson. "Music of the Spheres." *Village Voice* 38, no. 10 (9 March 1993): 69, 72.

Wilson, Matthew. "The Advent of 'The Nigger': The Careers of Paul Laurence Dunbar, Henry O. Tanner, and Charles W. Chestnutt." *American Studies* 43, no. 1 (spring 2002): 5–50.

Wilson, Olly. "Black Music as an Art Form." *Black Music Research Journal* 3 (1983): 1–22.

———. "The Heterogeneous Sound Ideal in African-American Music." In *New Perspectives on Music: Essays in Honor of Eileen Southern,* ed. Josephine Wright, 327–38. Warren, Mich.: Harmonie Park Press, 1992.

Wilson, Peter Lamborn. "Shoot-out at the Circle Seven Koran: Noble Drew Ali and the Moorish Science Temple." *Gnosis,* no. 12 (summer 1989): 44–49.

Wimsatt, William (Upski). *Bomb the Suburbs.* 2nd ed. New York: Soft Skull Press, 2000.

———. *No More Prisons.* New York: Soft Skull Press, 1999.

Woodyard, Jeffrey Lynn. "Africological Theory and Criticism: Reconceptualizing Communication Constructs." In *Understanding African American Rhetoric: Classical Origins to Contemporary Innovations,* ed. Ronald Jackson and Elaine Richardson, 133–54. New York: Routledge, 2003.

X, Malcolm [Malcolm Little]. *The Autobiography of Malcolm X.* As told to Alex Haley. New York: Ballantine Books, 1964.

———. *Malcolm X Speaks: Selected Speeches and Statements.* Edited by George Breitman. New York: Pathfinder, 1989.

Yasin, Jon A. " 'In Yo Face! Rappin' Beats Comin' at You': A Study of How Language Is Mapped onto Musical Beats in Rap Music." Ed.D. dissertation, Columbia University Teachers College, 1997.

———. "Rap in the African-American Music Tradition: Cultural Assertion and Continuity." In *Race and Ideology: Language, Symbolism, and Popular Culture,* ed. Arthur K. Spears, 197–223. Detroit: Wayne State University Press, 1999.

Aceyalone. *Accepted Eclectic.* Ground Control 7045, 2000.
Big Daddy Kane. *It's a Big Daddy Thing.* Cold Chillin' 25941, 1989.
Black Moon. *Enta da Stage.* Nervous 2002, 1993.
Brand Nubian. *Foundation.* Arista 19024, 1998.
——. *In God We Trust.* Elektra 61381, 1992.
——. *One for All.* Elektra 60946, 1990.
Busta Rhymes. *When Disaster Strikes.* Elektra 62064, 1997.
Digable Planets. *Blowout Comb.* Pendulum Records 30654, 1994.
——. *Reachin' (A New Refutation of Time and Space).* Pendulum Records 61414, 1993.
Eric B. and Rakim. *Let the Rhythm Hit 'em.* MCA 6416, 1990.
Freestyle Fellowship. *Inner City Griots.* 4th & Broadway 444050, 1993.
Ghostface Killah. *Ironman.* Columbia 67729, 1996.
Grand Puba. *Reel to Reel.* Elektra 61314, 1992.
Gravediggaz. *The Pick, the Sickle and the Shovel.* Gee Street 63881, 1997.
GZA. *Liquid Swords.* Geffen 24813, 1995.
Killarmy. *Silent Weapons for Quiet Wars.* Priority 50633, 1997.
King Sun. *Righteous but Ruthless.* Profile 1299, 1990.
Lakim Shabazz. *The Lost Tribe of Shabazz.* Tuff City 571, 1990.
——. *Pure Righteousness.* Tuff City Records 5557, 1988.
Micranots. *Obelisk Movements.* Subverse Music 1598, 2000.
Mobb Deep. *Hell on Earth.* Loud Records 66992, 1996.
Nas. *Illmatic.* Columbia 57684, 1994.
——. *It Was Written.* Columbia 67015, 1996.
Pete Rock and C. L. Smooth. *Mecca and the Soul Brother.* Elektra 60948, 1992.
Poor Righteous Teachers. *Black Business.* Profile 1443, 1993.
——. *The New World Order.* Profile 1471, 1997.
——. *Righteous Groove's.* BMG 44957, 1999.
Rakim. *The 18th Letter.* Universal 53113, 1998.
Scaramanga. *Seven Eyes, Seven Horns.* Sun Large Records 777, 2000.
Self Scientific. *The Self Science.* Landspeed Records 1007, 2001.
Wu-Tang Clan. *Wu-Tang Forever.* Loud Records 66905, 1997.

# Index of Songs and Performers

# Music Credits

This list constitutes an extension of the copyright page.

The publisher gratefully acknowledges the following for permission to reprint material in this book.

Lyrics from "Mystery (Who Is God)." Words and Music by William Griffin, Ervin Drake, Dan Fisher and Irene Higginbotham, © 1997 Sony/ATV Tunes LLC, Lindabet Music, EMI Blackwood, The Eighteenth Letter. All rights on behalf of Sony/ATV Tunes LLC administered by Sony/ATV Music Publishing, 8 Music Square West, Nashville, TN 37203. All rights on behalf of 18th Letter controlled and administered by EMI Blackwood Music, Inc. All rights reserved. Used by permission.

Lyrics from *Wu Revolution* by Robert F. Diggs, Jr. /Pete Cuffie/David Turner © 1997 Wu-Tang Publishing (BMI) / Diggs Family Music (BMI). All rights obo W-Tang Publishing (BMI) administered by Careers-BMG Music Publishing, Inc. (BMI).

Lyrics from "Ain't No Mystery." Words and Music by Christopher Kenner, Derek Murphy and Lorenzo DeSchaelus, ©1993 EMI Longitude Music and Rushtown Music. All Rights Reserved. International Copyright Secured. Used by Permission. (Contains elements of "Something You Got" by Christopher Kenner)

Music from "Suicide Is Painless." Words and music by Michael B. Artman and John Mandel © 1970 WB Music Corp. All Rights Reserved. Used by Permission of Warner Bros. Publications U.S., Inc., Miami, FL 33014.

Lyrics from "Allah and Justice." Words and music by Lorenzo DeChalus, Derek Murphy, Terrence Perry, Jerry Ragovoy, and Mort Shuman.© 1992 Unichappell Music, Inc. All Rights Reserved. Used by Permission of Warner Bros. Publications U.S., Inc., Miami, FL 33014.

Lyrics from "The Lost Tribe of Shabazz" by Lakeim Sharik. Performed by Lakim Shabazz. Courtesy of Tuff City Records. Published by Street Tuff Tunes (ASCAP). Featured on TUF CD 0571: Lakim Shabazz / *The Lost Tribe of Shabazz* www.tuffcity.com

**FELICIA M. MIYAKAWA** completed her Ph.D. in musicology at Indiana University. She is currently Assistant Professor of Musicology at the Robert W. McLean School of Music, Middle Tennessee State University.